FUTURE PROFITS

Empowering Youth to Make Wise Decisions About Life and Money

Dedication to Drs. John and Vera Mae Perkins
and the community of East Palo Alto, California

Written by
NORTHERN CALIFORNIA URBAN DEVELOPMENT
A Publication of the
CHRISTIAN COMMUNITY DEVELOPMENT ASSOCIATION

iUniverse, Inc.
New York Bloomington

FutureProfits
Empowering Youth to Make Wise Decisions About Life and Money

iUniverse books may be ordered through booksellers or by contacting:

iUniverse
1663 Liberty Drive
Bloomington, IN 47403
www.iuniverse.com
1-800-Authors (1-800-288-4677)

ISBN: 978-1-4502-5272-0 (pbk)
ISBN: 978-1-4502-5273-7 (ebk)

Library of Congress Control Number: 2010912170

Printed in the United States of America

iUniverse rev. date: 8/14/2010

Acknowledgements

Author: Northern California Urban Development Corporation
Executive Editor: John Liotti
Lead Writer: Jenni Ingram
Writers: Makenzie Gallego, Doral Miller, and Gilbert Chaidez
Content Editor: Sonia Stewart
Design Editor: Jim Berkman
Layout: Joy Miller
Layout Assistant: Michael Crampton
Cover Design: Salvador Jimenez
Cover Art Director: Noel Castellanos

Thanks to: NCUD Board of Directors and Advisors, Silicon Valley Community Foundation, Youthworks Foundation, CCDA Staff, Board and Advisors, Dr. Randy and Eileen Scott, Noel Castellanos, Dave Clark, Dr. Luis Carlo, Keisha Woods, Cynthia Ruiz, Menlo Park Presbyterian Church, Peninsula Covenant Church, The Highway Community, Vineyard Christian Fellowship of the Peninsula, Ann and Bob Ingram, Amy Joh, Leneita Fix, Crissy Brooks, Juanita Irizarry, Marie Turks, Debbie Favaloro, Maite Rodriguez, Donna Perkins, Phil Durden, Matthew Watson, Georgina Aubin, Grace Chu, Mark Chesney, Chris Nutter, Susan C. Bobb, Amy Nesbitt, Christina Lee, Deidre Elerath, Marilyn Early, Dorothy Emily Wu, Vicky Evans, Luke Seerveld, Anthony Gallego, Blanca Medina, and Kirsten Devlin

FutureProfits Table of Contents

Foreword

I wish *FutureProfits* had been available when I was growing up. If any of my early mentors had been equipped with a resource like this to teach me about money and finances, I am certain I would have been better prepared as a man, a husband, and a leader.

Growing up, financial instability was a constant reality for my family. I was born in southern Texas, a few miles from the Mexican border, to parents who spent most of my early years as farm workers, traveling around the country picking fruits and vegetables of every variety. While this is not an unusual starting point for many low-skilled, Mexican-American workers, my parents were fortunate to eventually find jobs that paid better and enabled them to provide a very adequate, working-class upbringing for our family. My father's employment at General Motors allowed our family to purchase a home in Northern California and has, to this day, provided my parents with both a pension and health-care in their retirement – benefits that many of us working today can no longer take for granted.

As a kid, I knew we were not rich. We qualified for free lunch most years, shopped often at second-hand stores, and ate our share of welfare cheese (which made great quesadillas, by the way). We never lacked food or shelter. But I learned quickly that working hard was not an option, but rather a requirement to survive.

It's no surprise that I had started working by the time I was thirteen years old. I sold newspaper subscriptions door-to-door and then in high school, I worked at a gas station. One summer, while home for summer-break during college, I landed a job at a canning factory cleaning up under the fruit cocktail conveyor belt (which was quite messy), and then I spent two other summers working in construction. Along the way and with the help of my parents, I saved enough money to buy a car, and I learned to take responsibility for earning the spending money I needed. This lessened my dependence on my parents for my needs and wants. Hard work and earning my own spending money were two values I learned early on. What I did not learn however, was how to save, invest or manage my money particularly well.

Like many young people today who have struggled with poverty, I have had to fight a compulsion to overspend – buying things as a way to build my self-esteem. Early in my marriage, I caused my wife great anguish due to my indulgent use of credit cards that lead to debt with outrageously high interest fees. Finally, I had to admit I had a problem with managing money. I was able to get some counseling support and I made some major changes that have led to a much less stressful and financially stable life.

As I reflect on my experiences with finances, I know I would have benefited from going through a practical and easy to understand class related to money: *how it works, how to manage and invest it effectively, and how to live in such a way that does not make me a slave to materialism and debt.*

As the CEO of the Christian Community Development Association, I am personally committed to providing excellent and relevant tools that our CCDA leaders and others working in under-resourced communities can use to empower young people in a wholistic manner. CCDA uses wholistic with a "w" to emphasize a whole person approach to youth development. Few things are more important than providing our indigenous youth with the knowledge and skills necessary to thrive in today's economic reality.

I am thankful for the leadership of John Liotti, Jenni Ingram and the staff at Northern California Urban Development in developing this *FutureProfits* curriculum. My desire is that you will use this material as an effective resource in your own community and you will also recommend it enthusiastically to others who are investing in the lives of young people growing up in challenging environments. Together, let's work to develop a new generation of leaders who are passionate about their faith and are fully committed to restoring under-resourced communities.

Noel Castellanos
CEO, CCDA

Introduction

Northern California Urban Development (NCUD) was established in 2004 with the mission of combating the causes of systemic and generational poverty through economic empowerment and community development. Its founders were deeply impacted by the philosophy of the Christian Community Development Association (CCDA) and the teachings of Dr. John Perkins. One of CCDA's core philosophies is the "Three R's" of Reconciliation, Redistribution and Relocation. NCUD primarily focuses on "Redistribution" which is defined not as socialist or dependent approach, but one of empowerment that gives students the tools and resources to work their way out of poverty. Our goal is to enable students to take responsibility for their well being by making wise choices regarding life and finances.

In the fall of 2007, NCUD began developing a comprehensive youth program, now called *FutureProfits*, focused on teaching students life skills, sound financial principles, career and life decision-making skills, the value of "giving back" to their community and the power structures that influence today's society. Our premise comes from research showing that in order to break the generational effects of poverty, it is critical to reach young people before they begin to make wrong financial decisions. We aim to give them a fresh, healthy perspective that will benefit them throughout their lives. We accomplish this through providing students with a greater understanding of how making right choices every day regarding career and money will assist them in making better decisions throughout their lives. We call this approach **Life Economics**. The 24 lessons you have in front of you are an entry point or an on-ramp to greater understanding of how money works in our American system. This curriculum has greater value when coupled with mentoring and direction from caring teachers and adults. Our hope is that it is used not only to teach, but also to change directions of students' lives for generations to come.

The format and perspective of this curriculum is modeled in a way that addresses the needs of volunteers during the school day. This curriculum has been used in the San Francisco Bay Area in local schools during the school day. Our classes are mainly taught by volunteers or people untrained in classroom management or curriculum development. Therefore, our hope is that this curriculum will serve the needs of two groups: 1) community-based organizations, civic groups and worshipping communities who desire to engage with and train students, and, 2) professional teachers and administrators who desire to implement this into an educational setting. Walking that middle ground can be precarious; our hope is that we found a fair balance.

Why do I need to teach these concepts?
According to the 2005 Finance Project (www.financeproject.org) report *Providing and Funding Financial Literacy Programs for Low-Income Adults and Youth:*

"Making effective financial decisions and knowing how to manage money are skills critical to enjoying a secure financial future. Yet many individuals and families lack the knowledge necessary to make sound financial choices, as evidenced by falling savings rates, mounting consumer debt, and a growing dependence on alternative banking institutions. These indicators suggest that **access to financial literacy programs is a pressing need in our society, especially for groups such as youth** *(emphasis mine)* and families transitioning from welfare to self-sufficiency."

Statistics from the financial and governmental sector support their findings:

- About 10 million low- and moderate-income households are "unbanked," that is, they do not have accounts in any mainstream bank.

- More than one million Americans filed for bankruptcy each year between 1990 and 2000; during this period, total bankruptcy filings, including businesses, increased 90.6 percent.

- On average, adults scored 57 percent on tests of basic economic knowledge, according to the Standards in Economics Survey.

- Three-fifths of U.S. households stated that their expenses were higher than their income, according to the Federal Reserve Board's 1998 Survey of Consumer Finances.

As indicated by these statistics, there is a tremendous need for a relevant and wholistic curriculum that focuses on financial health, banking skills, the entrepreneurial attitude, understanding how to gain the power for self-determination and civic responsibility. There have been several financial institutions, government entities, and non-profit organizations that have developed financial literacy curricula for youth; however, their curricula do not account for all that factors that have plagued under-served communities.

Many of our students are coming from single-parent homes or from undocumented, immigrant families. Most families, given the high cost of living, are living from paycheck to paycheck and their children are only exposed to managing money in a constant crisis-like state in which saving becomes entirely unknown. This is coupled with a pervasive attitude, fostered by media culture, which prizes spending money on material things and seeking immediate gratification. Cultural forces that enforce distrust of institutions exacerbate the problem. Latest reports indicate between 60-75 percent of our students will drop out of high school, placing them in the work force sooner rather than later. Ultimately, these factors leave our students with a greatly underdeveloped understanding of finances and without the ability to manage their lives and budgets in a healthy manner. This gap in life skills, coupled with a sense of despair due to poverty along with the lack of vision for their lives, leaves our students and families prey to financial predators, check cashers and credit card companies. To the extreme, we are finding college-aged students already in financial bondage that severely limits their choices for their future. The goal of the *FutureProfits* curriculum is to affirm each student's cultural identity while challenging the negative paradigms that inhibit under-resourced students from making wise choices regarding life, career and money.

The *FutureProfits* Approach

NCUD believes that financial literacy goes far beyond banking and budgeting. We have attempted to develop a wholistic curriculum that addresses the cultural issues of low-income, at-risk youth. Due to a number of issues, schools in under-resourced communities are struggling to give students all the tools that will empower them to move out of the generational or situational poverty that mires them now. The *FutureProfits* curriculum fills this education gap with relevant, all-encompassing activities that teach youth about the implications of poverty and how to take tangible steps to begin the upward movement out of it.

The goal of this curriculum is to guide youth toward understanding all aspects of poverty, including its historical ramifications, the affects it has on a community, how youth can move out of it through an entrepreneurial attitude, and how youth can be agents of systemic change.
The curriculum is based on our foundational mission to combat systemic poverty and is culturally appropriate for low-income, at-risk youth. Our objective is to equip under-resourced youth before they reap the consequences of poor decisions. This curriculum will build financial skills, while promoting a deeper understanding of how the financial system is structured and the consequent implications for individuals and communities. It gives students a greater understanding of life—the cost of living and the benefits of completing their education or career training successfully.

We hope this curriculum becomes as much of an invaluable resource to the students you serve as it has become to ours. It has been created with much prayer, research, evaluation and modification over a three-year period. Ultimately we believe the *FutureProfits* curriculum approach will play a part in helping students and their families break destructive cycles while giving them the opportunity to choose whatever lifestyle is congruent to their personal and cultural values.

Many have helped create these lessons. However, special thanks must be given to Drs. John and Vera Mae Perkins, Dr. Randy and Eileen Scott, Christian Community Development Association, the Youthworks Foundation, the Silicon Valley Community Foundation, and the current and former staff, board and advisors of Northern California Urban Development in East Palo Alto, California. Without their hard work, leadership, support and inspiration this could never have been accomplished.

Rev. John Liotti
Executive Editor
CEO and President – Northern California Urban Development
July 2010

Guide to Using the *FutureProfits* Curriculum

The *FutureProfits* curriculum is designed to impact students in low-income communities by teaching them practical and relevant financial concepts, and more importantly, how these concepts directly relate to their daily life and future success. It includes 24 lessons total, divided into four units and six lessons per unit. The curriculum is multi-layered, with basic concepts being introduced and built-upon, and then presented in a manner that is relatable and holds students attention. Upon examination, the teacher will find a number of different types of sections, with inserts for each section. This guide will provide clarification on the purpose and function of each section.

Basic evaluation instruments are provided online for optional use with this curriculum. These resources include: a demographic questionnaire, a class feedback form, and a pre/post-test for each unit. If teachers plan to utilize these instruments, schedule additional time at the beginning and end of each unit. An explanation of how to use the evaluation instruments is also provided online. See www.futureprofitsresources.org.

Unit Description

The Unit Description is found at the beginning of each unit, and serves to provide a philosophical description of the unit, along with an understanding of the overall flow of the lessons. This includes a description on how each lesson in that unit builds upon each other, and identifies any advance preparation that is crucial to know before beginning the unit. Also communicated are the main concepts students will learn during the unit.

Elements Found Within Individual Lessons:

Quote

The quote at the beginning of each lesson is provided for two reasons:

1. First, it ties into the overarching theme of each lesson. The teacher/facilitator can write the quote on the board, to which the students can look back as a reference.
2. The quote can also be used as a journal entry or to facilitate discussion at the beginning or end of each class session. Discuss with students the meaning of the quote and how it relates to their lives.

Key Concepts

This section usually consists of two to three main points the students should grasp by the end of the lesson. Sample evaluation tools, which will help to track whether or not the students have understood these key concepts, are provided online (see www.futureprofits.org).

Keep in Mind

This section is intended to identify background information that is relevant about students in low-income communities, or possible perceptions they may have in regard to the topic being covered. It will prepare the teacher to interact and relate with their students efficiently while the lesson is being taught.

Note to Teacher

> **Note to Teacher**
>
> *Each Note to Teacher will look similar to this note. This element serves to give teachers a quick hint or reminder while they are teaching a particular section. The information provided in this section is very important, so make sure not to overlook this small section.*

Lesson Plan Break Down:

Each lesson plan moves fairly quickly from section to section, making use of different teaching styles. This is designed to help keep the students' attention, and will more effectively reach a variety of different learning styles.

Each section has an approximate length of time that it should take. This time allotment will help to guide you while preparing for the lesson so you do not run out of time or go through the lesson too quickly.

In the lecture and discussion sections of some lessons, narratives are provided. These serve as models of how to present the information. It is not intended for the narrative to be repeated verbatim. Teachers should use their own unique personality, experiences, and skills to tailor the delivery of the information in each lesson. The lesson plans should act as a guide for the teacher to ensure that the major topics are clearly communicated, however, every class is unique and should be treated as such.

Sections by Type:

Review

This icon represents any material that must be reviewed from the previous lesson. The first lesson within each unit does not include a review section, however each subsequent lesson in that unit will. This reinforces the foundation of knowledge learned in the previous lesson, and allows the student to continue to build on those key concepts throughout the unit.

Introduction

This icon represents the introduction of the lesson. Every lesson begins with an introduction, and is intended to grab the students' attention about the topic. The teacher should take the opportunity to display enthusiasm about the topic being covered and to communicate its importance, as students will often reflect the enthusiasm that is encouraged of them from the teacher.

Discussion

This icon represents a discussion section built into the lesson. When done properly, discussions help to build a class culture that honors each other's opinions, and builds an expectation for students to verbally participate in the topic being covered. This section typically consists of questions to engage the students and help them think in practical terms. It also gives the students an opportunity for their thoughts and opinions to be heard. Discussions are meant to help keep students' attentions, and provide for interaction where the students can learn from each other, as well as the teacher. This section also helps the teacher to build rapport with the students, as they listen and validate students' thoughts and points of view. Because of this, it is important to verbally affirm students for sharing when they do, even if one disagrees with their perspective. Allow other students to disagree with each other, but make sure that the common rule of respecting each other is firmly held to.

Lecture

This icon represents a lecture in the lesson. This section provides the teacher time to communicate and reinforce the main points of the lesson to the class. By this point in the lesson, students should be engaged and willing to listen to your lecture. The section is intentionally shorter than the others in order to make sure the students' attention is not lost. The discussion section will usually set up the lecture, and then the activity will usually reiterate the lecture's main points. Be sure to command attention during this time so students aren't distracted and miss important information.

Activity

This icon represents an activity in the lesson. Activities are meant to be fun and interactive opportunities for the students to engage with the key points shared in the lecture portion of the lesson, and provide another way for students to grasp the information being taught. This will especially help to communicate the key concepts to students who are more visual or kinesthetic learners.

Wrap Up

This icon represents the wrap up or closure for each lesson. Some talking points are provided to conclude the lesson, but feel free to use your own words. Some lessons may not go according to plan, so this is your opportunity to end the class on a positive note. This section also gives the teacher one last chance to drive home the key concepts of the lesson. This will particularly help when new concepts are introduced, as repetition is key to helping students to remember these points.

At the End of Each Lesson:

Additional Resources

There are many additional resources that provide information through web links and other materials to aid the teacher in understanding the specific topic of each lesson. While preparing to teach each lesson, it is recommended to look through the additional resources to help gain a broader understanding of the topic. These can be found online at www.futureprofitsresources.org.

Vocabulary

This section includes new vocabulary taught during the lesson. Students should know and remember the meaning of each of the vocabulary terms. These terms are listed at the end of each lesson, and will be valuable by many students when written in their notes. The definitions of these words can be found in the lesson and in the glossary in the appendix.

Classroom Management Tips

Classroom management is a topic that is widely discussed among educators. A teacher who effectively manages his or her classroom will have a successful class. Some basic classroom management techniques are provided for the optimum success while teaching this curriculum. Implementing these techniques will help a teacher to communicate effectively and have an enjoyable experience. Whether being a paid facilitator or a volunteer, success in the class will depend on the effectiveness with which one manages the classroom. The strategies presented here are simple to apply regardless of previous teaching experience. The techniques that are encouraged through this curriculum are appropriate and effective with the target population of low-income communities.

Most people can recall being in school and having "good" teachers and "bad" teachers. Most people can also recall classes where the students had control and classes where the teachers had control. There were the classes in which good behavior was expected and classes in which bad behavior was tolerated. The same student who is completely disruptive in one teacher's class will be completely compliant in another teacher's classroom. The ways in which a teacher manages his/her classroom will contribute to the way the students act in the class. All teachers and volunteers are encouraged to embrace the following characteristics of an effective classroom manager.

Effective classroom managers will:

1. **Believe they have the ability to influence the behavior of an entire classroom.**
   Teachers who embrace their role as an educator and influencer will be the most successful. Every teacher sets the tone of a classroom. Therefore, the students take their cue from the teacher. Teachers must make an intentional decision to influence students toward a high standard of behavior.

2. **Teach policies and procedures on the first day of class.**
   The number one priority of successful teachers is to clearly communicate all the rules and expectations of the class (see suggested general rules and expectations). It is crucial to lay a strong foundation of classroom expectations during the first class meeting, regardless of whether the teacher is with students for one hour a day or one hour a week. Reiterate the rules and expectations at least two times and leave opportunity for students to ask questions. Whether or not the students realize it, they appreciate being given high expectations. They

do not respect teachers who are too relaxed in their approach to discipline. Many teachers and adults put low expectations on students of color; meanwhile, these students gravitate toward adults who have high expectations. They will not respond positively to an adult that is considered too "soft."

3. **Motivate all students to quickly follow directions.**
   Students will stay on task if expected behavior is clearly communicated. Provide positive feedback to students who meet the expectations and take corrective action with students who do not meet the expectations.

4. **Build relationships with the students.**
   Students — especially from a low-income background — will appreciate teachers who take an interest in who they are as individuals. The teachers who will have the biggest influence in their lives are teachers they know care about them. Commit to learning all the students' names and greet them when they enter the classroom. Create a positive environment where students feel comfortable. Stay consistent in having a positive attitude toward the students.

   Reach out to distrusting and/or "difficult" students. Due to possible life experiences, some students do not trust teachers. As a result, these students usually have a conflicted relationship with teachers. It is extremely important to intentionally reach out to these students. It will take time to build relationships with them, but if a teacher is successful in convincing a student that he/she is on the student's side, it can dramatically decrease the number of disruptive classroom incidences.

5. **Be prepared to fill up your entire classroom time.**
   Have enough structured activities to keep a good flow of time. The less structure given, the more room is left open for students to misbehave. Do not give your students time to misbehave.

6. **Use explicit directions instead of vague directions.**
   Students will best respond to directions that are clear and explicitly communicated.
   - Example of vague direction: I need everyone to pay attention.
   - Example of explicit direction: I need everyone's attention. That means your eyes are on me, there is nothing in your hands except your pencil, and no one is talking.

7. **Be conscious of your facial expressions, gestures, eye contact, and voice.**
   All these things send unintentional signals to a class. A stone face sends the message that the teacher is cold and indifferent. An open face sends the message that the teacher is enthusiastic and cares about what they are teaching. A projected voice can command the students' attention. Yet, if the teacher has the students' attention and adjusts to speaking in a softer voice, this can also help to command attention, causing students to listen harder for the teacher's instructions.

8. **Always be ready to give positive feedback to your students.**
   There are two types of positive feedback: individual and class-wide. Every time a student is doing something right, the teacher should make sure to acknowledge him or her at that time. In addition, the entire class should receive positive feedback when they are on task and following directives. Remember, students do not appreciate phony or artificial praise. They will see through that and believe the teacher does not care about them. All positive feedback should be genuine, immediate, and appropriate to the situation.

9. **Always be willing to give corrective action.**
   When a student breaks a rule that was clearly communicated, be sure to immediately give corrective action. This should be done within close proximity of the student and not in an angry or frustrated tone. Tell the student what they did wrong and what they should be doing. Remember to be as clear as possible. When trying to regain the attention of a class, it is important to address students directly by their names, or have a call back to attention that the whole class knows.

Dealing with Disruptive Behavior

It is most important to know the school's policy for disciplining disruptive behavior and implement it accordingly. Some students will try to challenge the teacher's authority. They should not be allowed the opportunity to challenge a teacher in front of the entire class. For example, if a student is asked to do something and he/she refuses to do it, the teacher should not continue to ask him/her to follow the instruction. This will result in a lost battle, and possibly lack of respect from other students in the class, if the disruptive student is set on standing his/her ground. Some tips to remember:

- Never escalate or get in a back-and-forth argument with a truly defiant student.
- Simply remind the student of the consequence of the inappropriate action and follow through on that consequence if the student continues to misbehave.
- Never threaten a student with a consequence that will not actually be enforced (either due to willingness or ability to enforce).

Ultimately the teacher has no authority to make a student do anything. If the student is truly defiant the teacher should call for an administrator to remove that student from the class. At a later time that day, the teacher should follow up with the student and explain why they had to bring in someone else to deal with the situation. They should emphasize their desire to help the student succeed in the class. If there is not additional support from other school personnel, the teacher should develop a plan for handling the student.

If these nine management techniques are implemented, it will greatly increase the teacher's effectiveness and ability to teach. It will also greatly reduce the number of disruptive behaviors while teaching. Review these nine techniques before the first day of class. It may take time to remember and practice all of these techniques, but these simple techniques will benefit you and your students.

Suggested General Rules and Expectations

We suggest that a teacher keep the general rules and expectations simple and clear to prevent disruptive behavior, rather than providing a long list of "do's" and "don'ts." The two most basic behavior rules, which cover most behavior issues, are:

1. Be respectful.
2. Behave appropriately for the classroom setting.

If a student does something inappropriate for the classroom setting (whether or not they know it is inappropriate), calmly tell him/her which of their behaviors was inappropriate and that it should not be repeated.

Depending on the class context, the teacher may want to implement specific rules on attendance and electronic devices, but these two basic rules will cover most behavior issues.

Each group of students is different. There may be additional classroom management techniques that can help teachers effectively manage their individual classes. Research and implement any other techniques that may be appropriate for each class.

This unit is the first unit of the *FutureProfits* curriculum because it sets up an understanding of why money is so important and applicable to our lives, both today and in our future. Many choices made are directly related to money — choices based on available money or lack of money. Money often influences available choices. The amount of money one has or has access to, combined with the amount of knowledge about how the financial and power structures in our society work, will impact the choices and opportunities in life. Ultimately, having access to resources and information increases choices and opportunities, and having a greater range of choices increases the ability and freedom to control one's own future, which is the most essential form of power.

This unit establishes a foundation for the *Life Economics* curriculum with the understanding that most choices made about money are influenced by one's surroundings and background. The unit will help the students analyze the attitudes and assumptions they may bring with them, and break down any negative information they have received, opening the way for new information taught in later lessons that can help the students make healthy choices for their future.

Through this unit, students will...

- Gain confidence, knowledge, and insight, equipping and empowering them to take control of their life directions
- See that they do have options and opportunities
- See that there are ways they can leverage their choices now to increase their options and opportunities in the future
- Experience a sense of power, and be equipped to use their power for good in both their own lives and their communities

Youth are at a critical age. They can set themselves up for financial stability and success through the education and the financial training they receive. Most students have a clean slate financially, as they have not yet made decisions that would establish a pattern of debt, damage their credit history, or trap them in other ways. The financial understanding they attain now will inform them as they make key financial choices about saving, loans, and college, so they can navigate the financial system to their advantage and break the cycle of systemic and generational poverty.

Lesson Plans:

This unit begins by addressing power, and how the world has created systems that distribute power unequally. Youth in low-income neighborhoods often feel the effects of this, but do not necessarily grasp the bigger picture that would help them understand the system and navigate it more effectively. Many of these students come from situations where the cards are stacked against them. From their perspective, the system in the United States seems to predetermine the success of an individual, completely dependent on where an individual was born or what resources the individual possesses. In order to influence or break out of that system, students need to develop a deeper understanding of how the system perpetuates itself, and identify the ways that the system affects them individually.

Lessons 2 and 3 of this unit are set up to hear from the students. The activities are designed to establish a foundation for the FutureProfits classes by building rapport with the students. By acknowledging that students are the experts on their communities, the students become the teachers, increasing understanding by providing their perspectives and experiences. Additionally, this unit facilitates a process through which students can recognize how these perspectives and experiences will impact their financial lives. Students are given time to identify important aspects of their community (who are the shot-callers, what are the struggles, where is the community pride, what change they want for their future, etc.), and what their role is in their community. Further, students identify the messages about money that they are receiving, so they can make a conscious decision about which messages they want to incorporate in their own outlook on money.

Student success is critical — not only for them to sustain their lives, but also for them to be active contributors and leaders in the world. In order for students to succeed, they will need to understand how to engage with the power structures that exist in their community and the larger society, and how to position their lives for success within those structures. Lessons 4 and 5 address these power systems, individual choice within them, and how they impact lives presently and in the future. For students to succeed, they will also need to develop both their critical thinking skills and a vision for who they want to become, and then use their skills and vision to guide choices that build toward a positive future. Lesson 6 addresses making choices, specifically why it is important to consider how those choices impact the future. Students learn they can choose to increase power in their lives by making careful and informed decisions now.

Outline:

Lesson 1 – The Bean Game
Lesson 2 – Tell Me About Your World
Lesson 3 – Money Messages
Lesson 4 – Whose Life Would You Choose?
Lesson 5 – Power Spread
Lesson 6 – Choosing Power

Vocabulary:

- resources
- power
- powerlessness
- privilege
- *optional: capitalism*
- fast money

POWER

Power at its best is love implementing the demands of justice.
–Dr. Martin Luther King, Jr., Civil Rights Leader

Materials needed:

- 300 beans
- 30 Dixie® cups (one cup for each student)

Key Concepts:

1. A direct relationship exists between access to resources, financial status and power in our society.
2. Resources and power are distributed unequally, creating a cycle from one generation to the next.
3. Choices can be made that will help to break out of these cycles by developing our resources and increasing our power.

Prep Time: 10 minutes

Advance Preparation Tasks:

- Buy beans and Dixie cups
- Distribute different amounts of beans into each of the Dixie cups (between 3 and 15 beans per cup)
- Stack the cups so they are ready to pass out to students randomly and so that the beans are distributed disproportionately

Keep in Mind

- Be sensitive about the power dynamics drawn out by the game.
- When discussing power dynamics, be aware that community pride and personal image are strong forces in underprivileged communities.
- Bottom line: having real power is when an individual has the ability to make choices about his or her own destiny.

Some students may feel uncomfortable experiencing the power dynamics that the Bean Game draws out. Students may have strong reactions particularly to the position of "servant," either because they don't like being subject to another student's control or because they may react to the title itself as an affront to their personal image. Pride is often a strong force and motivator in underprivileged communities. For some, personal and family pride may be their most valuable possession, and maintaining that pride is crucial in sustaining them in the face of daily challenges. As issues of generational and systemic poverty come up throughout this lesson, be cautious about making statements that "label" their community as poor.

Pride can often act as a powerful motivator, driving students to succeed and reflect positively on their community. However, it can also be a street mentality that causes someone to be so protective of their persona that they would sacrifice anything else to protect it, even their own or someone else's life. This kind of pride can often hinder people from listening to any advice, which could help them improve their situation. Because pride is such a powerful force in low-income communities, a deliberately light tone should be set for the game, emphasizing that the game does not reflect actual status. It is an opportunity for students to observe power dynamics, and then process their observations and feelings about having or not having control.

Future lessons will help to provide an understanding that having real power is when an individual has the ability to make choices about his or her own destiny. This includes having a range of opportunities, with the freedom to choose among them, and be successful pursuing them. This game and the other activities and discussions throughout Unit 1 will help students to recognize and understand the power structures at work in their lives, so they can make choices about how to increase their power in existing systems.

Lesson Snapshot

Setting the Tone (5 minutes)
- Give brief background and why you are excited about class
- Share story about a significant financial experience
- Give an overview of the FutureProfits curriculum
- Establish expectations and ground rules for the class

Introduction (4 minutes)
- What does it mean to have power?
- What role does money play in having power?
- Introduce the Bean Game

Activity: Bean Game (20 minutes)
- Distribute beans in Dixie cups disproportionately and explain rules
- Play game for the remaining time of the activity, ideally allowing all of the beans and servants to become concentrated among only a couple of players

Discussion: Game Debrief (15 minutes)
- Process experiences and feelings from the game
- Process how this game is similar to or different from systemic power dynamics
- Focus on relationship between resources and opportunities or power

Lecture: The Relationship Between Resources and Power (5 minutes)
- Share stories of Adrianna and Michael to show the relationship between resources and power through the resource of education
- Explain how one can make choices to break the cycle
- Add any other examples of how power and money are related
- The cycle of power does not automatically determine their future or their ability to take control of what their future could look like

Wrap Up (1 minute)
- Understanding the system is the first step to changing it
- Continue to explore the concept of power and resources in upcoming lessons

Setting the Tone (suggested time: 5 minutes)

If you are beginning with a new group of students with whom you do not have existing relationships, spend a few minutes introducing yourself, giving an overview of the *FutureProfits* curriculum, and establishing expectations and ground rules for the class.

Begin with giving students some brief background information about yourself and about why you are excited about this class. You may want to share a story about a significant financial experience or lesson from your life that illustrates why it is so important to learn financial literacy. Consider a story about a first job, a lesson learned, credit cards, a major purchase, etc.

Draw from the following to introduce the curriculum: "The *FutureProfits* curriculum gives students a framework that empowers them to understand the importance of good decision-making, especially regarding educational, career, and personal financial choices. The curriculum teaches 'life economics,' which includes financial literacy through the lens of the specific experiences, attitudes, and needs of students who have been reared in a low-income environment. It gives students a deeper understanding of how the choices they make today will affect the life they lead tomorrow. Lessons include topics such as understanding power, building life skills, and achieving goals, in addition to the standard financial basics like budgets and banking."

Finally, give an overview of your expectations for every student. Do this as a collaborative process in which the class establishes expectations for themselves, for each other, and for you as the facilitator, or prepare a list of ground rules in advance, explaining them to the students now. Allow time for questions, and be sure that everyone understands the expectations.

Introduction (suggested time: 4 minutes)

This lesson will help students explore how power works, particularly in relationships between people with more power and people with less power. Ask the students, "What does it mean to have power?" and "What role does money play in having power?" These ideas will be examined through an activity called "The Bean Game." Emphasize that the game is for fun. The purpose of the lesson is to understand the idea of power. The game talks about servants to help prove a point. It does not mean that anyone in this class is actually a servant in real life. The game will be followed by a discussion about what feelings students experienced during the game.

Activity: Bean Game (suggested time: 20 minutes)

The purpose of the Bean Game is to help students understand the importance of the amount of resources they have when they enter the workforce. The beans signify resources in real life. There are certain factors outside of their control that influence the amount of resources they have (i.e., the elementary school district in which they grew up, the safety of the neighborhood in which they live, coming from a single-parent household, having a mental disability, or the education of their parents). But it is the intention of this curriculum to ultimately help students understand the importance of the choices they make today. Their personal ethical choices, educational and career paths, and the influence of the relationships around them (good or bad) will impact the amount of beans (or resources) they have when they enter the workforce. This will, in turn, impact their amount of opportunities in life, i.e., their power.

1. Give each student a Dixie cup with a predetermined amount of beans (between 3 and 15 beans). Pass out the cups of beans to each student, with the beans being disproportionately distributed. This reflects the uneven distribution of resources in society. Pass out beans, randomly in different amounts. Students who receive smaller amounts should not feel intentionally singled out.
2. Instruct the students that the goal is to increase their pile of beans by taking beans from their classmates. Beans are obtained by playing Rock, Paper, Scissors. (Remember Rock beats Scissors, Scissors beats Paper, and Paper beats Rock.) The winning player takes a bean from the losing player. However, there is a catch.
3. If students have equal bean wealth, the winner takes a bean from the loser. If students have unequal bean wealth, the student with more beans only has to win once before he or she can take a bean from the loser. The student with fewer beans has to win two times consecutively before he or she can take a bean from the loser.

4. When a losing player does not have a bean to give the winning player, he/she becomes the winning player's "servant." The player with no remaining beans must place a hand on the right shoulder of the person with beans and follow them around the classroom for the rest of the game.
5. If a player with servants and beans loses, he or she must give up the servant before giving up a bean. A servant is equal to one bean for trading purposes.
6. The game should go on for at least 15-20 minutes, ideally allowing enough time for all of the beans and servants to become concentrated among only a couple of players.

Discussion: Game Debrief (suggested time: 15 minutes)

The goal of this discussion is to help students process their experiences in the game, particularly any negative emotions brought up by the power dynamics they have just experienced. Discussion should also help students to examine how this game is similar to or different from systemic power dynamics in our society. Particular emphasis should be placed on comparing the beans to money and other resources. Take time as well to discuss the relationship between having access to resources and having power. Select from the following questions to stimulate discussion:

- Do you think the game was fair?
- How did it feel to start off with an advantage over others?
- How did it feel to start off with a disadvantage?
- How did it feel to be someone else's servant?
- How did it feel to have a servant or servants?
- Did anyone start off with a lot of beans and lose everything? How did that feel?
- Did anyone start off with very few beans and work your way up to having servants? How did that feel?
- Do you think this game is similar to or different from the way things work in our society? What is similar or different?

Note to Teacher

One primary goal of this exercise is to help students go beyond feelings of frustration or anger when confronted with unequal distribution of wealth. Realizing that education, employment, and housing impacts a person's level of personal power will help students better understand generational cycles of wealth and poverty, and how their choices continue or break the cycle in which they currently exist.

It will be important to direct students' negative feelings toward the system, and not toward individuals who have resources and power. Point out that some people who start with more resources will choose to help others in need. Bill Gates is one good example. You may also point out that the system itself gives people with more resources the advantage to gain wealth, and that in the process those individuals may not be purposely trying to take away from people who have less.

- What could the beans represent in our society? (What do people start out with different amounts of that gives them an advantage? Answers might include education, money, skill, connections, food/nutrition, medical care, transportation, type of housing, type and stability of employment, etc.)
- Do you think it is possible to change your position in society? Is it possible to start off with a lot and lose it, or to start off with very little and make it grow?
- What was the relationship between the amount of beans you had and the amount of power you had in the game? (What is the relationship between money/resources and power in society?)
- Does this experience change your perception of society? Do you feel sympathetic toward any particular groups of people?
- Did anyone develop a specific strategy for getting more beans? Do you think that is similar to or different from how people try to get resources and power in real life? (For example, a student with 10 beans might have realized that he should try to play Rock, Paper, Scissors only with students who had less beans, so that he was always in the position of power.)
- What might have happened if several people who started out with five beans decided to combine their resources and work together in the game? What are ways to do this in real life?

Conclude the discussion by giving the students the definitions of resources and power that will be used throughout FutureProfits. Write these definitions on the board.

- **Resources** are the supply of money, education, connections with people, transportation, health care, or personal skills and capabilities that can be drawn on in order to function effectively.
- **Power** is when an individual has the ability to make choices about his or her own destiny.

Then move on to the lecture to explain the relationship between resources and power.

Lecture: The Relationship Between Resources and Power

(suggested time: 5 minutes)

The purpose of this lecture is to communicate how resources and power are deeply related. To help explain this relationship, the cyclical relationship between wealth and education is outlined through the stories of two characters. Although this example is recommended, there are other examples of resources and power you can use, including the following:

- *The ability to choose the neighborhood in which you live and to own your own home*
- *The ability to choose a career (including the location of employment, convenience of work schedule, amount of physical strain, etc.)*
- *The ability to build savings and stay free of debt, and to choose a low-interest rate lender when obtaining a loan*

- *the ability to access high-quality health care, including preventive care, and to be protected from environmental health hazards in your neighborhood*

Decide how many of these to explain, based on available time and your students' level of understanding.

Teach the following example of the relationship between wealth and education to explain the relationship between power and resources. *Draw the following diagram on a white board or flip chart paper while lecturing:*

Wealthy Income and Education Cycle

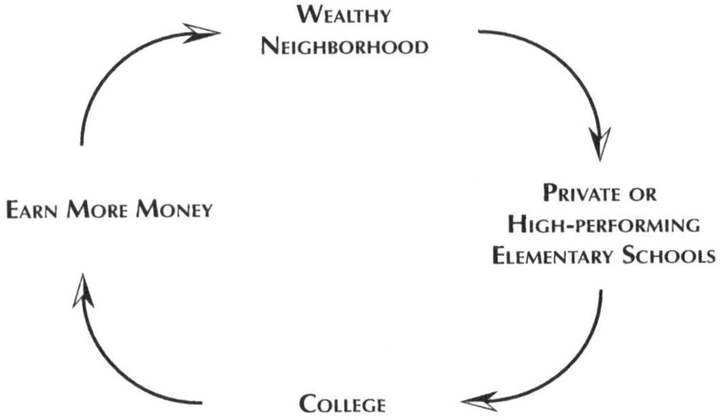

The following is a suggested script for the lecture:

Education is a key example of the cyclical nature of the system. Let's look at the story of Adrianna. Adrianna grew up in a neighborhood that was relatively safe and secure. Both of her parents had college degrees and made enough money to buy a house in a wealthy neighborhood. The property taxes of the homes in these neighborhoods go toward the schools to provide students like Adrianna with a great education. Her parents spent time reading with her every night when she was in elementary school, and helped her with her homework in middle school. Because of this, she worked hard and got good grades. Adrianna learned from an early age that she could be anything she wanted to be. Her parents expected her to go to college, and set up tutors and extra-curricular activities to help her get good grades and have a good standing among her classmates. Adrianna had been prepared to go to college, where she could get the education she needed to get a job with enough money to be able to buy a house in a wealthy neighborhood. She would most likely meet a nice man, get married and have kids. Her kids would then have the same opportunities that her parents gave her. This is an example of the cycle that can continue because of wealth and education.

The cycle is similar in low-income neighborhoods. *Draw this second diagram on a white board or flip chart paper while lecturing:*

Low Income and Education Cycle

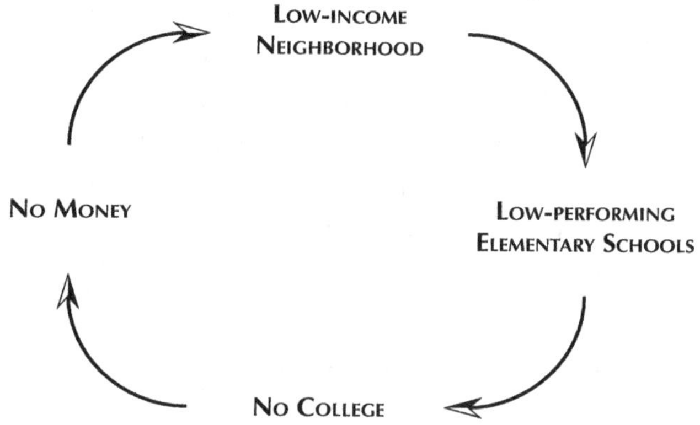

Now let's look at the story of Michael. Michael grew up in a low-income neighborhood. His mom was a single mom and had to work three jobs to make ends meet. Because his mom was so busy throughout the day, and preoccupied with concerns of day-to-day survival, she wasn't able to read with Michael at night or help him with his homework. By the time Michael turned 12, he was expected to provide childcare for his younger brother and sister, so he didn't really even have the time for homework. He started to get bad grades and although his teachers helped him for a while, he continually regressed, so they eventually stopped trying to help him improve. He didn't know of any after-school programs that could help. Because his mom didn't go to college, and was working three minimum wage jobs, he didn't view college as a realistic option for himself. After struggling through high school, he eventually got whatever job was available, regardless of how much it paid. He just had to get some income to help out his family. Because Michael never got a college degree, he struggled to get jobs and make enough money to live comfortably. He had to borrow money, which limited his choices as to how to spend his income, because once he got it, he had to pay back the money he borrowed as soon as possible. Michael eventually had limited choices as to where he could live when he started a family, and the cycle continued with his children as well.

Note to Teacher

School systems in lower-income areas are often not as strong as those in wealthy areas. This is compounded by the fact that the realities of survival for lower-income families may cause education to be less of a priority in the home. Because of this, be sensitive not to put down anyone's family when describing this cycle.

However, education is also a perfect example of a way individuals can make choices to break the cycle. Some students who went to high-performing elementary schools like Adrianna may choose not to take advantage of the educational opportunities they receive, and they won't be as successful as their parents. Other students like Michael whose parents did not go to college may choose to work hard in school, even amidst their responsibilities at home, or access helpful resources around them like after-school programs. This may position students to choose college or professional training, which may lead to having a higher income, thus enabling them to give their children an advantage within the system. The cycle has successfully been broken. Instead of being stuck in either of the cycles in which Adrianna or Michael were stuck, students may be able to live in a system that can be more healthy. *Draw the following diagram on a white board or flip chart paper:*

Alternative Income and Education Cycle

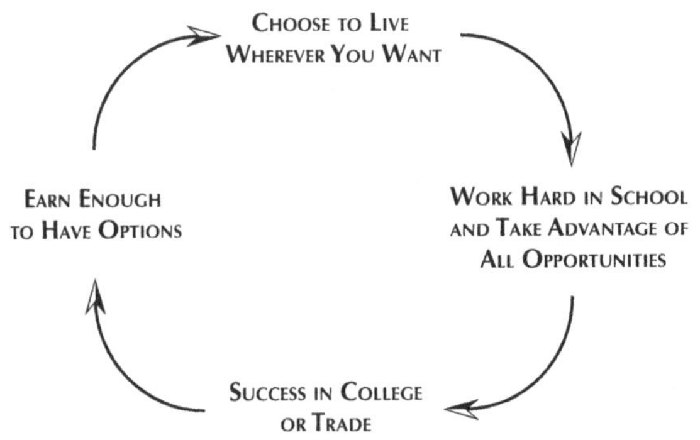

These are some of the cycles covered over the next six lessons with discussions about how money revolves in your neighborhood.

End the lecture by emphasizing that the cycle of power does not automatically determine their future or their ability to take control of what their future could look like. Every person has the potential to change his or her position within the system. Like in the Bean Game, starting out with a lot of beans probably does make it easier for that individual to gain even more beans. Emphasize to the students that they are at a place in their lives right now where their choices will impact the amount of beans they have when they enter the workforce, which will help them to increase their beans, no matter how many they may have started with. The information that is taught in *FutureProfits* will help students build their skills, tools, and knowledge so they are better able to understand the system and to gain power over their own futures.

Wrap Up (suggested time: 1 minute)

This lesson intends for students to leave class feeling empowered by any new understanding they may have gained, not discouraged by the unequal distribution of resources in society. Remind students that the first step to changing a system is to understand how the system currently works and how it could or should work differently. In working to develop their understanding of how power works in society, they have already taken a step toward increasing their ability to change their own position and role within that system.

Looking Ahead:

- Continue to explore concepts of power and resources
- Encourage students to look for relationships between power and resources in their own lives
- Examine the communities in which students live

Thank students for their participation.

Vocabulary:

- resources
- power

Preservation of one's own culture does not require contempt or disrespect for other cultures.
–Cesar Chavez, Civil Rights Activist

Materials needed:

- 7 sheets of poster or flip chart paper, labeled with headings
- Post-it® notes (7 per student, plus extras)
- *Optional Activity: Word Association Game – 1.2.1**

Key Concepts:

1. The students are experts on their own communities.
2. It is important to recognize any assumptions taken for granted about power systems and our role in those systems.

Prep Time: 10 minutes

Advance Preparation Tasks:

- Prepare Post-it note posters (see Activity: Post-it Note Brainstorm)

Note to Teacher

If your students are fairly active in discussion, the Post-it Note Brainstorm Activity will be sufficient to receive information from the students about their community. However, if students are less engaged, the Word Association Game is an optional activity to download online that will help them come up with ideas to contribute for the Post-it Note Brainstorm Activity. Consider adding it before the Post-it Note Brainstorm Activity.*

*For all additional resources, including handouts, video links and helpful websites, see www.futureprofitsresources.org

Keep in Mind

- This lesson will help students learn through participation and observation.
- Listen to their opinions and do not try to correct them if you disagree.
- Establish good rapport with the students by listening and validating their experiences and perspectives.
- Students may share vulnerable perspectives. Therefore, set a strong rule of respect so all students feel valued.

This lesson serves two main purposes. The first is to give students the chance to begin examining the power structures and systems with which they are most familiar—those in their communities. Students are probably already making assumptions about how the world works and how they see themselves fitting into that world. Unfortunately, some students may not have healthy models of how power is attained. **This is not the time to directly correct or contradict students' opinions or assumptions.** Students should begin developing an awareness of how power functions in their community, so they can become better equipped to make more informed personal choices (in regard to power, influence, pride, their future, etc.).

The second purpose is to begin establishing good rapport with students. Before expecting students to respect and trust the information provided, it is important to take the time to learn from them first. Teenagers have plenty of adults who tell them what to do, but may have less experience with adults who value their experiences and perspectives. If you are not from the same background as your students, asking them to educate you about their world will help to show that you do not consider yourself an expert who expects to solve problems you may not truly understand. You may be offended by what you hear. There could be opinions mentioned about their community and surrounding communities that may seem rude or in need of correction. For example, students may have a negative view of the police because of a past experience. However, it is really important to allow students the freedom to express themselves freely without correction. Strive to understand how the students may feel, keeping your personal emotions or reactions retained.

Many of the lessons rely heavily on discussion, and establish you and the students as collaborators in the learning process. In this lesson, they are teaching you and each other, and there are no right or wrong answers. Your role is that of a facilitator. As a facilitator, you are allowing the opinions of the students to sit out in the open. Try to guide conversations so that students listen to each other and begin to realize why they view their community the way that they do. If your class is diverse, with a mix of ethnicities and / or socioeconomic backgrounds, this lesson will be more delicate, as the students may describe more than one community. Some tensions may exist. Set the tone by explaining that everyone is both teacher and learner, and it is important to act as both respectfully. Students will say things about their community that reflect their perspective. Whether the statements are objectively true or not, they are real from the students' perspective. Even if students are joking about something they say, there will still be an element of truth to their comments. Encourage students to be real in their reflections, but to also respect each other in discussing topics on which they may disagree.

Lesson Snapshot

Review (5 minutes)
- Review the bean game and ask about the relationship between resources and power

Introduction (5 minutes)
- Share a story about your background and the community that you came from
- Learn from students about their community
- Set up ground rules of respect

Activity: Post-it Note Brainstorm (20 minutes)
- Give each student 7 Post-its and have them write on each and place them on the 7 large poster/flip chart papers around the room

Discussion: Post-it Note Brainstorm (15 minutes)
- Pick one to three Post-it note responses from each poster that would be productive and/or edifying to discuss
- Ask the class to stand up if they agree that the statement accurately describes their community and why
- Discuss a couple of the responses from the students
- Draw out some of the main things the students have identified about their community that will continue to shape their understanding of how money revolves in the community

Wrap up (5 minutes)
- Next Lesson:
  - Who has influence on us?
  - What messages do we receive from different people in our lives?

Review (suggested time: 5 minutes)

Remind students of the Bean Game, which helped students to start thinking about the relationship between resources and power in our society. Ask a few student volunteers to share the following:

- What was something new you learned from the Bean Game and our discussion last time we met?
- Did you notice any examples of the relationship between resources and power in your life or in the society around you since our last class?

Introduction (suggested time: 5 minutes)

This lesson depends on the students sharing with you and with each other their perceptions about the communities they come from. It is generally helpful, before asking the students to be vulnerable, if the instructor is the first one to take that risk. Start today's class by sharing a story about your background and the community you come from, so the students can get to know you a little.

Note to Teacher

Even through your background might be different than your students', it's important to present yourself in a way that is still relatable to them. Don't pretend to know what life is like in their community, or what struggles they have faced. Instead, draw out similarities about your communities, or share about a struggle your family or community has faced. If you share about struggles, choose ones that will be credible with students so you are not dismissed as not knowing what a real struggle is. Remember, no matter what your background is, be genuine about your story. For instance, if your upbringing was more privileged than theirs, acknowledge this and admit that you don't know the challenges they face. Your students will respect your honesty and willingness to admit what you don't know.

Following are a couple of examples of the stories our staff share about themselves:

An example of a story if you are from the same community as your students:
"I grew up in East Palo Alto, California, like many of you have. It was a little tough growing up in my neighborhood. There was gang violence, my parents didn't have a lot of money, and there were a lot of negative influences. But, on the other hand, there were also a lot of great places and a lot of great people around to help me to stay focused on success and out of trouble. I was taught to have a lot of pride in my neighborhood, and to give back to my neighborhood when I was able. And once I graduated from college, that's exactly what

I did. From the financial knowledge that I've gained from college and through the network I have built since college, I got the opportunity to teach in the same community where I grew up. I was able to give back the knowledge I've learned in order to change lives in the community to which I am loyal. I feel like you can relate to me because I understand the community, I look like the community, and I've experienced some of the same things you may be dealing with today. I hope that you can see the fact that I'm young, and this is definitely something you can do. You can follow your passions at a young age, and get paid for it."

An example of a story to share if you are not from the same community as your students:
"I grew up in Flagstaff, Arizona. Flagstaff is a small college town full of forests. The closest city is a 20-mile drive away, and the closest large city is a two-hour drive away. So as you can imagine, it's very different from what you all may experience as the city life. As I've been a part of your community, I've learned so much about the differences and even seen some similarities. Each community has its own character, and so although I'm from a different background, I really appreciate being able to learn about the character of your community. Later we'll be talking about the struggles going on in this neighborhood. One of the struggles going on in my community growing up was that there was nothing to do in Flagstaff. Now looking back, I could have gone hiking during the summers or snowboarding when it snows during the winters, but when I was a teenager, all we did was go to the movies and play pranks on friends. A lot of people got into drugs and partying, too, since it felt like there was nothing else to do. A darker struggle in this community was suicide. We have train tracks that run right through the middle of town, and it's usually freight trains that come through the town. I knew or knew about some of my peers who committed suicide on the tracks. This was definitely a struggle in my neighborhood, and though it was more drastic than the struggle of having nothing to do, both of these struggles are important in their own ways."

RESPECT

Explain to the students that the purpose of the lesson today is to learn from each other about how we view our community. Tell the students that you hope they will agree to be your teachers. Give them the stage, and tell them there are no wrong or right opinions. Set up some ground rules for the students so it is a safe environment for students to be honest. RESPECT should be the main rule which means the following:

1. Listen to each other's opinions.
2. It is okay to disagree, but do not put another person in the classroom on the spot.
3. Do not make or write comments that attack other people. Comments that insult a particular race or other group of people are not appropriate.

Ask the students if there is anything else that they would like to include.

Activity: Post-It Note Brainstorm (suggested time: 20 minutes)

Write the following headings on seven pieces of poster paper or flip chart paper. Then hang the posters on the walls, spaced around the room. You can choose to write the entire question on each poster, or write only the shortened headings, and then read the expanded questions aloud to help students think about each heading.

Note to Teacher

During this exercise, students may include racially degrading or disrespectful comments on their Post-it notes. If this happens, say that you appreciate the honesty and willingness to express their opinion, but that you are taking the comment off the poster to help maintain a safe environment of respect for everyone. Be aware that your students may believe false stereotypes of people from different ethnic or socio-economic backgrounds.

1. Shot Callers (Who calls the shots or has the most influence in your neighborhood?)
2. Who's Looked Down On? (Who receives the least amount of respect within your community? To whom do you feel superior?)
3. Struggles (What struggles does your community face?)
4. What's cool? (What is popular in your community?)
5. Community Pride (What gives you pride about your community?)
6. Change for the Future (What do you want to change in your community? What are your hopes for the future? How will you change these things?)
7. Your Role (What is your place in the community? How do you make a difference?)

Pass out seven Post-it notes to each student and provide extras at the front of the class. On each Post-it, students should write their personal answers to each of the seven questions. Students should complete at least one Post-it for each poster, but they can get extra Post-it notes from you if they want to provide more than one answer to some of the questions. Emphasize that this activity is anonymous, so they should not write their names on the Post-its and they can feel free to be honest about their opinions. They should stick their completed Post-it notes underneath the heading on the corresponding poster paper.

Discussion: Post-it Note Brainstorm (suggested time: 15 minutes)

End class with a brief discussion about some of the opinions students have contributed to the posters. Pick one to three Post-it note responses from each poster, and read them aloud, one at a time. For example, you might say (based on the information written on the student's Post-it), "Rent prices getting higher is a struggle facing this community," or "The murals in neighborhood parks are a source of pride in this community." After reading each one, ask the class to stand up if they agree that the statement accurately describes their community. Ask students who are standing to share why they agree, and ask those who remain sitting why they do not agree. Move around the room, briefly discussing a couple of responses to each of the seven questions. Though you will not have time to have the class react to every statement on each poster, you and your co-teachers should review the posters later to get additional insight into students and their perspectives on their community.

Note to Teacher

It's suggested that you only pick one to three Post-it note responses from each poster for discussion. When selecting notes, try to pick ones that provide insight into the community as a whole, versus ones that might single out a particular student. Also, look for notes with different handwriting, to ensure that you select ones from a variety of students, as well as ideas that appear more than once. This will allow you to discuss the most common perspectives within the community.

After the discussion has finished, ask the students if any of them have gained a different perspective of their community by listening to each other. Draw out some of the main things the students have identified about their community that will continue to shape their understanding of how money revolves in the community. For example, did the students find that the shot-callers are the ones with a lot of money? Did they find that the people identified as "looked down on" were generally without money? Identifying this information about the community and the students' roles within it will help them understand how money and power function in the community, and will help them to make more informed choices for how they want to live their lives.

Note to Teacher

Save the "Shot Callers" and "Who's Looked Down On" posters created in this lesson for use again in Lesson 4.

Wrap up (suggested time: 5 minutes)

Thank students for sharing their input about their communities and setting the foundation for much of the learning ahead.

Looking Ahead:

- Who has influence on us?
- What messages do we receive from different people in our lives?

Vocabulary:

None

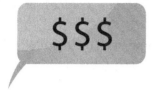

Your beliefs become your thoughts.
Your thoughts become your words.
Your words become your actions.
Your actions become your habits.
Your habits become your values.
Your values become your destiny.
–Mahatma Gandhi,
Political and Spiritual Leader

Materials needed:

- 3 envelopes containing prepared materials for Puzzle Pop game
- 5-7 "Agree" and "Disagree" signs – 1.3.1*
- *Optional: Prizes for Puzzle Pop game*

Key Concepts:

1. We are constantly receiving messages about money from various people around us, and it is important to be aware of who is communicating what message.
2. Each of us must decide for ourselves about which messages we agree and disagree, and how much we will allow those messages to influence our decisions.

Prep Time: 30 minutes

Advance Preparation Tasks:

- Prepare materials for Puzzle Pop game (see specific instructions in the Puzzle Pop Activity)
- Prepare "Agree" and "Disagree" signs by copying signs and cutting in half
- *Optional: Buy prizes for the winners of the Puzzle Pop game*

**For all additional resources, including handouts, video links and helpful websites, see www.futureprofitsresources.org*

Keep in Mind

- This lesson gives students the opportunity to begin examining both the positive and negative perspectives they hear about money.
- Encourage students to make deliberate and conscious choices about which perspectives they adopt for themselves.
- Attitudes common in low-income communities come from the mentality that says, "Get it by any means," or "I deserve to have something good, and I should give it to myself."

Similar to Lesson 2, the main objectives of this lesson are for the students to experience being heard and for you to understand more about where the students are coming from. This continues to build a foundation for future lessons, and additionally gives students the opportunity to begin examining the perspectives they hear about money. Hopefully this lesson will encourage them to make deliberate and conscious choices about which perspectives they adopt for themselves. Your students may come from backgrounds that are very different from your own, and may have attitudes that you might find difficult to understand or accept. Validate students for sharing openly, and affirm that there are no right or wrong answers in this discussion. As students gain new knowledge and skills in the coming lessons, they will have opportunities to reexamine whether they want to adopt different perspectives about money. For this lesson, the focus is on learning about students' perceptions of money without influencing them one way or another.

One attitude you may encounter is the philosophy of "Get it by any means," which can come from the experience of constantly living in survival mode. Teens from high-risk communities often do little long-range planning, either because traumatic experiences have taught them that the future is uncertain, or because encountering frequent barriers has taught them that they shouldn't bother trying. Either experience can lead teens to live for the moment, seeking short-term relief, without considering long-term goals or avoiding activities that could have negative consequences for their future. Additionally, the mentality of "I deserve to have something good, and I should give it to myself" can develop, while living in poverty. Because later lessons will directly address this attitude through a variety of activities and discussions, do not attempt to change students' perspectives during this lesson.

Lesson Snapshot

Review (5 minutes)
- Recap what you learned from students last class about their neighborhood

Introduction (5 minutes)
- Tell the focus for the lesson
- Share a story about who has influenced the way you think about money

Activity #1: Puzzle Pop (7 minutes)
- Split class into 3 groups and give each group a prepared envelope
- First group to unscramble lyrics and artist's name moves to the prize round
- Prize Round: Correcty name the title of the song...and win!

Discussion #1: Puzzle Pop (8 minutes)
- Ask the class what each song lyric tells them about how that particular artist views money

Activity #2: Representing Perspectives (15 minutes)
- 3-4 students per group; assign groups to a people group to represent; give each group two signs (agree and disagree)
- Read aloud a statement and have groups raise their signs
- Ask students why their people group would agree or disagree
- Repeat this process, discussing as many statements as time allows

Discussion #2: Personal Perspectives (5 minutes)
- Read 5-6 of the statements that could be considered controversial, and ask students whether they agree or disagree with each statement
- Tell students that we each have a responsibility to choose the messages with which we agree about money because these messages impact how we make our choices with money

Wrap up (5 minutes)
- Thank the students for sharing their input
- Encourage students to decide whether they agree or disagree with the "money messages" they hear throughout the day

Review (suggested time: 5 minutes)

Recap what was discussed during the last lesson about their neighborhood by doing the following:

- Reaffirm their perspectives about their community and thank the class for their participation in the discussion about their community
- Highlight some of the new things learned about community strengths and areas of improvement

Introduction (suggested time: 5 minutes)

Focus for this lesson: Examining how our backgrounds and communities influence us; looking specifically at what influences the ideas we have about money and where we get those ideas.

Before moving into the lesson, share a story about who or what has influenced the way you think about and handle money. One option is to talk about a person who taught you about money when you were growing up and how your life is different because of that person (this could be a family member, a singer, a teacher, etc.). Another option is to tell a story about a person who handles money in a way you admire and explain why. An example of each type is provided below:

Who taught you about money: "I first discovered that saving money makes your money multiply in about the 7th grade when I started getting an allowance, so the process of saving became one of my joys. I kind of took it overboard though, and became a penny pincher. Basically I was saving money just for the fun of being able to say I had a lot of money. So when the time arrived for the new Madden video game to be released, naturally I didn't want to spend my money. So I asked my mom to buy it for me, and she began to teach me a very valuable lesson about money. She told me that she wasn't going to buy the video game because I had enough money to do so. She went on to tell me that money has no true value; it is the individual who gives money value. Saving is good, but you should have a purpose for saving money, instead of saving it just to admire it. When you have money to spend, use it as long as you are spending wisely. After all, it's only useable while we're alive, and you can't spend it when you're dead. That taught me how to be responsible with my money, and also the value and purpose of money."

Someone whose approach to money you admire: "The person I always admired for the way he dealt with money when I was growing up was P. Diddy. He has risen from a poor section of New York all the way to Fortune 500 success, but on his journey to success, one story always stood out to me as a kid. When he was 13, he wanted a job to make money that he could call his own. He was told that he needed to be 14 to have his own paper route, but he wanted that particular job, so the rules didn't stop him. First, he negotiated a deal with one of the paperboys for him to split the profit 50/50. After that deal was successful, he negotiated more deals with the paper boys around the neighborhood until he monopolized the paper route. He ended up making $600 a week at the age of 13 before he was even able to qualify for a paper boy position! This story taught me that entrepreneurship starts young, and that success can always be obtained, but is not always a given. It starts with you."

Activity #1: Puzzle Pop (suggested time: 7 minutes)

This game encourages students to recognize that they are hearing messages about money from popular culture all the time without necessarily realizing it. Do not make judgments, positive or negative, on those messages, but continue to let the students teach about their world. Facilitate an experience that fosters awareness about how the songs students regularly listen to contain messages about money. Encourage students to make informed decisions about which of those messages they adopt for themselves.

Advance Preparations:

1. Choose a lyric from three popular songs that contain messages about money. The main theme of the whole song does not necessarily have to be about money as long as the line contains a clear message about money. Choose any song with which your students are familiar. For suggestions, see www.futureprofitsresources.org.
2. Write the words from the song lyric, and the artist's name, on flashcards, with only one word on each card. Use a total of 12-15 flashcards.
3. Shuffle the completed cards and place them in an envelope.
4. Prepare three envelopes, one for each song.

In-Class Directions:

1. Divide the students into three groups.
2. Provide each group with a prepared envelope.
3. Tell students that they have to put pieces of the song lyric and the artist's name in the correct

order. The first group to put them in order correctly enters the prize round.
4. For the prize round, instruct the winning group to name the song title that corresponds to their lyric. If they don't name the song correctly, then the next group to correctly order their lyric has the opportunity to steal by naming the correct song title corresponding to their lyric.
5. The first team to enter the prize round and correctly give their song title wins the game. If no group is able to correctly name their song, the group that put their lyric in order fastest is the winner.

Discussion #1: Puzzle Pop (suggested time: 8 minutes)

Ask the class what each song lyric tells them about how that particular artist views money. Consider asking:

- Does the artist view money as good or bad?
- What emotions does the artist express in relation to money?
- In your own words, how would you summarize the message the artist is communicating about money?
- What reasons might the artist have for viewing money this way?
- Is the artist's view of money similar to or different from your own view of money?

Activity #2: Representing Perspectives (suggested time: 15 minutes)

This activity is designed to identify what students think that people who might have influence over them would say about money.

Directions:
1. Divide the class into groups of 3 or 4 students.
2. Assign each group of students a "people group" they will represent. Suggested groups are:
    - parents or guardians
    - themselves
    - hip hop culture
    - billionaire investors (Bill Gates, Warren Buffet, Oprah Winfrey Steve Jobs, Donald Trump)
    - your neighborhood culture
    - advertising companies
    - religious leaders
    - mentors and teachers
3. Give each group two signs: "AGREE" and "DISAGREE."
4. Each statement is a message about money that will be read out loud. Each group will decide

whether the person or group they are representing would agree or disagree with the statement. After they discuss as a group, one person from the group will hold up either the "AGREE" sign or the "DISAGREE" sign (see below for a list of statements).

5. After the students, answering from the assigned perspective, indicate whether their group agrees or disagrees with the statement, have two to three groups explain their choice. Why does the group representing parents think that parents would agree with the statement? Why does the group representing local neighborhood culture say they would disagree?
6. Repeat this process, discussing as many statements as time allows.

Choose from the following statements about money or come up with your own:

- The most important thing in life is money.
- Your value is based on how much you make.
- Make as much money as you can with as little work as possible.
- Get your money any way you can.
- A penny saved is a penny earned.
- Money doesn't grow on trees.
- Teenagers are old enough to bring in money for the family.
- Hard work pays off.
- Get rich or die trying.
- If you don't work, you don't eat.
- Parents should give their kids money for anything they request.
- You can use money to make money.
- Don't work hard for money. Make your money work hard for you.
- The poor are getting poorer while the rich are getting richer.
- The more money you give, the more money you receive.
- Money should be used to help people.
- If you don't grind, you don't shine.
- Money is power.
- Money makes the world go 'round.
- The best things in life are free.

In a Spanish-speaking class, you can also use the following:

- No puedes sacar sangre de una piedra. (You can't get blood out of a rock.)

- No tengo ni un centavo para acer rezar un ciego. (I don't even have one cent to make a blind man pray.)

Discussion #2: Personal Perspectives (suggested time: 5 minutes)

This discussion will give the students an opportunity to represent themselves. Choose five to six of the statements that may be controversial and likely spark discussion among the students. Ask students by a show of hands who agrees or disagrees with each statement. Ask students from each group to explain why they agree or disagree, and write down key points on the board.

Note to Teacher

Remember, this exercise is a chance for your students to express their current opinions about money, without being corrected. Later lessons are designed to help them reexamine their views and perspective on money. Try and make this discussion an open environment where they can put the ideas they have into words, and where you can listen to how they currently view money.

Explain that everyone takes in a lot of different messages from the people and media around them. It is unlikely they will agree with all the messages received from any one person. It is important to take responsibility for examining the messages received and then develop your own opinions. We tend to agree with the messages we've received from people whom we trust and respect. In the end, though, each of us has to decide for ourselves which messages we agree with and want to live by, and which messages do not fit the way we want to live our lives.

Wrap Up (suggested time: 5 minutes)

FutureProfits lessons will introduce a lot of messages about money. Some messages will match with messages they have heard in the past, and other messages may conflict with things they have learned from other people in their lives. The curriculum will serve to inform students so they are equipped to make positive decisions for themselves as it relates to money. Encourage students to pay attention to the messages they hear throughout the day about money and to think about whether they personally agree or disagree with each message.

Thank the students for their participation and for sharing their opinions about money. Tell them that next time we meet, we will examine the lives of two men to see how their different perspectives on money influenced the decisions they made in life.

Vocabulary:

None

Additional Resources:

For possible songs to use for the Puzzle Pop activity, go to www.futureprofitsresources.org.

Whose life will you choose?

Materials needed:

- Chris Gardner biography – 1.4.1*
- Felix Mitchell biography – 1.4.2*
- "Whose Life Would You Choose" worksheet – 1.4.3*
- "Shot Callers" and "Who's Looked Down On" posters from Lesson 2 (both the original posters and summarized versions)

Everyone thinks of changing the world,
but no one thinks of changing himself.
–Leo Tolstoy, Author

Key Concepts:

1. It is important to examine the reasons why we think certain people are the shot callers and/ or certain people are those on whom others look down.
2. The amount of power an individual has is related to the choices a person makes.
3. Your choices now affect the outcome of your future.

Prep Time: 15 minutes

For all additional resources, including handouts, video links and helpful websites, see www.futureprofitsresources.org

Advance Preparation Tasks:

- Make 6 copies of the Chris Gardner biography and cut into Part 1, Part 2, and Part 3
- Make 6 copies of the Felix Mitchell biography and cut into Part 1, Part 2, and Part 3
- Make a copy of the "Whose Life Would You Choose" worksheet for each student
- Using the information students provided during the Post-it notes brainstorm in Lesson 2, build a list of "Shot Callers" and a list of "Who's Looked Down On" on new posters with writing large enough for the class to read

Keep in Mind

- In under-privileged neighborhoods, "negative" role models often appear to have the most power, and therefore, may be appealing to students.
- Urban culture and popular media does not often glorify or encourage examples of people who obtained power through healthy avenues.
- Through observing power in two men's lives, students will understand that sometimes less glamorized roles of power are actually more stable and offer greater freedom.

In under-privileged neighborhoods, "negative" role models can end up being highly respected. Gang leaders and drug dealers may appear to have more resources and power, and therefore, more success than anyone else in their communities. They also may contribute to their communities in positive ways that younger community members look up to. An example of this is Felix Mitchell, who is discussed during this lesson. Meanwhile, teens may not see many examples of people from their community who became successful through healthier avenues because they may not be as highly visible or glorified by urban culture and popular media. Many teens believe that the system is stacked in such a way that it will never allow them to change their circumstances. Given this sense of discouragement, the apparently glamorous and successful lives of rich and powerful gangsters are understandably appealing and may seem like the best path to moving beyond a subsistence income. Students will gain a more informed and complete perspective on the pros and cons of different life choices.

For the purposes of this lesson, power is defined as the ability to make choices about one's own circumstances and destiny. **The goal is not to glorify the kind of power that can be used to control other people.** The impression that becoming a corporate executive is the only way to succeed should also not be reinforced. Students are encouraged to make choices that will lessen their feelings of powerlessness. The goal of this lesson is to help students understand that sometimes less glamorized roles of power are actually more stable and offer greater freedom. The discussion and lecture in this lesson are crucial to communicating a new perspective. Make sure that Chris Gardner's story is lifted in high esteem, and shown as an example of someone whose choices consistently maintained and increased genuine power.

However, this understanding will have more impact if students are enabled to discover it for themselves. Avoid lecturing students on the "right" decisions for their lives, which will communicate that you do not actually believe they can be trusted to make choices for their own futures. Instead, try to facilitate a process through which students recognize for themselves (and in discussion with each other) that having the appearance of power is not necessarily the same as having genuine power. Help them see that having power is first and foremost about being in a position to make choices that will determine your own path.

Lesson Snapshot

Review (5 minutes)
- Ask students to share the messages with which they personally agree or disagree the most

Introduction (2 minutes)
- Remind the students of the categories discussed from the Post-it Note Brainstorm Activity, specifically "Shot Callers" and "Who's Looked Down On"
- Today's Lesson: Power vs. powerlessness

Lecture #1: Defining Power and Powerlessness (5 minutes)
- Connection between money and power
- Definition of power and powerless
- Share a personal story about power or powerlessness with the definitions given
- "Shot-Callers" vs. "Who's Looked Down On" — Are they connected to power and powerlessness?
- Understanding why people do or do not have power can help us learn how to develop genuine power in our own lives
- Examine and discuss the reasons why we see people as powerful
- Tell students the following activity focuses on understanding power through the lives of two men

Activity: Whose Life Would You Choose? (20 minutes)
- Break the class into six groups
- Give each student a "Whose Life Would You Choose" worksheet
- Give each group Part 1 of each biography; students read both biographies and complete Part 1 of the worksheet; discuss each question from worksheet.
- Repeat with Part 2 of the biographies
- Ask the class, "Where do you think these men's lives go from here?"
- Repeat with Part 3 of the biographies

Discussion: Whose Life Would You Choose? (5 minutes)
- Discuss the outcome, success, and power of each man's life
- Discuss other examples of choices in which the consequences of the decision would have a significant impact on the outcome in life

Lecture #2: Having Genuine Power (8 minutes)

- Tell the students a personal story about a person you admired when you were their age, and the ways you patterned your life after that person
- When choosing whom we admire, it is important to consider the question, "Are we admiring the appearance of success, or real and long-lasting success?"
- Recap stories of two men, focusing on the following:
  - These two men had similar backgrounds and similar financial struggles, but different outlooks on how to achieve success
  - Negative power is not true power
  - Our choices now impact the outcome in our lives years down the road
  - Seek positive power and persevere in times of struggle

Wrap up (5 minutes)

- Refer back to the Lesson 2 list of the people whom students considered to be the shot callers and those looked down on, and evaluate the "outcome" of their choices now
- Next lesson: How our power can be affected by our circumstances

Review (suggested time: 5 minutes)

Thank the students for their participation last class and remind them of some of the messages discussed about money. Ask students if they recognized any other messages they received from their surroundings since the last class. Ask a few students to share one to two messages with which they personally agree the most and those with which they disagree the most.

Introduction (suggested time: 2 minutes)

Remind the students of the categories discussed regarding their neighborhood from the Post-it Note Brainstorm Activity in Lesson 2. Two of the categories were "Shot Callers" and "Who's Looked Down On." Today's lesson will go more in depth with these categories and explore what it means to have power and to be powerless.

Lecture #1: Defining Power and Powerlessness (suggested time: 5 minutes)

1. Begin by reminding the students why power is related to money so they will easily make the connection in their mind. The concept was introduced through the Bean Game in Lesson 1, and depending on their level of understanding, may need a more thorough explanation now. The explanation should refer back to the experience of the Bean Game and cover the following:

- Review the relationship between money and power.
- Introduce the definition of **powerlessness** as "having a lack of opportunities and choices about your future." (Write the definition on the board.)
- Review the definition of **power** as "having the ability to make choices about your own destiny." (Write the definition on the board.)
- One of the goals of *FutureProfits* is to increase your knowledge so you will understand how to use your resources and can increase your power.

Power vs. Powerlessness

For ideas, draw from the following:
Think about the first lesson, when we played the Bean Game. What was frustrating for some of you? *(Allow a few responses.)* It was frustrating that the students who started out with more beans could take beans more easily than the people who started out with less. Those who had the most beans clearly had the advantage. When you started out with few beans, it was harder to win, and you probably ended up as a servant, under someone else's control. "Having a lack of opportunities and choices about your future" is the definition of **powerlessness**, and it is very frustrating to feel like you don't have much of a choice in what happens to you. The choices and opportunities you will have are impacted by two things: the amount of resources, particularly money, that you have or to which you have access, and the amount of knowledge you have about how to make the system work for you. Having control over resources and having knowledge about how best to use those resources will give you an advantage, similar to starting the game with more beans.

If being powerless means having a lack of opportunities and choices about your future, what do you think power means? (Allow a few responses. If students suggest that power means controlling other people, ask if it is necessary to control others to have power, and ask whether there is a step in between being controlled and controlling other people. Then offer the following definition.) The most basic form of **power** is "having the ability to make choices about your own destiny." If you are able to make your own decisions about where you go in life, you have power. The more resources and knowledge you have, similar to the more beans you had in the Bean Game, the more likely you will be in a position to control of your own future. One of the goals of *FutureProfits* is to increase your knowledge so you will understand how to use your resources and can increase your power. We want you to be able to have power and use it for good. And having more choices and opportunities is directly related to money.

2. It will help make this concept less abstract and more accessible if an example is provided. Consider sharing a personal story about a situation in which having resources increased your choices or a situation in which lack of resources forced you to make an undesirable choice. If you cannot think of a personal example, remind students of the examples from Lesson 1.

(To review, Lesson 1 gave the examples of Adrianna and Michael. Adrianna had more money, which allowed her to choose the neighborhood and environment in which she wanted to live; more education allowed her greater choice in type, location, and convenience of employment; more money allowed her to choose where and how her children would be educated. For Michael, his mom having less money gave him a lack of choice in what he did after school: instead of doing his homework, he watched his brother and sister; he had to get a job to help support the family; borrowing money controlled how he would spend his income while repaying the debt, and having less money made it more likely that he would have to borrow again; etc.)

3. Put up the "Shot Callers" and "Who's Looked Down On" posters from Lesson 2. Point out that students probably named people as "Shot Callers" because they saw them as having power. Ask the students how many of the people they named as "Who's Looked Down On" are powerless, according to the definition of lack of choices and opportunities. Explain that sometimes we do not examine our reasons for thinking one person is powerful and another person is not. However, understanding why people do or do not have power can help us learn how to develop genuine power in our own lives.

4. Ask the students why they view certain people as powerful. Their answers may include reasons like being rich, well respected, highly religious, or having other qualities the students admire and want to develop in themselves.

5. Today's activity will focus on understanding power through the lives of two men. Looking at their stories will lead to the discussion about the best way to obtain power, to maintain power, and to take pride and responsibility in the power you get.

Activity: Whose Life Would You Choose? (suggested time: 20 minutes)

The purpose of this activity is to show the students the direct connection between their early choices in life, and the ultimate outcomes that stem from those choices. This is accomplished by examining the lives of two real men, Felix Mitchell and Chris Gardner. They started from similar backgrounds but made drastically different choices in life, leading to totally different outcomes.

1. Break the class into six groups.
2. Give each student a "Whose Life Would You Choose" worksheet.
3. Give each group Part 1 of the Felix Mitchell biography sheet, and Part 1 of the Chris Gardner biography sheet.
4. Have each group read Part 1 of both biographies, then complete Part 1 of the worksheet.
5. Once each student has circled their choices, read each question aloud to the class and ask the students to raise their hands if they chose Chris Gardner. Then ask the

Note to Teacher

It is important to take this activity one step at a time. By going consecutively, step-by-step, it will help students to reexamine their initial assumptions about money.

students to raise their hands if they chose Felix Mitchell. Finally ask a few volunteers to share why they made the choices they did for each question in Part 1.

6. Repeat steps 3-5 with Part 2 of the biographies.
7. Before handing out Part 3 of the biographies, ask the class, "Where do you think these men's lives go from here?" Allow for some discussion among the students.
8. Repeat steps 3-5 with Part 3 of the biographies.

Note to Teacher

The questions on the worksheet are focused on having your students select answers based on their personal beliefs. Therefore make sure that each student circles his/her answers before hearing what others have selected. The discussion will be the key part of the activity, and will help students understand the difference between the appearance of power and making choices that give them genuine power.

Discussion: Whose Life Would You Choose? (suggested time: 5 minutes)

- Was it possible for you to predict the outcomes of each subject's life? Why or why not?
- How did the men's decisions relate to their ultimate outcomes?
- Were both men successful? Why or why not?
- Who was more powerful? Why? (Depending on how students respond, you may want to point them back to the definitions of power and powerlessness that you wrote on the board. Ask the students which man had more choices in the direction his life took.)
- If Chris Gardner's story ended with him making $150,000 a year as a reasonably successful stockbroker, would that change your opinion about the two stories?
- What are other examples of the type of choices in which the consequences of the decision would have a significant impact on the outcome of your life? Students should name such things as teen pregnancy, infection with a sexually transmitted disease, driving while intoxicated, and engaging in fights or violence.

Note to Teacher

Students may challenge that Felix Mitchell was more powerful at the end of his life. Allow his life to speak for itself. Since his life is over, you can point out that he has no choices or future opportunity, and therefore, no power.

Lecture #2: Having Genuine Power (suggested time: 8 minutes)

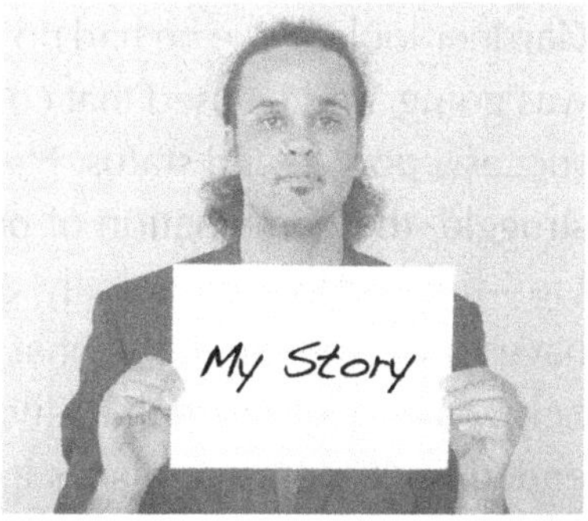

Tell the students a personal story about a person that you admired when you were their age, and the ways you patterned your life after that person. This will give students a realistic picture to help them realize that when people admire someone, they pattern their lives after that person to a certain extent. Point out that when we choose someone as an example for how we want our own lives to go, it is important to think about whether we have a good understanding of the reality with which that person lives. Are we admiring the appearance of success, or real and long-lasting success?

After sharing your story, recap the stories of the two men, focusing on these main points in your lecture:

- These two men had similar backgrounds and similar financial struggles, but different outlooks on how to achieve success.
- Negative power is not true power. That type of power can be extinguished at any time.
- Our choices now impact the outcome in our lives years down the road.
- Seeking positive power and persevering during times of struggle are key to a successful life.

You can say something like the following:

Today we looked at two examples of people with similar backgrounds. Both came from difficult circumstances, and they even had similar financial struggles, but they had two different outlooks on how to achieve success: one saw getting power through being a gangster, and one saw getting power through being a businessman. In the middle of their stories, it seemed like the gangster was the one who had achieved his goals. He had a lot of money, influence, and status, which seemed to come easily, while the aspiring businessman was unable to provide a home for his son despite working extremely hard.

But the ultimate outcome was that the gangster was dead at 32 and the aspiring businessman is now a CEO and a multi-millionaire with a stable life and a family. Both men had similar determination, but they looked at obtaining power differently. These two men give an example to show why it is important to examine who actually has power in a given situation. Felix Mitchell looked like he had a lot of power, but because of the choices he made, he was always at risk of being arrested or killed. With either of those a very real possibility every day, Mitchell was not actually in control of his own destiny. Chris Gardner looked like he had no power, and yet he was almost always in control of where his life was going, and he used that control to make smart choices that brought him to a place of huge success, power, and status. His life is an example of how even in the midst of great pain and struggle, the combination of perseverance and making positive choices leads to a successful life—financially, emotionally, and physically. When you think about your own future, you will have to decide carefully what kind of power you want to have, and make choices that will help you work toward that kind of success. Felix Mitchell and Chris Gardner could easily have ended up in opposite places if each had looked up to different power structures as examples. It's all about your outlook and mindset.

As we mentioned before, Chris Gardner did not come from the best circumstances. However, he did his best with what he had, and he was rewarded more in return. You can never change your background, where you have been born and raised, but through the proper amount of hard work and positive choices, you will gain knowledge and ability. As you obtain this knowledge and ability, you will be faced with decisions that will either have a positive or negative effect on your life. The choices you face may not be about dealing drugs. They may be other types of decisions that will significantly impact your future. It is up to you to decide what kind of power you will seek and what direction your life will take.

Wrap Up (suggested time: 5 minutes)

1. Refer back to the lists of "Shot Callers" and "Who's Looked Down On" that you made from the students' Post-it notes.
2. Repeat the point that they probably named people they see as having power as "Shot Callers." Ask the students if there is anyone listed on the "Shot Caller" list who does not control his or her own future, that is, anyone who does not have genuine power.
3. Ask if there is anyone on the "Who's Looked Down On" list who is making the kind of choices that will likely help them to have choices in their own future.
4. Also ask the students what they think the outcomes of each of those people's lives will be, based on the choices they are making now.
5. Thank the class for their participation.
6. Next Lesson: Exploring the concept of power vs. powerlessness more by looking at the power that exists in our lives even now, and how our power can be affected by our circumstances.

Vocabulary:
- powerlessness
- power

Additional Resources/Information:
For more information on Felix Mitchell and Chris Gardner, go to www.futureprofitsresources.org.

Materials needed:

- Power Spread Statements for Character Cards – 1.5.1*
- Power Spread Statements for Students as Themselves – 1.5.2*
- Power Spread Character Cards – 1.5.3*
- Whiteboard and pen, or chalkboard and chalk, or poster paper and pen

This will be the day when we bring
into full realization the American dream...
a dream of equality of opportunity,
of privilege and property widely distributed.
–Dr. Martin Luther King, Jr.,
Civil Rights Leader

Key Concepts:

1. The amount of power we begin with is determined by our circumstances, but we can increase our future power by making smart choices now.
2. There are systems in place that impact our power in society, and understanding how those systems affect us is a key first step in taking control of our own futures.

Prep Time: 30 minutes

Advance Preparation Tasks:

- Copy and cut the Character Cards to hand out to the students

For all additional resources, including handouts, video links and helpful websites, see www.futureprofitsresources.org

Keep in Mind

- Many students do not know how to articulate the sense of injustice they feel in their lives and communities.
- Many students may have a victim mentality, which stems from their experiences.
- The goal of this lesson is for students to identify: 1) how the system has impacted their position in life, and 2) opportunities to make choices that can change their position within the system.

Many students are aware of power and privilege all around them, but they don't necessarily have the words or understanding to articulate the sense of injustice that stems from what they see and experience. They may live daily with the effects of injustice, such as growing up in an under-performing school district, or living without health care or proper nutrition, which leaves them without a sense of hope and the potential for change. For some students, this may have fostered a victim mentality, which may look like a belief that the system is stacked against them, that it is impossible to change their position in the system, or that the system owes them to make up for any disadvantages they have experienced.

This lesson facilitates the beginning of a conversation to help students begin to articulate their feelings of power or, more likely, lack of power. Students will be encouraged to move beyond a defeated mindset, towards a hopeful one where they can see choices they make can impact their future. The goal is for students to develop enough understanding of power systems to be able to identify: 1) how the system has impacted their position in life, and 2) opportunities to make choices that can change their position within the system. It is important to recognize, acknowledge, and validate the students' perceptions that the system treats them unfairly. However, they should also be empowered to develop an understanding of the system and how to navigate it to increase their advantages. Every individual has the power to make certain choices that will alter how the system impacts his or her life.

These complicated concepts will likely require time for the students to grasp thoroughly. Don't feel that you have to complete the conversation or bring students to a point of resolution in this one lesson, as it will also be addressed in subsequent lessons.

Lesson Snapshot

Review (5 minutes)
- Chris Gardner and Felix Mitchell recap; review definition of power; discuss what makes a good role model

Introduction (7 minutes)
- Brainstorm people in their community whom they view as powerless
- Share a personal story of powerlessness if applicable, and ask students to share
- Define privilege; explain that power is affected both by privilege and choices

Activity: Power Spread (20-25 minutes)
- Give character cards to students and give them time to read their card and "become" that person
- Clear room and have students line up in the middle of the room, all facing one side of the room and explain activity to students
- Read each statement and have students move accordingly (break between statements to ask the students whom they are representing)
- When finished, have each student report their name and title to the class, record their name and place on the board, then move into a circle for discussion

Discussion: Power Spread (8 minutes)
- Ask questions to process the activity and how their position made them feel
- Ask questions to see how students understand power in society and what this activity showed them about what power looks like in society

Optional Lecture: The Capitalistic System (5 minutes)
- *Define capitalism*
- *Biggest advantage: rewards hard work and initiative*
- *Biggest disadvantage: relies on cheap labor and cheap resources to survive*
- *Emphasize the importance of the decisions that students make now in order to have power in the system in the future*

Wrap up (5 minutes)
- Repeat what you've heard from the students, drawing out the key concepts
- Next lesson: Our choices determine our power despite our circumstances

Review (suggested time: 5 minutes)

Briefly discuss Chris Gardner and Felix Mitchell. Ask the students:

- Who remembers our definition of power? (The most basic form of power is "having the ability to make choices about your own destiny.")
- Did anything stand out to you about either man's life or choices?
- What do you think makes someone a good role model?
- Can you think of any examples of good role models from your community?

Note to Teacher

Students are encouraged to share honestly, and some students may name an unhealthy role model. If that happens, ask them what they look up to about that person. You might also ask whether they think this person has the power to control his/her own destiny.

Introduction (suggested time: 3 minutes)

Ask the students to brainstorm a list of people from their community whom they see as powerless. This list may overlap a lot with the earlier list of "Who's Looked Down On," but there may be some significant variations. For example, police may be looked down on but also perceived as having power. Write this new list on the board. Then ask the students to share what they think it means to be without power. Again, this curriculum defines powerlessness as an individual lacking opportunities and choices about where his or her life is going. In this time, it is important to hear how the students perceive what it is like to be without power, and also to give them the opportunity to express some of the frustration they may feel about their experiences of powerlessness.

Think of a story that you could share with the students about a time that you felt powerless, and share how it felt and how you handled it. Be thoughtful in selecting a story, however, particularly if your background is very different from your students' backgrounds. If you share a story about your parents not letting you go to a concert or receiving a lower grade than you wanted as an example of feeling powerless, students are likely to perceive you as having no idea what it is like to deal with the kind of struggles that they encounter regularly. Your experience of feeling powerless may have been no less real, but the students will disengage unless they can relate to the situation. After sharing your story, give the students an opportunity to share about a time in their lives when they felt looked down on, or without power. This is a personal question, so if no one answers, that is okay.

Ask the students how they think people get power. Allow for responses, and then point out that it often seems like people who have power started off with a certain kind of privilege. **Privilege** is when certain people start with advantages due solely to circumstances outside of their control. Often privilege is connected to money. Having access to money usually gives people more choices and more control of their situations. This lesson looks at privilege and at how power is affected both by privilege (circumstances outside our control) and by choices (circumstances within our control).

Activity: Power Spread (suggested time: 20-25 minutes)

This activity is set up to demonstrate a distribution, or spectrum, of power that resembles what is experienced in life. Looking a certain way may influence the way people treat each other. Being born into a certain family may determine access to opportunities. Low-income teens are often aware that they feel disadvantaged, but are not necessarily aware of the systemic nature of privilege. Understanding the system is a key element of being equipped to navigate the system more effectively. This is an honest examination of how circumstances outside of our control affect the amount of power we feel like we have. Further, the choices we make also affect the amount of power we have.

1. Shuffle the pre-cut "character cards" and hand out one card randomly to each of the students.
2. Have the students read over their cards to become familiar with the characters they are going to be representing for this activity. Encourage them to really try to enter into the life of that person—to think through what kind of choices this person would make, what this person's life would really look like, and what this person's background might mean about their future. Tell the students that they will be pretending to be this "character."

Note to Teacher

There are 30 character cards. If there are less than 30 students, please use cards from front to back (use the first and second pages first, then add the third page, and so on, until you have enough cards for every student). This will ensure that the ultimate distribution of power will reflect the broadest possible range of characters and experiences. There are an even number of men and women in the first four pages (men in the left column and women in the right column), and the last page contains all extra men.

Note to Teacher

This activity makes use of character cards that allow your students to represent people across a wide spectrum of power. This wide spectrum may facilitate greater insights and a more interesting discussion. Students will be spread across the room based on how much power their character has in given situations. The character cards are used so that students won't be required to reveal information that could be too personal or embarrassing. While the use of cards is normally recommended, this can be a powerful experience if your students have built maturity and trust to participate as themselves without using cards. If you choose to do this, begin with Step 3.

3. Clear the room so there is empty space and room for the students to move around. Have all the students stand in a line in the middle of the room, all facing the same direction, so that they all begin from the same starting point.
4. Explain that you will be reading a list of 30 different statements that describe a person's character or lifestyle. Some describe characteristics that are outside of our control, and some describe choices that we can control. As you read through each of the statements, the students will decide whether or not the statement describes or applies to their character. If their character card does not tell them, they should take a guess. If the statement does not apply to their character, they should remain in place. The students will follow the movement directions corresponding to the statements, stepping forward or backward six inches. Tell the students that their movements forward reflect something that indicates a character has power in society, while their movements back reflect something that indicates a character lacks power in society. As the students move forward or backward in response to each statement, they will spread themselves across the room in a way that creates a visual representation of the power or powerlessness experienced by different individuals in our society, and how others treat them. Where an individual ends up in the spread depends on a combination of the privilege they received and the choices they made.
5. Read each of the statements from the "Power Spread Statements" document (see 1.5.1 for Character Cards or 1.5.2 for Students as Themselves), pausing after each statement to have the students step forward or backward as appropriate. Ask students to notice any patterns they see as you go through the statements. After a statement is read, you may want to stop and ask the students who took a step to share about the character they are representing. Ask the students to give the character's name and a short description. You may also want to ask the class if the people who took a step are all similar in some way, or how the people who took a step seem different from the people who did not take a step.
6. After reading through all 30 statements, have each student say the title of the character he or she was representing in the activity. Ask the students to take note of who ended up

where in the room. The students will have spread themselves out along an imaginary line moving from least privileged / powerful to most privileged / powerful. Create a chart on the board that captures an image of the power distribution. Divide the board into five sections. Each section represents a section of the room. Write the title of each character in the section on the board that corresponds to where they were standing at the end of the activity. (Section 1 includes the characters who took the most steps forward, Section 3 includes the characters who stayed relatively close to the starting point, Section 5 includes the characters who took the most steps backward, and so on.) It will be useful to have a visual record to which to refer during discussion.

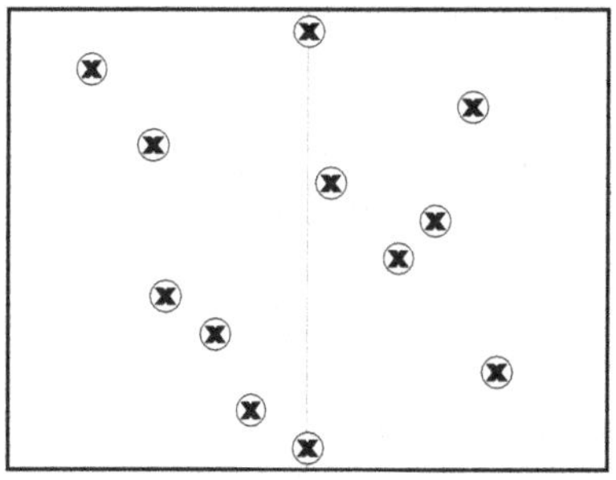

7. Then have the class sit in a circle and move on to the following discussion.

Discussion: Power Spread (suggested time: 8 minutes)

Before starting the discussion, thank the students for participating, and tell the students that every character who was represented is unique and brings a valuable perspective about life to the United States, regardless of how much power he or she had. This discussion will focus on the power or lack of power in their lives.

Focus on the following key concepts:

- Privilege can affect the amount of resources you have.
  - Power or lack of power is the result of choices. Sometimes we have made these choices for ourselves, but often we experience the effects of choices that other people have made. These other people may be close to us, like family members, or they may be people we have never met, like politicians, historical figures, business executives, etc., who affect the systems in place in our society. When we benefit from other people's choices, we have privilege.
  - Lack of power means that we have fewer choices or opportunities than someone with power, or we may have to work harder to get choices or opportunities. That is generally the experience of those who start out without privilege.
- Although some elements of power are completely dependent on factors outside of our control, where we will end up in the power spread can often be impacted by the choices we make now.
- The way students view their education, money, and resources now will impact the resources they have when they are ready to enter the workforce.

- The more resources you have, particularly when you enter the workforce, the greater number of choices and opportunities you have.

Note to Teacher

It is crucial to engage with your students' responses to the questions in this discussion. Pick up on key words they say to help draw out their conclusions and ask follow up questions that can lead them toward reaching broader conclusions. For example, if the students stated that they felt "confident" when stepping forward, follow up with, "What about stepping forward made you feel confident?" Remember, the best solutions are the ones that your students come up with on their own, since the goal is for them to be able to relate these conclusions to the decisions in their own lives.

As your students draw conclusions ask questions to confirm what you've heard them say. For example, you might say, "Can we conclude that it helps us feel positive about our future when we feel like we have something valuable to offer, such as being able to speak two languages?" Or, after the students have named some factors that they feel keep them trapped, you could ask, "Do you feel like our environment defines what options we have in life?" These kinds of questions will help make sure that you understand the students properly, and help confirm the conclusions they have reached on their own.

Move through the following questions with your students:

(The first set of questions assumes that you have used the character cards. If the students participated in the activity as themselves, use the alternate discussion questions instead.)

- Raise your hand if you would want to be your character in real life. What are your reasons for wanting to be this person?
- Raise your hand if you would not want to be your character in real life. What are your reasons for not wanting to be this person?
- Who feels like their character was trapped by certain circumstances in his or her life? What circumstances limited this person's power or opportunities?
- How would you have wanted your character's life to be different? What is one thing that the person could do to improve his or her life circumstances?
- What are any other factors you think would keep you trapped in life?
- What are some ways that people have privilege that is outside of their control?
- How did other people in your character's life influence where your character ended up standing in the end?
- What are some ways that people choose power or lack of power in their lives?
- Think about where you would end up standing if you answered these questions as yourself. Do you think you would be in a similar place to your character or a very different place? How do you feel about where you might have been standing?

Alternate discussion questions:

- How did it feel when you stepped forward?
- How did it feel when you stepped back?
- How do you feel about where you ended up in the room?
- Did any of the statements surprise you? Was there anything for which you were asked to step forward or backward that you think is not related to power?
- Have you had experiences in life where you think someone acted a certain way towards you based on the amount of power they assumed you had? Is anyone willing to share an example?
- How do you think circumstances beyond your control have influenced where you ended up standing?
- How do you think other people in your life influenced where you ended up standing?
- How do you think your choices have influenced where you ended up standing?
- What is one thing you could do to improve your life circumstances?
- What systems may work against you? What are some ways you can counteract their impact on your life?
- What systems may work for you? What are some ways you can use these systems to increase your advantage?

Optional Lecture: The Capitalistic System *(suggested time: 5 minutes)*

The systems to which this lesson refers mainly stem from the capitalistic system of America. Define **capitalism** for the students. A basic definition is, "an economic and political system that determines how the businesses in a country operate. The prices, production, and distribution of goods are determined mainly by competition in a free market. The country's trade and industry are controlled by private owners for profit, rather than by the state." It is not the intention of this curriculum to elevate or look down on the capitalistic system, but it can be helpful to give a brief explanation of the advantages and disadvantages that come from the capitalistic system, as with any system. Understanding this system can help students see the importance of their choices today, specifically how they will impact their ability to thrive later in life.

- The biggest advantage of the capitalistic system is that it rewards hard work and initiative, giving the individual the ability to make choices to determine his/her future. For example, when a person graduates from high school, they have the choice to pursue other options for education that would potentially give that person a higher paying job in the future. Another example is how a person can move up in their position at work. Even if they start at one of the "lower positions," they are able to move up through working hard and taking initiative.

In a capitalistic system, both the advantages a person starts out with and the amount of initiative that they exhibit impact their ability to progress in their chosen profession or career.

- The biggest disadvantage of the capitalistic system is that it relies on cheap labor and cheap resources to survive. As people progress in their profession or career, other people are needed to work what is deemed as "the lower positions" in society.
- Therefore, the choices students make now impact the amount of resources and opportunities they will have in the future. Referring back to the Bean Game, the choices they make now impact the amount of beans they will have when they are ready to enter the workforce. When an individual has the resources such as education, skill, connections, money, transportation, and health care, they will also have more of a choice in determining their own destiny. Some students may have to learn to overcome their lack of privilege through the choices they make today that will impact their future. If students understand the importance of working hard and making wise choices, they can increase the amount of resources or beans they have in the future.

Wrap Up (suggested time: 5 minutes)

Recap the key points shared by students during the discussion, highlighting what they expressed about how power is distributed in society. Acknowledge that there are systems that definitely cause each of us to start out with advantages or disadvantages. Many of these advantages and disadvantages are directly related to financial status. Often, starting out with less money limits our choices. Encourage students, however, that there are also opportunities to make choices that change where we stand in the power spread. The circumstances we start out with do not have to be the circumstances we end up with. Remind the students of the cycles discussed in Lesson 1, and the fact that each individual has the power to make his or her own cycle instead of being controlled by the cycles that society sets up. The next class session looks more closely at what it looks like to navigate the systems of power in our lives.

Vocabulary:
- privilege
- *optional: capitalism*

You are never strong enough that you don't need help.
–Cesar Chavez, Civil Rights Activist

Materials needed:

- Computer with internet connection, projector, and speakers
- Two Struggle Video Clips*
- One Success Video Clip*
- *Optional: Struggle / Success Video Scripts – 1.6.1**
- Whiteboard and pen, or chalkboard and chalk, or poster paper and pen

Key Concepts:

1. The choices we make now help determine how much power we will have in the future. Some choices increase our positive opportunities, while other choices put our futures at risk.
2. When we are in a hard situation in life, it is important to explore all our options, and to consider how our choices will impact our future.

Prep Time: 10 minutes

Advance Preparation Tasks:

- Bookmark the two Struggle Video Clips on YouTube (see Activity #1 for specifics)
- Bookmark the Success Video Clip on YouTube (see Activity #2 for specifics)
- Watch the video stories beforehand so you are familiar with the stories and what kind of discussion will come from it

**For all additional resources, including handouts, video links and helpful websites, see www.futureprofitsresources.org*

Keep in Mind

- The way people perceive and handle money often comes from their surroundings and often it is internalized before it is examined.
- It is important for students to make informed and conscious choices about how their perceptions of money guide their behavior.
- The pursuit of fast money is common in low-income communities. It often starts from a "survival mentality" and turns into greed.
- Focus on options that can help in the present without putting the future in jeopardy.

The overall goal of Unit 1 was to develop awareness that will empower students to make informed decisions. Whether realized or not, the way people perceive and handle money often comes from viewing how money is used by family, friends, and community. Often people internalize these perceptions without examining them more closely. Therefore, it is important to make informed and conscious choices about how these perceptions should guide our behavior. We also are all subject to large systems that heavily impact our individual experiences with power and money. Understanding how these systems function and how they shape our personal experiences is crucial to learning how to successfully navigate them. This unit has attempted to provide opportunities for students to unpack: (1) the attitudes about power and money they have adopted from their families and communities, and (2) the systemic nature of power and the relationship between successfully navigating power systems and financial success. Having built a basic understanding of these concepts lays the foundation for future units, which go into more detail on financial concepts. This foundation will help students to be more receptive to topics that they otherwise might choose to ignore.

This process has facilitated an opportunity through which students can examine the attitudes they observe regarding money and power and those which they may possess themselves – attitudes that may appear effective but ultimately perpetuate the cycle of poverty. This lesson directly addresses one of the most pervasive of those attitudes, which is seeking "fast money." When resources are severely limited and people have immediate needs such as food and shelter, most will do whatever it takes to survive. The pursuit of fast money often starts from this "survival mentality" of doing anything necessary to survive, regardless of the morality or long-term consequences of the action. Although fast money may answer an immediate need, it often puts an individual's future in jeopardy, because it usually involves significant risk and potentially severe consequences. Particularly for individuals who have seen people around them work hard for seemingly little in return, the lure of fast money may start with survival, but turns into greed. The desire to accumulate more can lead to thinking we deserve to have more, rather than just wanting enough to survive. Many of your students will be familiar with ways that people get fast money and may understand the appeal; this attitude is acknowledged in the lesson. However, the emphasis is on the options that can help in the present without putting the future in jeopardy.

Lesson Snapshot

Review (5 minutes)

- Ask students to share about last class
- Make a list of circumstances which made people feel trapped or feel like they have limited power

Introduction (2 minutes)

- Today's Lesson: Choices we can make in order not to be trapped
- Choices are an opportunity to exercise power

Discussion: Fast Money (8 minutes)

- Define "fast money"
- Give examples of, along with advantages and disadvantages to fast money
- Discuss motivation for fast money — survival or greed

Activity #1: Struggle Video Stories (20 minutes)

- Show each video and break for discussion in between
- List the person's possible options or choices (positive or negative)
- List how each option could affect the individual's future

Lecture: Choosing Power (5 minutes)

- Fast money comes from mindset of survival or mindset of greed
- Often a short-term solution in an emergency turns into a habit that is hard to break
- Use example of Fred choosing to sell drugs puts his future at risk
- Slow down the decision and think strategically: consider resources...not only money but people, too
- Ask for help from people who are concerned with the outcome, or the long-term effect, that the solution will have on the family
- Do not sacrifice long-term stability with short-term solutions
- Return to the cycles discussed in Lesson 1

Activity #2: Success Video Story (5 minutes)

- Show video and discuss
- Ask about the choices he made to gain power in his future

Wrap up (5 minutes)

- Learning through observation is key in being able to make wise decisions for the future
- Access to money and resources, along with the choices made about money and resources, can determine what choices and opportunities are available, which determines how much power one has

Review (suggested time: 5 minutes)

Ask one of the students to summarize the last class. After someone describes the Power Spread activity, ask the students to list some of the characteristics and experiences that contributed to some people having their power limited and seeming trapped by their circumstances. Make a list on the board. Thank each of the students for sharing.

Introduction (suggested time: 2 minutes)

After looking at some of the circumstances that seem to trap us, this lesson looks at the ways to make choices that help us to move out of being trapped. Along with every circumstance comes a choice, and every choice influences the direction in which we are heading. The choices we make will either trap us or help us move out of the traps that hold us back. This is particularly true dealing with money. Money can be used as a tool to avoid traps and increase our future opportunities, but some methods of pursuing money can lead us into traps and decrease the opportunities we have in the future. Because each choice represents an opportunity to control the direction of our future, each choice is an opportunity to exercise power. Let's look at some choices that people make when they experience feeling trapped by circumstances.

Discussion: Fast Money (suggested time: 8 minutes)

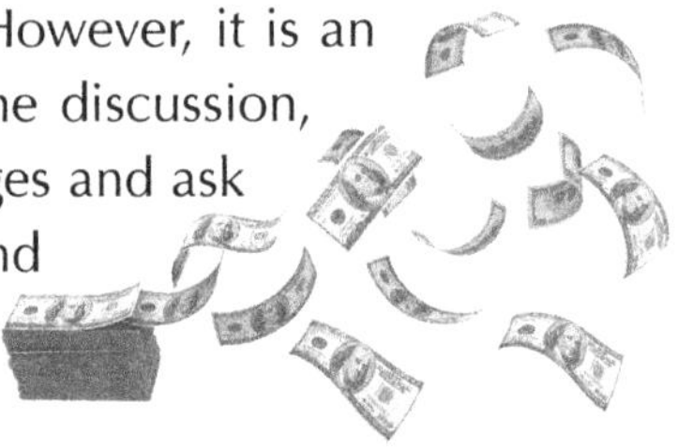

Fast money may look to students like the best and easiest option, or even the only option, when faced with very difficult circumstances. However, it is an option that will keep them trapped in the long run. During the discussion, define fast money, ask for examples, state the obvious advantages and ask for possible disadvantages, then ask about the motivation behind fast money.

1. Introduce the discussion by saying the following, "Most of us want hopeful futures and more opportunities in our lives to do and be everything in our dreams. However, those dreams often seem far away, while the problems we have right now can be urgent. Some circumstances have to be fixed right away, and it can be difficult to figure out a positive solution. Let's take a look at fast money."
2. Write "fast money" on the board, and ask a student to define what fast money means. The definition used here for fast money is, "Trying to make money quickly and by any means necessary, usually because of a desperate need."
3. Ask students to list ways that people get fast money. Some examples are selling drugs, selling

your body, robbery, credit card scams or bank money scams, stealing, gambling, etc.

4. State that the obvious advantage of fast money is that you get the money you need, and you get it quickly.
5. Ask the students what they think could be possible disadvantages to fast money. One example is that you could get caught for doing something illegal and go to juvenile hall. Another disadvantage is that most ways of getting fast money takes advantage of other people. It doesn't just meet your needs; it often takes something from or hurts someone else.
6. Finally ask the students if they think that most people who try to get fast money are motivated by survival or greed. After receiving feedback, tell the students that we will be returning to this conversation later, but now we are going to look at a couple of real life stories and discuss what options these people may have in their circumstances.

Activity #1: Struggle Video Stories (suggested time: 20 minutes)

The purpose of this activity is to help students start to think about the different options they might have when they feel trapped and would be tempted to make negative choices. Students learn how to think critically about difficult situations in order to make choices that can address the circumstance now and have a positive future outcome.

Overview:
Students will be hearing the stories of two people who have felt trapped by circumstances in their lives. After hearing about their situations through watching the following video clips, stop and discuss the clip with the students. Ask them if they see this person as powerful or lacking power, then brainstorm what options the person may have. Lead the students through a process of asking the following questions to evaluate their options:

1. What are the resources I can use around me?
   a. Money — How can I get money? Is it legal or safe?
   b. People — Who are the people who can help me?
2. How could this choice affect my future?

Directions:

1. Show Struggle Video #1 (a scenario in which the individual has the cards badly stacked against him). Go to www.futureprofitsresources.org for a link to this video.
2. Ask students if they see this person as powerful or lacking in power, and why.
3. Ask students what they might do in Fred's situation. Options that may be mentioned by students include:
   - He can go sell drugs to make money.
   - He can find a job to make money.

- He can ask a teacher or family member for help.
- He can ask a church for help.
- He can rob someone to make money.
- He can report his mother to child services.

4. Ask students how they think the options they mentioned would affect Fred's future if he followed through on them. Here are examples that students may give about how the above options could affect his future:
   - He can go sell drugs to make money or rob someone to make money.
     - This could result in fast cash return, jail time, and/or death.
   - He can find a job to make money.
     - This could give him a stable and consistent source of money. Getting job experience now may help him get a better job in the future. However, it could also take time away from his schoolwork and affect his grades negatively.
   - He can ask a church, a teacher, or a family member for help.
     - This could result in positive help, a change in environment, financial assistance, or educational assistance. If handled badly, it could make the situation worse. For example, if those parties refuse to help or give the wrong advice, it may push Fred into the negative alternative because at that point he may see it as the only option.
   - He can report his mother to child services.
     - This too could result in positive help, a change in environment, financial assistance, or educational assistance. Depending on how child services responds, Fred may be placed in a group home, and group homes can be tough around rough neighborhoods. Fred also might be worried about what will happen to his mom if he isn't around to watch out for her.

Repeat Steps 1-4 with Video #2.

1. Show Struggle Video #2 (a scenario in which a teenage girl, Michelle, starts with power, but makes choices that lead to difficult circumstances). Go to www.futureprofitsresources.org for a link to this video.
2. Ask students if they see Michelle as powerful or lacking in power, and why.
3. Ask students what they might do in Michelle's situation. Options that may be mentioned by students include:
   - Get an abortion and dump Ronny.
   - Keep the baby and dump Ronny.
   - Ask a third party who is an adult but not a family member for help on the decision.
4. Ask the students how they think the options they mentioned would affect Michelle's future if she followed through on them? Here are examples that students may give about how the

above options could affect her future:

- Get an abortion and dump Ronny.
  - This could make all her problems go away in the short term, but could also lead to depression and lifelong regret. She did say she wants to keep the baby.
- Keep the baby and dump Ronny.
  - This could cut the abuse out of her life, but the dad may be absent from the child's life and the child may never know Ronny. She may not be able to receive child support, especially if Ronny is in jail.
- Ask a third party who is an adult but not a family member for help on the decision.
  - This may help her clear her mind, vent, and make the right decision. The adult could offer a perspective she may not have thought about. If she asks an adult who tries to convince her to do a certain thing, she may feel forced into a decision.

Lecture: Choosing Power (suggested time: 5 minutes)

The purpose of this lecture is to reinforce that students can make positive choices to cope with their current situations while still setting themselves up to succeed in the future.

1. Return to the topic of obtaining fast money and the motivation that drives the desire for fast money. Discuss the beginning survival mindset, which frequently turns into greed.
2. The way to combat the need for fast money is by slowing down to think about the decision and switching to a position of strategy.
3. Address the fear of asking for help and explain the importance of asking trusted people.
4. Trusted people consider what is best for your present and your future.
5. Thinking about the long-term effects is a crucial step in evaluating solutions. If we sacrifice long-term stability for a short-term solution, we are more likely to find ourselves back in a position of struggle continually throughout our lives.
6. Return to the cycles discussed in Lesson 1 to drive home the point of long-term effects from choices made now.

Here is an example of wording you could use:
When we talked about fast money earlier, some of you said that looking for fast money comes out of a mindset of survival ... doing whatever you can to get money to survive the situation you are in. It's like the example of a starving beggar who steals bread from a store. He just needed some food in his stomach ... who could blame him? Some of you think that looking for fast money comes more from a mindset of greed ... you want money, and more of it, so you'll

do the easiest thing possible to get the money, regardless of whom it hurts. Well many times, getting fast money begins from a survival mindset at first, and then often turns into greed. It starts as an emergency but often becomes a habit that is hard to break. For example, let's look at Fred's situation and imagine he chose the option of selling drugs. Doing it just once and only because he has no other way to pay the rent could make him feel like he might as well keep doing it so that he can stop worrying about money. But people who sell drugs are in danger of getting arrested or killed. We've seen it happen before ... it's more common than we would like it to be. Even if Fred only sells drugs one time, he is already putting his future at risk.

So how do we make choices that can be positive for our future while still finding money to survive here and now? One of the most important things to do is to **slow down the decision.** When we feel like we are in a crisis, we feel like we have to solve it right away and we don't take time to think about our options. If we can switch to a position of strategy, we may be able to make wiser decisions that protect a more safe and comfortable future. As we think through difficult situations in advance — not when we are in the middle of the emotions of crisis — we can think through our options more carefully so we are likely to make a more solid decision. Each of us will face difficult situations in our lives, but if we figure out what we want to stand for and what direction we want our lives to go, it will help us make positive choices.

When we consider strategy to help our struggles now, it's important that we consider not only the money that is a resource available to us, but also the people who could help us. Although it can often be difficult to ask for help, everyone needs help, especially when it comes to situations that are outside of our control. It is scary and uncomfortable to ask for help because we may feel like it will embarrass our family by exposing the situation. But when we ask the right person, we can often find healthy solutions that we couldn't have discovered on our own. How do we know who the right people are? One of the ways to determine that is to ask yourself if the person really has your best interests in mind. An appropriate person should be concerned with the outcome, or the long-term effect, that the solution will have on the family. Thinking about the long-term effects is a crucial step in evaluating solutions. Asking for help may lead to options that have positive long-term outcomes, whereas trying to deal with the situation by yourself may provide temporary relief but cause more stress for you and your family in the long run.

You have such valuable lives and often what can be best for your family is thinking about your long-term success. For example, let's return to the cycle of education and power that we talked about in Lesson 1. In our lives, if we were to make the choices that lead to college or professional training to be able to get a higher paying job in the future, it is likely to put us in a better position to support our families and cope with the struggles we may face. If we sacrifice long-term stability for a short-term solution, we are more likely to find ourselves back in a position of struggle continually throughout our lives.

Now we are going to watch one more video clip of a person who grew up with struggle and probably felt trapped at times. Look for examples of the choices he makes and how those choices affect his future.

Activity #2: Success Video Story (suggested time: 5 minutes)

1. Show Success Video of Noel Castellanos (a story of success in the midst of hard struggles). Go to www.futureprofitsresources.org for a link to this video.

Noel Castellanos is the Chief Executive Officer of Christian Community Development Association (CCDA), which works to equip leaders working among the poor. He was appointed to serve on President Obama's Council for Faith and Neighborhood Partnerships, and is a highly sought after speaker, motivator, and mentor to young leaders throughout the USA. He has a deep passion to serve and invest in the lives of leaders committed to serving the poor, and has worked in Latino, urban communities since 1982.

His story is one where he came from a past that wouldn't naturally lend him power, but he made choices to propel his life forward and to choose success. Now he is using his power for good, to help bring hope and power to the powerless and poor all over the states. He has positioned himself so that his voice can be heard throughout America.

2. Ask the students what stood out to them in Noel's story. Ask the students what choices he made in order to gain power in his future. Reinforce the fact that he ends up with power because he made choices to put himself in that position. He had healthy resources around him that he took advantage of, and he thought through the impact his choices could have on his future.

Wrap Up (suggested time: 5 minutes)

This is the last lesson about Money in Your Neighborhood. Point out to the students that the way we have been learning about money in our neighborhood is all through the exercise of observing. Observation is key in being able to make wise decisions for the future. It is important to recognize what is going on around you, because it will help you to make conscious decisions about what you let influence you. When you know what is going on around you, and whether or not you agree or disagree with that, it will help you to make choices that are the best for your life.

These topics show that money is all around us and already influences our lives every day. Most decisions made in life have something to do with money. Sometimes the relationship is obvious, like deciding how to spend money or how to make money. But money also affects a lot of other types of decisions, because access to money and resources can determine what choices and opportunities are available. One of the most important reasons to learn about managing money is to help prevent situations where power is taken from us. The goal of Future Profits is to prepare you to use money in ways that improve your life and increase the power you have over your own future. You've all heard the saying, "Money is power." Power means having control over your own choices and opportunities, and money is a tool to increase those choices and opportunities. Therefore, the choices we make with money in our lives, and the way we position ourselves for success, will help determine the amount of power we have, and help us to use that power for good.

Vocabulary:
- fast money

This unit is specifically designed to teach students the important concepts of budgeting and managing their money. It starts with the very basic concept of showing students the money they have flowing through their lives even today. Recognizing that money is already flowing in and out of their lives will help them better appreciate and relate to future lessons in this curriculum. Five of the six lessons in this unit are devoted to a budget simulation. This simulation will not only teach students about budgeting, but will also give them a realistic picture of what life looks like financially for an adult. Some students may come to a deeper understanding of what their parents or guardians go through in providing for the family's needs and wants. The budget simulation also gives students a broad picture of some different jobs that are out there, and how much a starting income at those jobs would be. This unit is meant to inspire students to dream about their future through this simulation. Some students will see jobs that they or their classmates receive, and be inspired to pursue that job in the future. In a later unit (Unit 4), we will look at the specific goals that students can make in order to pursue some of these jobs.

Lesson Plans:

After a general introduction to budgeting in Lesson 1, the budget simulation begins in Lesson 2. It starts out by giving the students a job with a set income, and giving them an opportunity to make a first draft of their budget. In this first draft, we expect that the students will not have a very practical idea of what certain expenses cost. The following lesson (Lesson 3), students will learn about the realistic cost of living in their location. Students should be surprised at the costs, and this experience will hopefully cause them to begin thinking more carefully about how they spend money, both now and in the future. At the end of this and each of the following lessons, the students will readjust their budgets in order to reflect the new information they have learned.

After students have a realistic understanding of the cost of living, we want to address the issue of instant vs. delayed gratification. Many students have already bought into one of the two mindsets based on how they grew up, but it is important for students to recognize and understand these two mindsets in regard to money. Lesson 4 encourages them to make an informed decision about which mindset they want to affect their choices with money. Because delayed gratification requires patience and perseverance, which do not necessarily come naturally, students must see the benefits that can come from this mindset.

Finally, in Lesson 5 students receive different emergencies that they have to deal with financially. This element should be a surprise during the simulation. Many students have experienced emergencies in their lives, so it may be familiar to deal with the emotions and physical hindrances that often result from emergencies. Therefore, it is important for students to experience the financial impact of these emergencies during this lesson. After all of the steps, the simulation ends in Lesson 6 with a thorough class discussion, in which all students have an opportunity to share with each other and learn from each other.

This unit is different than other units in this curriculum in the sense that it involves more preparation on the teacher's side. The timing of the lessons can fit into 50 minutes, but if the class size is larger, or if the students need help with some of the math in this lesson, you may want to provide for more time to go through each lesson. It will also help to have additional volunteers to help the students with individual questions as they make drafts of their budgets.

Outline:

Lesson 1 – Cash In – Cash Out
Lesson 2 – Life at 25
Lesson 3 – How Much Does Your Life Cost?
Lesson 4 – Delayed vs. Instant Gratification
Lesson 5 – Emergencies!!
Lesson 6 – Budget Simulation Debrief

Vocabulary:

- budget
- income
- expenses
- positive/negative cash flow
- simulation
- annual income
- monthly income
- take-home income (or net income)
- tax brackets
- needs
- wants
- cost of living
- utilities
- delayed gratification
- instant gratification

A budget tells us what we can't afford, but it doesn't keep us from buying it.
–William Feather, Author

Materials needed:

- Computer with internet connection, projector, and speakers
- Whiteboard and pen, or chalkboard chalk, or poster paper and pen
- Budgeting Pennies pages – 2.1.1*
- 200 pennies per class

Key Concepts:

1. Money flows into and out of your life regularly, and it is important to keep track of it.
2. It is important not to have more money going out than coming in.
3. Budgeting requires making choices about how to spend your money.

Prep Time: 30 minutes

Advance Preparation Tasks:

- Bookmark "Sitcom Clip - Regular People" (visit www.futureprofitsresources.org)
- Make 6-7 copies of the Budgeting Pennies pages
- Cut pages through the middle on the dotted line (make sure to use a paper clip to group each set of papers together)
- Make sure to have at least 200 pennies for the activity

**For all additional resources, including handouts, video links and helpful websites, see www.futureprofitsresources.org*

Keep in Mind

- Living without money can lead to negative feelings for students, so be sensitive.
- Help students realize they probably make money choices daily or weekly.
- Making wise choices with money can help to give them control over their future.
- Students should gain awareness of their current choices, and see how important it is to prioritize where and how they spend their money.

Money can be a delicate topic for low-income students. It is often associated with frustration, disappointment, or anxiety, as many have experienced times when their families struggled to make ends meet. Many students feel they are forced to do without, a position especially frustrating when they are bombarded with media messages for the latest products. When students live in low-income communities that are located near wealthier neighborhoods, this sense of wanting will likely be especially strong. Some students will believe they deserve more, and can direct the resulting anger at their parents/guardians, at others with more money, or at an unfair society. This perception can lead toward a victim mentality, and strong negative feelings about their situation. This can foster an attitude of oppression because they feel society will always keep them down. Another symptom is the belief that they shouldn't have to work to change their situation because society owes them a more fair distribution of resources. While acknowledging students' perspectives, our goal is to help them to feel empowered by seeing that they do have choices about money, and that making these choices wisely can allow them to take control of their future.

Though money is often tight, most students spend money on a daily or weekly basis. However, they are often unaware of how often money passes through their hands. Many don't realize their purchasing power, or that they are even constantly making financial decisions. Since many students do not have jobs, they may believe they have no access to, or control over money. Recognizing that they already have purchasing power will help them better appreciate and relate to lessons on bank accounts, budgeting, etc. The goal is to identify the money students do have, and to help them be aware of what they do with it. Even if they purchase a bag of chips or can of soda, they are making a decision about how to spend their money and about where they spend it. This curriculum will often touch on the choices of how and where one spends money. Students should be led toward an awareness of their current choices, and to be more deliberate in the financial decisions they make in the future. Students should see that they already have power in how they use money, and grasp that this will increase as they have more to spend in the future.

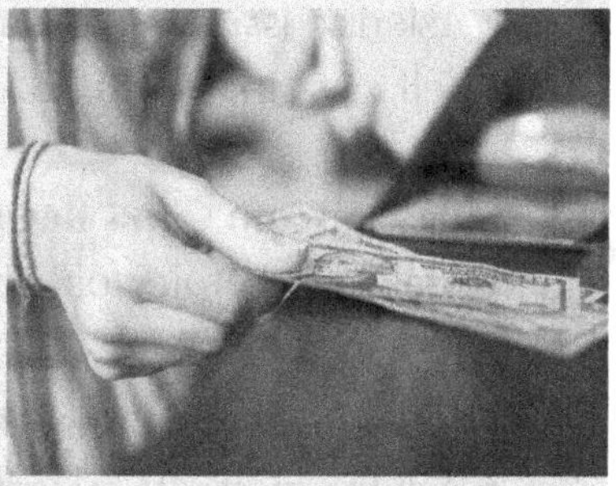

This lesson includes an activity that introduces the basic idea of budgeting, and that creating a budget involves making choices about how to divide money into categories. In the next lesson, students will go though a realistic experience of budgeting, however for this week, simply focus on the concept that making a budget requires setting priorities and making decisions about how to spend the money we have. Although budgeting concepts aren't specifically defined yet, students should begin to experience that: (1) spending money in one category is a choice that takes away their ability to spend money in other categories, and (2) some categories are absolutely essential, like housing and food, even though students may not realize the cost of these items if their parents/guardians are providing it.

Lesson Snapshot

Introduction (3 minutes)
- Ask discussion question about budget
- Tell class that we'll be learning about budgeting the next six weeks

Video: Sitcom Clip - Regular People (5 minutes)
- Make sure projector and speakers are connected ahead of time and show clip

Discussion: Why Budget? (5 minutes)
- Ask the class, "Why is it a good idea to have a budget?"
- Write student responses on white board
- Highlight importance of a budget

Activity #1: Cash In – Cash Out (7 minutes)
- Write "Cash In" and "Cash Out" with arrows on board and have student stand in the middle
- Track volunteer student's specific expenses and sources of income
- Total both sides

Lecture: Budget (5 minutes)
- Referring to the previous activity, define "income" and "expenses"
- Referring to the previous activity, define "positive cash flow" and "negative cash flow"

Activity #2: Budgeting Pennies (23 minutes)
- Split students into groups of 3-4
- Pass out pennies and Budgeting Pennies sheets
- Give students 15 minutes to decide where they would spend their pennies
- Have each group report

Wrap Up (2 minutes)
- Highlight the importance of making choices in regard to a budget

Introduction (suggested time: 3 minutes)

Begin the class by asking students, "How many of you know what a budget is?" Allow students to respond, then ask, "How many of you want to get the most you can out of your money?" Presumably, students will respond positively. You can then explain that budgets are one of the best tools we can use for getting the most from our money. For the next six weeks, we will be learning about how budgeting works.

Video: "Sitcom Clip - Regular People"

(suggested time: 5 minutes)

This clip offers a great and humorous introduction to the concept of monthly income and expenses. Show the first four minutes. Go to www.futureprofitsresources.org and look for the sitcom clip.

Note to Teacher

Theo's assumptions may be very similar to the way some of your students think about money. Watch this clip in advance to give yourself an idea of where some of them may be coming from. It is not uncomon for students to be unaware of how expensive their lives actually are.

Discussion: Why Budget?

(suggested time: 5 minutes)

Tell the students that a simple definition for a **budget** is "a tool or plan for how an individual will spend his / her money." Write definition on the board. Ask the class, "Why do you think it might be a good idea to have a budget?" Allow for a variety of responses. Since the concept of budgeting may be unfamiliar to many students, they may not have a lot of ideas. Prompt students with questions like:

- Is it important to know how much money you spend each month? Why?
- Do you think you need to know if you are spending more money than you have in a month? Why?
- What do you think would happen if you spent more money than you actually had in a month?
- Why would it be helpful to keep track of where you spent that money or what you spent that money on?
- What will help you decide how to spend your money each month?

After each question, allow for student input and reaction. Students will generally respond better and pay more attention to information communicated through discussion rather than through lecture. At the end of discussion, highlight the following:

- Spending money is about making choices.

- If we think carefully about the ways we spend money, we can make choices that help us get more out of our money.
- Spending more money than we have will quickly limit the choices we have in the future, and cause us to get less out of our money.
- Knowing where our money is going allows us to have more control over how we are spending it and to plan ahead to make the purchases we really want.
  It is helpful to provide an example here. You might explain that keeping track of money could help us realize that we are spending $2 every day to buy Hot Cheetos and a soda. That's a total of about $60 a month. Knowing we have $60 a month to spend allows us to plan ahead and decide whether we want to keep spending the money on Cheetos and soda or whether we would prefer to save it to buy a new video game or pair of jeans.

Activity #1: Cash In – Cash Out (suggested time: 7 minutes)

The objective of this activity is for students to see and understand that there is money coming into and out of their lives all the time.

1. Ask for a volunteer who has spent some money in the past seven days to come to the front of the classroom and stand next to the white board.
2. On the white board, draw one arrow on the left pointing toward the student.
3. Write "Cash IN" next to that arrow.
4. Draw another arrow on the right pointing away from the student.
5. Write "Cash OUT" next to that arrow.
6. Ask the student what is one item that he/she spent money on during the last seven days,

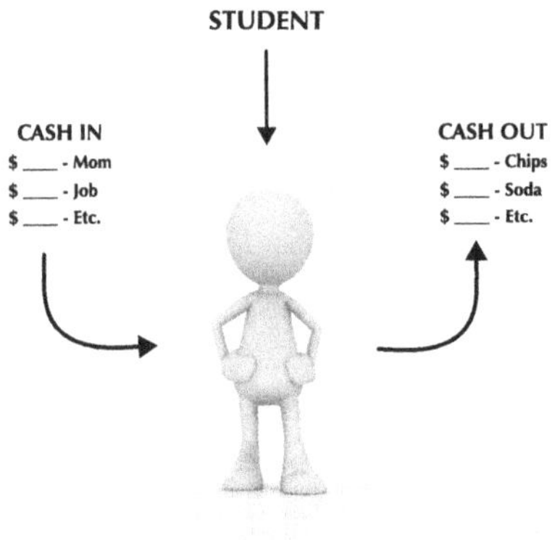

and how much money he / she spent on that item. Encourage the student to think about even the smallest purchase. For example, they may have bought a bag of chips, a candy bar, a song downloaded from iTunes®, or a bus fare.

7. Write each purchase under the "Cash OUT" arrow, along with the approximate amount the student spent on that purchase.
8. Then ask the student where he / she got the money for that particular purchase.
9. Write their answer(s) under the "Cash IN" arrow, along with the actual amount they received from that source.
10. Repeat the process for each purchase mentioned. REMEMBER: The key is to have the students visually understand that there is a source of income for every purchase made.
11. After the student has recalled all purchases, add up the total amount spent during that seven-day period.
12. Ask if the student received any money that he or she did not spend, and add up the total amount received during that seven-day period.
13. Repeat the process with another volunteer student (if you have time).

Lecture: Budget (suggested time: 5 minutes)

Explain that a budget has two main parts: **income** and **expenses**. "Income" is the same as "Cash IN," meaning the money coming into our lives from any source, like parents, friends, or a job. Generally when we hear the word "income," people are talking about the money they make from a job, but money can come into our lives from other sources as well. "Expenses" is the same as "Cash OUT," meaning the money exiting our lives when it is spent. The term "expenses" is used more frequently to talk about the costs that are not chosen, like utilities, housing, and transportation, but it should also include the more fun ways that money is spent, like entertainment.

Ask the students if they would want the Cash IN side to be bigger or smaller than the Cash OUT side, and why. After receiving answers, explain that in order to keep a positive budget, our income, or cash in, must be greater than our expenses, or cash out. It is a good thing when there is more money coming into our lives than going out of our lives. This is called **"positive cash flow."** It is a bad thing when we have more money going out than we have coming in. This is called **"negative cash flow."** You can point out whether the students from the previous Cash IN – Cash OUT activity had positive or negative cash flow (it should always be positive unless they still owe someone money). You can also mention that negative cash flow happens when we borrow money, although the specifics of borrowing money will not be discussed until a later unit.

Conclude with the following statement: "When you don't have a budget sometimes it is hard to tell how much you have going out. It is easy to spend money faster than we realize if we don't keep track. If we don't plan ahead, we may not have money left for the more important purchases, or we may spend more than we have coming in. Spending money is all about making choices. Is it more important to me to buy lunch at McDonald's with my friends, or am I willing to eat lunch at home so that I can spend that money on music for my iPod® instead? Later on, when you are financially responsible for yourselves, you will be making bigger decisions, but the idea is the same. Am I willing to share a studio apartment with a roommate so that I can save money for a car, or would I rather live alone and ride the bus? Every dollar that comes into our lives represents a choice that we get to make about how to use it."

Activity #2: Budgeting Pennies (suggested time: 23 minutes)

The purpose of this activity is for students to experience the process of making decisions about how to divide their income (the pennies) in order to cover all of their expenses. Students will begin to recognize that they will have to choose less expensive options in some categories, but will also realize that they have power in making choices.

Tell the class that they are going to do an activity that will help them better understand the concept of budgeting. They will have to decide how to divide up their money (pennies) based on what expenses they think are most important.

Game rules: Students only get 25 pennies per group. They have to decide as a group the best way to spend their pennies. Each group must account for every category on the "Budgeting Pennies" sheets, and to do so they will likely have to choose the "free" option for at least a few categories.

> **Note to Teacher**
>
> *You can use pennies, beans, M&M's®, or anything else that is small and cheap to get in large quantities.*

Directions:

1. Divide class into groups of 3-4 students per group. Give each group 25 pennies.
2. Give each group the "Budgeting Pennies" sheets that will guide them through this activity. The sheets list multiple options for each category, with options ranging in cost from zero to eight pennies, approximating the idea that we all make choices about whether to meet our various needs in cheaper or more expensive ways.
3. Tell the groups that they will have to decide how to spend their pennies according to the sheets. They should assume that they are adults, responsible for their own financial support.

They should decide how many pennies to use for their transportation, their cell phone, their cable bill, their rent, etc. They cannot spend more pennies than they have (so no more than 25), and they have to account for all the categories on the sheets.

4. Have groups explain their reasons for how they spent their pennies. Have students display their findings on the board or poster paper to be discussed during the group discussion time.

Note to Teacher

To make the game more exciting, you can add some type of emergency to each group during the game that will result in them having to give you some pennies. For example: tell one group that their car broke down unexpectedly and that they have to pay you two pennies to fix their car. You can also reward groups that have chosen to put a lot of pennies into savings by giving them an extra penny or two.

Possible group discussion questions:

- Why did you choose to divide your pennies the way you did?
- What was one category that was difficult for your group to decide on together?
- Why might you want to save some pennies?
- What did you learn about budgeting from this activity?
- Would you be happy making those same choices in real life when you become an adult? (For example, if they chose to spend no money on housing and live with their parents, would they be willing to make that same choice as an adult?)
- How would it change if you had more pennies? Less pennies?

5. Note similarities and differences between the ways different groups spent their money.

Wrap Up (suggested time: 2 minutes)

Finish class by telling students that many people end up going broke and owing money to others because they either do not know how to make a budget, or they do not know how to follow one. Making a budget may seem boring to some, but it allows us to decide where it's most important to spend our money. Planning ahead for those decisions results in more choices with our money. Then we will likely use the money to get the things that are most needed or most important to us. Budgeting can keep us from constantly feeling like we are "living without" by enabling us instead to feel that we are in control of our money and to look forward to the purchases for which we may be saving.

The pennies game isn't completely realistic, but it gives an idea of what it means to make a budget. Every month each of us has to decide how much money we can spend on various items. We will always have a limited amount of money that we receive each month, and we have to make choices about the wisest way to spend that money. That generally means making sacrifices in some areas in order to have enough for what we need and want in other areas.

Thank the class for their attentiveness and participation.

Vocabulary:
- budget
- income
- expenses
- positive cash flow
- negative cash flow

*Never spend your money
before you have earned it.*
–Thomas Jefferson, Former U.S. President

Materials needed:

- Budget Simulation Worksheet for each student – 2.2.1*
- Job Cards ready to hand out – 2.2.2 or 2.2.3*
- Income for Students Outline – California – 2.2.4*
- Taxes on Paycheck (project or hand out to each student) – 2.2.5*
- Students' names on slips cut up and ready to draw out of a hat
- A hat or bowl/cup
- A calculator for each student
- A pencil for each student

Key Concepts:

1. Making a budget involves choosing how much money we want to spend in different categories.
2. Budgeting helps us to avoid spending more money than we have.

Prep Time: approximately 60 minutes

Advance Preparation Tasks:

This lesson sets up the budget simulation, which is central to the next five lessons. In our experience with the curriculum, this simulation provides one of the most powerful learning experiences for the students. The simulation does require a fair amount of preparation, which is key to its success. Please allow plenty of time to familiarize yourself with all the materials and to make the necessary preparations. If you are unfamiliar with this lesson, it can end up taking longer than the allotted 50 minutes. We suggest having additional volunteers to help the students with any individual budget questions.

**For all additional resources, including handouts, video links and helpful websites, see www.futureprofitsresources.org*

Advance Preparation Tasks (cont.)

If you come from a city where the cost of living is similar to San Jose, CA or New York, NY use the included "Job Cards for students," and skip down to #2. If your students live in any other region, follow step #1 to create your own Job Cards. To compare the cost of living in your city to San Jose, CA, you can use the comparison tool at http://www.bankrate.com/calculators/savings/moving-cost-of-living-calculator.aspx. Compare your local area to "San Jose-Sunnyvale-Santa Clara Metro." If the figures are fairly similar, you can use the included Job Cards. If not, we strongly recommend going through the process of creating Job Cards that accurately reflect your local economy. The students will get the most out of the simulation if they are able to directly relate their experience in the simulation to their daily life experience with money and expenses. Using inaccurate salary figures can skew their perception about realistic income in proportion to realistic expenses.

1. **Research salaries for local area and update Job Cards.** We have provided a set of fill-in-the-blank Job Cards that can be adapted to your local area. The job titles and notes are included, but you will need to fill in the annual and monthly income for most jobs (a few are already completed). Use these websites to look up average salaries for jobs in your local area:
   a. www.salary.com
   b. www.payscale.com OR see www.futureprofitsresources.com for additional websites
   Using the "Job Cards for Students – blank," write in the amount for annual income, then divide the annual income by 12 to figure out the amount for monthly income, and write that in as well.
2. **Print and cut Job Cards.**
3. **Prepare students' names on slips of paper to draw out of a hat.**
4. **Print Budget Simulation Worksheet (one for each student).**

Keep In Mind

- Students may not be familiar with the concepts of saving and budgeting money. It challenges the mentality they may have adopted from experiencing trauma and unpredictability.
- Let the students discover the challenges of budgeting themselves during this exercise. The experience will be more powerful than a lecture.
- The early lessons in this unit may seem very basic, but are designed to lay a foundation for more complex concepts that come up later in the unit.

Budgeting may be new and unfamiliar for some of your students. Many may come from families that are focused on immediate financial needs. They may be caught in a cycle of living paycheck-to-paycheck, without necessarily creating a budget or saving for future emergencies and large purchases. Some students may not know anyone who saves money. In those families that do have a budget, the parents/ guardians may not share that information with their children, so the teens may be unaware of the decisions their parents / guardians make regarding money. You may find that many of your students have unrealistic concepts of monthly spending, financial decision making, and long-term planning. **Do not correct them yet.** This unit will allow them to experience some of the realities of budgeting firsthand. It is critical that your students be allowed to discover these realities for themselves. Practicing budgeting through the simulation should provide a much stronger impact on the students than anything taught in a lecture. It is important not to appear condescending or judgmental about their perceptions of or experiences with money. Allowing students to learn about budgeting through the simulation empowers them to begin to think about the financial choices they currently make, and the ones they will make in the future. Practicing budgeting will help students think about setting financial goals and working toward them, and exposes them to an alternative way of handling money that has the potential to break the paycheck-to-paycheck cycle. Budgeting also challenges the mentality of "live and eat today for tomorrow we might die," which is common in low-income communities where many students have experienced trauma and unpredictability.

The budget simulation can become overly complicated for the students if overlaid with too many details. In order to keep students engaged and interested, keep these lessons as simple as possible. The lessons are structured to move from basic to more complex concepts throughout the curriculum, so many concepts will not appear in these early lessons. For example, in real life, students would need to deal with higher costs as they transition toward independence, such as start-up costs like security deposits for rent, down payments for cars and homes, tuition and book payments for school, etc. These concepts will be covered in later units in order to make this unit as simple as possible.

Lesson Snapshot

Review (suggested time: 5 minutes)
- Review Budget and Cash Flow: Income and Expenses

Introduction: **Life at 25** (suggested time: 5 minutes)
- Give students time to imagine life at 25 years old
- Ask students to raise their hands if... (and go through list of scenarios)

Budget Simulation Intro (suggested time: 3 minutes)
- Explain simulation and tell students they'll be pretending to be 25 years old
- Explain that the students will be making a budget and continually adjusting it
- Pass out Budget Simulation Worksheet
- Make sure each student uses a pencil

Activity #1: Assign Jobs (suggested time: 10 minutes)
- Explain range of incomes and what to write on Budget Simulation Worksheet
- Call out job, then pick student's name, and give student the job card

Activity #2: Calculate Taxes and Take-Home Income (suggested time: 15 minutes)
- Give a general explanation of what taxes are:
  - overview of take-home income (or net income)
  - purpose of taxes
  - tax brackets
- Show students how to calculate their taxes on board
- Help students individually figure out taxes and monthly take-home income

Activity #3: **First Draft of Budget** (suggested time: 10 minutes)
- Explain the notes column and give students time to work individually on their Budget Simulation Worksheet
- Help individual students, but do not tell them the correct amounts for the different categories (encourage students to guess or ask a parent / guardian)

Wrap up (suggested time: 2 minutes)
- Next lesson: local cost of living

Review (suggested time: 5 minutes)

Remind students that last week we learned about how there is a flow of money in our lives. We all have cash moving in and out of our lives on a regular basis. Ask students who remembers the vocabulary word for cash coming in? (Income) For cash going out? (Expenses) We also introduced the idea of a budget. By playing the pennies game, we could see how there are a lot of different categories that adults need to consider when making a budget. Ask the question, "Who remembers what a budget is?" A budget is a tool for organizing your money, and figuring out how much you want to spend in certain categories. It is important to stick to a budget so we make sure we have enough money to pay for what we need.

Introduction: Life at 25 (suggested time: 5 minutes)

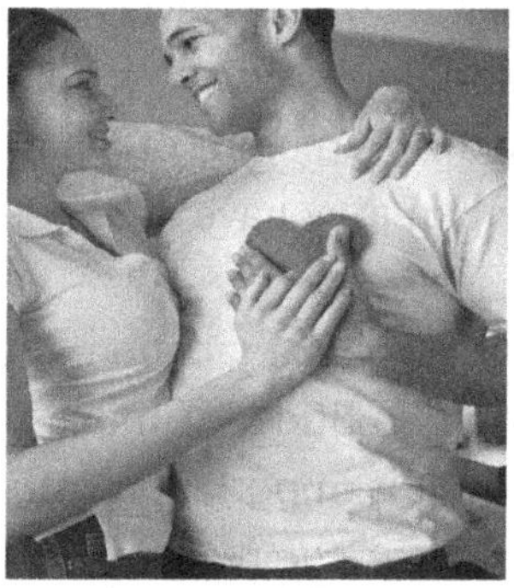

Have the students close their eyes and imagine what their life would be like at 25 years old. You might prompt them to think about work, family, and where they will live. Give them some time to imagine, then tell the students to open their eyes. Ask the students to raise their hands if:

...they live with their parents or guardians at 25.
...they are in college or grad school at 25.
...they are single at 25.
...they are married at 25.
...they own their own car at 25.
...they own their own house at 25.

Note to Teacher

Move through the questions quickly, but give the students time to look around and see what other students imagine for their lives. It is important to let the students respond to these questions before the budget simulation is introduced so that the teacher can learn more about the students and their aspirations before the simulation experience. Hopefully, this also will help foster an atmosphere of engagement with the simulation.

Budget Simulation Intro (suggested time: 3 minutes)

Inform students that for the next five weeks, they will be participating in a budget simulation. Ask the students if they know what a "simulation" is. After a few students have guessed, tell them a **simulation** is when people pretend to be someone or something other than themselves. Then tell the students that they will be pretending to be 25-year-old single adults. They will be randomly assigned a job and a corresponding income. Each of the students will have to decide how to use that income to pay for all of the monthly expenses they might expect to have as an adult. Covering all of the expenses will be easier for some students than others, depending on their assigned income, just like in real life. Students with lower income levels may have to make some difficult decisions about what is most important to them. Hopefully they will get a realistic picture of what they will have to think about in the future when they have an income to spend.

After the explanation of the budget simulation, ask if there are any questions so far. Then pass out the Budget Simulation Worksheet to each student and tell each student to pull out a pencil. It is important for students to use pencils since they will be adjusting their budgets several times in the next few weeks.

Activity #1: Assign Jobs (suggested time: 10 minutes)

It is now time to pass out "jobs." Before doing so, instruct the students that after they've received their jobs, they should write down the job title, the annual income, and the monthly income on the Budget Simulation Worksheet. Explain that the incomes range from a minimum wage income (the lowest legal income that a person working in the United States can have) to a star actor/actress. Also explain that there may be some additional notes for some of the jobs that students will need to copy onto their sheets. (For example, if the notes say that this person will be paying $425 in student loans, the student should write that amount in the line item for student loans.) Explain that **annual income** refers to the total amount of pay a person receives in a year. People usually receive paychecks either once or twice a month, so the amount they get paid each month is called **monthly income**.

> **Note to Teacher**
>
> *If you would like to track which student has which job, collect the Budget Simulation Worksheets at the end of class and make a list, or have a volunteer write down the names of students with their jobs as you go.*

Read a career/job from the Job Cards, along with how much the annual income is, and then pick a student's name out of a hat. Give each student the pre-cut slip that explains that job and income, and have each student copy the information down on their Budget Simulation Worksheet.

Activity #2: Calculate Taxes and Take-Home Income

(suggested time: 15 minutes)

Note to Teacher

It may be helpful to show your students a sample paycheck so that they can see the different types of taxes that are taken out of their pay. A sample paycheck is provided (see "Taxes on Paycheck" (2.2.5)) to make copies for your students, or download and project the image to show your students.

If any of your students have heard of taxes before, it may have been when their parents/guardians received a tax refund. Therefore, students may be surprised and confused to learn that taxes are something we pay to the government and not the other way around. Be prepared to address this question if it comes up.

After each student has received and recorded their job, annual income, and monthly income, they will now figure out how much money is going to be taken out of their income to pay for taxes. First, give a general explanation of what taxes are. This explanation should include an overview of **take-home income** (or net income), the purpose of taxes, and **tax brackets**.

You can say something like: "Whenever someone is offered a job with a certain annual income or hourly pay, this amount is always before state and federal taxes are taken out. The state and federal governments each take a percentage of your income in the form of taxes. The amount that you actually receive after taxes are taken out is called your take-home income (or net income). This is the amount that you get to choose how to spend. The government uses taxes to pay for all the programs and services it provides, including military spending, health care programs like Medicare and Medicaid, assistance for people living in poverty, interest on the national debt, government operations, public education, scientific research, environmental protection, and foreign aid.

"Taxes are a percentage of your income, but not everyone pays the same percentage. People with lower incomes pay a lower percentage, and people with higher incomes pay a higher percentage. These percentages are called tax brackets. Having different tax brackets helps

> **Note to Teacher**
>
> *Some students may struggle with this process and feel embarrassed about asking for help. Walk around the room to show your availability to answer questions. If a student acts out, or says something like, "This is stupid," he/she is probably feeling frustrated and really saying, "This is hard." Take some time to process the worksheet with the student until they have a better sense of how to continue on their own.*

people who have lower incomes take home more of their pay, so that they are more likely to have enough take-home income to take care of their basic needs."

The tax brackets are on the students' Budget Simulation Worksheet. Tell the students to find which tax bracket matches with their annual income and circle the tax bracket percentage. Then have students calculate how much tax is taken away from their monthly income to determine their monthly take-home income. This is described on the Budget Simulation Worksheet, but it may be helpful to go through a couple of examples with the class. You can write these equations on a board for the students to see: Monthly Income x Tax Bracket Percentage = Monthly Taxes; then Monthly Income - Monthly Taxes = Total Monthly Take-Home Income. You should also allow some time to help individual students. Use the worksheet, "Income for Students Outline – California" (2.2.4), as a reference when helping the students. Pass out calculators to each of the students so that they can calculate their monthly taxes and their total monthly take-home income.

Activity #3: First Draft of Budget (suggested time: 10 minutes)

Give the students 10 minutes to work on a first draft of their monthly budget. The Budget Simulation Worksheet lists the most common categories that might appear on an adult budget. Students will need to assign an amount of money to each category, based on how much they would expect to spend each month (for example, $750 for rent; $200 for groceries, etc.). There are a few lines that students might choose to fill in as "0," but they will need to account for most of the categories. They should explain their choices under the "Notes" column. For example, students might write "2-bedroom split with roommate" to explain their rent, or "bus pass" to explain their transportation. Tell the students to guess at prices. If they

> **Note to Teacher**
>
> *While students are working on their first draft, do not share the costs of specific categories if they ask. Instead, ask students how much they think it costs, and have them use that amount for now. Their first drafts may be unrealistic, but this should provide a powerful learning experience when they learn about the realistic cost of living. If students are unable to finish their first draft, they can complete their budgets the following class when it is time to make adjustments.*

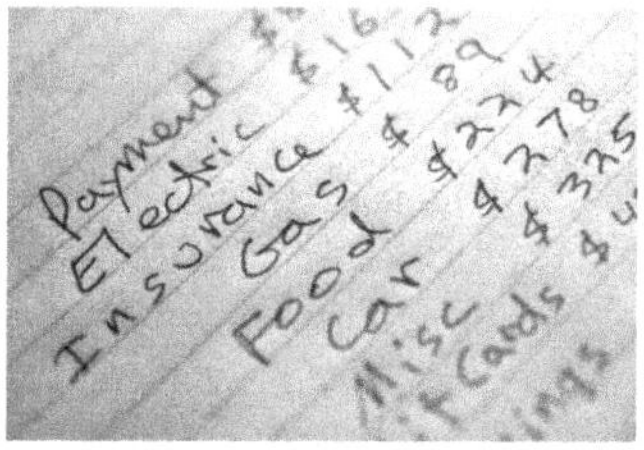

have no idea, tell them to think about what their parents/guardians might spend. Have them make their best guess for now, and encourage them to go home and ask their parents/guardians what they think is a practical amount for a single 25-year-old adult in their local area. They can also ask their parents/guardians if they have a budget and if so, how it compares to the students' first draft of their budget. The "Total Monthly Take-Home Income" and "Total Monthly Living Expenses" lines must equal each other. Have students use their calculators to make sure that the amounts are equal to each other. Students with higher expenses need to choose where they will cut back, and students with higher income need to decide whether they want to spend more in some categories or put the remainder in savings.

Note to Teacher

Depending on how responsible your students are, decide whether or not students should hold onto their budgets, or return them to you each week. If you decide to collect the worksheets at the end of each class, it will help with control and organization during this unit. If students are allowed to keep their worksheets, suggest that they show it to a parent or guardian. This can provide for valuable discussions in the home. If you choose this option, make sure to keep track of who had which jobs, in case any of the worksheets are lost.

Wrap Up

(suggested time: 2 minutes)

Finish the class by thanking the students for their participation, and telling them that next week, they will be learning about the realistic costs of living in this area (locally).

Vocabulary:

- simulation
- annual income
- monthly income
- take-home income (or net income)
- tax brackets

Additional Resources:

For additional resources on salaries and tax brackets, see www.futureprofitsresources.org.

Money is only a tool.
It will take you wherever you wish,
but it will not replace you as the driver.
–Ayn Rand, Author

Materials needed:

- Computer with internet connection and projector
- Whiteboard and pen, or chalkboard and chalk, or poster paper and pen
- Picture Cards for Comparison Pictures Activity #1 — 2.3.1*
- Additional images or examples of the "clothing" category for the Comparison Pictures (see Advance Preparation Tasks)
- Websites bookmarked in advance, or printed out to show class
- A pencil for each student

Key Concepts:

1. Healthy budgeting requires recognizing which expenses are needs and which are wants.
2. Students will be exposed to the average cost of basic expenses in their local area.
3. Understanding the cost of living will encourage students to begin thinking about what salary they want to earn as adults.

Prep Time: 1-2 hours

Advance Preparation Tasks:

- Print picture cards for Comparison Picture Activity #1 and cut along the dotted line on each page, creating 10 separate pictures
- Bookmark or print information from reality-check websites (recommended websites are provided at the end of the lesson)
- For "Activity #1: Comparison Pictures," provide images or examples of expensive brand-name clothing compared to less expensive brands of clothing. We suggest using similar-looking shoes or jeans that are commonly known to your students.

**For all additional resources, including handouts, video links and helpful websites, see www.futureprofitsresources.org*

Keep In Mind

- High school students usually have an unrealistic idea about the cost of basic expenses, and therefore an unrealistic idea about the amount of income that is necessary to live comfortably.
- It is important that students become aware of, and even surprised by, all the money it takes to provide their basic expenses.

Most teenagers do not have a realistic idea about the amount of money their parents or guardians spend to support their lifestyle. You may have noticed last lesson that many students made their expenses fit their incomes by assigning unrealistically low amounts of money to cover basic expenses like rent and food. Because students may not realize how expensive these necessities are, they also may be unaware about what level of income is necessary for a comfortable lifestyle in their area. In this lesson, it is important that students become aware of, and even surprised by, all the money it takes to provide their food, housing, cell phones, cable, internet, etc. If they begin to get a realistic picture about local cost of living, this may provide incentive for them to work toward the education necessary to achieve a higher income career. It is not the intention of this curriculum to communicate that being wealthy is the goal of life, but it is important for students to have a realistic picture of how much money it costs to cover the necessary expenses most adults pay for.

Lesson Snapshot

Review (3 minutes)
- Have a few students share about their experience creating a budget last class

Introduction (2 minutes)
- Learning realistic costs of expenses that were guessed last class

Discussion: Needs vs. Wants (7 minutes)
- Write "Needs" and "Wants" on board and brainstorm expenses that would go in each category
- Give definitions of needs and wants, and adjust lists on board if necessary
- Explain how sometimes a need becomes a want

Activity #1: Comparison Pictures: When Needs Become Wants (8 minutes)
- Show pictures for each category and have students determine need vs. want
- Discuss why some broader need categories can actually be wants
- Summarize needs vs. wants in their families and their simulation budgets

Lecture: Cost of Living (5 minutes)
- Definition of Cost of Living
- Explain how it differs from location to location, and give example

Activity #2: Cost of Living Comparison (5 minutes)
- Go to Cost of Living website and use students' salaries to compare locations

Activity #3: Local Reality Check (17 minutes)
- Go through bookmarked expense categories online so that students can see the actual cost for different categories
- Remind students of the choices they have for different options, and give them time to balance their budgets with their new expense costs

Wrap Up (3 minutes)
- Ask students about categories that surprised them and which expenses they had to change on their budgets
- Next lesson: delayed vs. instant gratification

Review (suggested time: 3 minutes)

Have a few students share something about their experience with creating a budget last week. You could ask:

- What was most difficult about making your budget last week?
- What decisions did you have to make in order to make your income cover all of your expenses?
- Did any of you ask your parents/guardians about their budgets, or for their advice on your budget? What did you learn from them?

Introduction (suggested time: 2 minutes)

Remind students that last week they had to guess how much they would need to spend in each category on their budget worksheets. Ask if anyone had trouble guessing what some items would cost. Tell them that this week we will be investigating how much different lifestyles really cost in our local community and adjusting our budgets to fit the local reality.

Discussion: Needs vs. Wants (suggested time: 7 minutes)

One of the most critical tools in deciding how to prioritize expenses in a budget is the concept of Needs vs. Wants. Introduce the topic by telling the students: "Everything that we spend money on can be categorized as either a need or a want." Ask, "What do you think are some items that people pay for that are considered needs?" If they need prompting, tell them to think of things they see adults pay for. Also tell them to think of some of the categories on their budget simulation worksheet. Write the students' answers on the board under the heading "Needs" so that all students can see what has been brainstormed.

Then ask the students, "What do you think are some items that people pay for that are considered wants?" Write the students' answers on the board under the heading "Wants" so that all students can see what has been brainstormed. Examples of wants can include items such as: cell phone, rims, iPod, flat screen television, entertainment, etc.

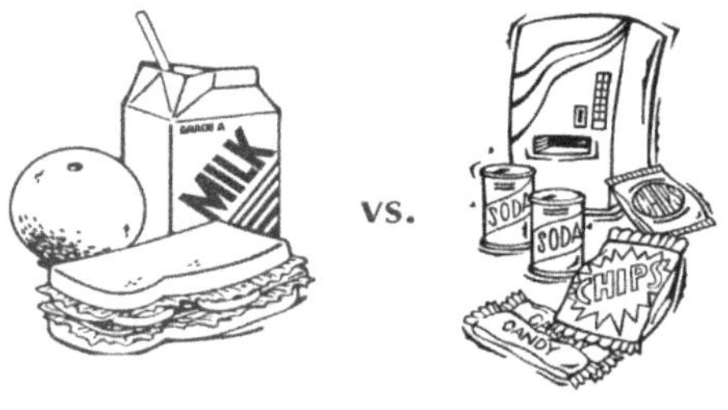

Ask the students, "What do you think the definition of a need is?" Allow for several responses, then give them the following definition: "A need is an item we spend money on that is necessary for the most basic level of survival. The following are examples of basic needs (add these to the list on the board if students did not mention them):

Note to Teacher

For the moment, go ahead and let the students brainstorm their ideas for both Needs and Wants without correcting them. They may list some wants as needs, but you will give them an opportunity to adjust their lists in a moment.

1. Food
2. Shelter
3. Clothing
4. Transportation
5. Communication

An item can also be a need if it is necessary to help us earn our income. This is why transportation is considered a need." Then ask, "What do you think the definition of a want is?" Allow for several responses, then give the following definition: "A want is any other item that we spend money on. Wants are items that may make our lives more comfortable, but if we had to survive without them, we could. In the United States, we are used to a high standard of living, particularly compared to many other parts of the world. We often say that we need something when we could actually survive without it." Ask if there are any items on the brainstormed lists that students think should move. If there are any wants that are still listed under the "Needs" heading, point them out, and ask, "What about this one? Is it absolutely necessary for us to survive?"

Once the lists are corrected, explain that sometimes our needs turn into wants. For example, we cannot survive without eating, so food is definitely a need. However, if a person goes out to eat in a restaurant every day, then that basic need becomes a want that is expensive to maintain. Also, there are foods we buy, like candy and soda, which do not help us get the nutrition we need. Although we eat them, they are not necessary for our survival and so they are wants.

Activity #1: Comparison Pictures: When Needs Become Wants

(suggested time: 8 minutes)

The purpose of the picture activity is to teach our students how to properly identify when needs turn into wants, and to understand the subjectivity that one deals with in determining a need. We will look at five specific "need" categories: Food, Shelter, Clothing, Transportation, and Communication.

Explain to students that they are going to practice identifying which expenses are needs vs. wants. Have the Picture Cards ready (see Advance Preparation tasks). There are 10 pictures, one pair for four of the five "need" categories, and a sixth pair to further express the subjectivity in choosing whether an item is a need or want. You will need to provide the images or examples for the clothing category. They should be set up in pairs:

1. A grocery store and a chain sit-down restaurant (Food category)
2. An apartment and a regular-looking house (Housing category)
3. A pair of less expensive shoes/jeans and a pair of expensive brand-name shoes/jeans (Clothing category) *(see Advance Preparation Tasks)*
4. A bus or bicycle and an average car (Transportation category)
5. A basic cell/home phone and a more expensive phone (Communication category)

Introduce and hold up each pair in the front of the class, then ask, "In the category of ______, which picture is the need and which picture is the want?" For each set you hold up in front of the class they must vote which picture would be a need or a want. Allow for debate among the students if there is disagreement, but make sure the students have a clear understanding of each pair before you move on. You may need to explain for an item like the expensive brand-name clothing that, while shoes/jeans are a need, there are a lot of options to buy that are much less expensive than the expensive brand-name version of those shoes/jeans. Since we can take care of the need in a more cost-effective way, choosing to spend the extra money on more expensive shoes/jeans is a want. It doesn't mean we can't decide that we will buy those more expensive shoes/jeans, but we do need to recognize that they are not a need.

Finally, show the extra pair of pictures:

6. A peanut butter and jelly sandwich and a double cheeseburger from the McDonald's dollar menu

Ask the class to vote on which picture would be a need or a want. After students debate over whether each of these pictures is a need or a want, point out two concepts to the students. First, comment that many of the choices we make daily are small purchases and may seem like they don't matter too much, but all the choices we make, even regarding small purchases, add up.

Second, comment that deciding between needs and wants often changes depending on the person or the circumstance. Choosing a want over a need is not bad, but we must recognize they are wants in order to determine what purchases are best for our budgets.

After the activity, summarize Needs vs. Wants using the following narrative:

"Different families have different needs and wants that they have to pay for. Some families have to pay for items for their children, while other families or people who don't have children will not need to pay for that. Based on an individual or family's income, sometimes families have to make difficult decisions about whether an expense is really a need or whether they can do without it. Certain expenses cannot be eliminated. Knowing which expenses are basic needs will help us figure out how much our lives cost and where we can make choices to have our lives cost less. By identifying which expenses are wants, we can see where we could choose to save money. When you look at your budgets later today, you will want to think about which items are needs and which are wants to help you make decisions about how to prioritize your spending. Sometimes we can choose to spend money on wants, but we should always make sure we take care of our needs first."

Lecture: Cost of Living (suggested time: 5 minutes)

Begin with asking the students this question "What do you think cost of living means?"

After you have received several responses, tell the students that the definition of **cost of living** is "the average cost of food, clothing, and other necessary or usual goods and services paid by a person" (you may want to write this definition up on the board and have each student copy it on a sheet of paper). Explain to them that the cost of living can be different, depending on where you live. Give an example that students may be familiar with, comparing the cost of rent or gas in two nearby cities or neighborhoods: "Have you noticed that the price for a gallon of gas is usually less in Neighborhood X than in Neighborhood Y, even if it is the same brand of gasoline?" Big cities generally have a higher cost of living than small towns and rural areas, and living on either coast is generally more expensive than living in the middle of the country. Today we are going to focus on the cost of living here in our local area.

★ Activity #2: Cost of Living Comparison (suggested time: 5 minutes)

This activity is to reinforce the concept of cost of living in a fun and interactive manner.

This website offers comparisons of salary levels and expenses in different cities across the United States.

1. Go to http://cgi.money.cnn.com/tools/costofliving/costofliving.html, and use the projector to show the website to the class.
2. Ask for a student to give his/her annual salary from the budget simulation. Enter that salary, and choose your state and your city (or the closest one available) for the initial city/state.
3. Ask the student you have chosen to name a state and city in the United States where they might be interested in living some day. Enter this into the destination slot.
4. Press the button to calculate and the website will give you a comparable salary and the major cost of living differences. Prompt the students to comment on or discuss the information. For example, "Housing is 65% less in Oklahoma compared to California. What do you think about that? Where would you rather live?"
5. Repeat these steps 3-4 times, comparing different areas of the country.

Note to Teacher

When selecting cities, it's most interesting if you compare different types of locations, so try to avoid comparing only major cities to one another. If your first volunteer chooses to compare your location to New York, suggest that the next student pick a smaller city in the South or Midwest for a different comparison.

Activity #3: Local Reality Check (suggested time: 15 minutes)

This activity will help the students readjust their budgets with realistic amounts for each category in their budget. The reality of making a budget has a much greater impact when students take into account the actual cost of items and aren't able to spend as much as they want on entertainment by shorting their spending on necessities like rent and food.

Note to Teacher

Use a computer with internet and a projector so the students will be able to see the cost of living websites first hand. Bookmark the web sites in advance. If you don't have access to this equipment, print the web pages that show local costs and ask students to read them aloud to the class. You will not have time to go through every category during class. Therefore, prioritize the categories, utilities, and car expenses. These are typically the categories for which students currently do not pay themselves. Choose from the suggested resources for every category provided in the Additional Resources of this lesson.

1. Pick an expense category. For each category, ask several students to share how much they guessed this category would cost. Remind them that it's okay if they are wrong, because the purpose of this activity is to be surprised and learn together what life really costs.
2. Show the actual examples for your local area from the web.
3. Direct students to adjust each category on their budget as you move through the categories.
4. After you have completed all of the categories, give students time to balance their income and expenses, taking into account their newly adjusted expenses. This may require some students to make changes like getting a roommate, moving to a studio apartment, changing to a less expensive form of transportation, eliminating certain optional expenses, etc. For students who have to make adjustments, remind them to think about which categories are needs and which categories are wants. Generally they will have much less flexibility in lowering their expenditures in need categories.

Wrap Up (suggested time: 5 minutes)

If you are collecting students' budgets, do so now. Ask the following:

- Who was surprised to learn the realistic cost of living?
- Which categories most surprised you?
- Was it difficult to balance your budgets with the realistic numbers for your expenses?
- What changes did you have to make to your lifestyle in order to balance your budget? (roommates, type of apartment, transportation, entertainment, etc.)
- Does this experience change your idea about how much money you need to make to live a comfortable lifestyle in our area?

You may also want to suggest again that students discuss with their parents/guardians what they spend in some of these categories. We often find that it is a powerful experience for students to learn how much it may be costing their parents/guardians to support their lifestyle. Thank students for their participation. Tell the students that next week, we will be using what we have learned about needs and wants to help us understand delayed gratification and instant gratification.

Vocabulary:

- needs
- wants
- cost of living
- utilities

Additional Resources:

See the list of Reality-Check Websites.

Reality-Check Websites

For specific links, see www.futureprofitsresources.org

http://www.bankrate.com/calculators/savings/moving-cost-of-living-calculator.aspx
This website compares the cost of living in two different locations (like the CNN website), but provides very detailed figures for the average expenditure on things like mortgage payments, apartment rentals, energy, and a range of grocery items. Other websites we suggest may provide a more engaging way to present the information (e.g. seeing actual rental listings is more interesting than seeing an average figure on a chart), but this is a good backup for information that you cannot find elsewhere.

Rent/Mortgage

You will need to research several examples of rental apartments and homes for sale. For rentals, we recommend finding listings for at least a studio, a 1-bedroom, and a 2-bedroom apartment. Students can then choose what type of apartment they want, and how many roommates with whom they will share. Use a website like www.craigslist.org to find up-to-date rental listings in your area. For students who want to buy homes and pay a mortgage, www.realtor.com has a mortgage-estimating tool that should be helpful. Search for listings in your city, then click on a particular listing and a link to mortgage rates will appear near the top of the listing. Again, we recommend having several levels of homes with a range of mortgage costs. You might consider homes of different sizes, condos vs. single-family, or homes in different neighborhoods. You might also consider picking up some "Apartments for Rent" and "Homes for Sale" books that are found outside grocery stores. These resources may be more realistic and familiar sources of information to the students.

Utilities

Students may be unfamiliar with the term "utilities," so first give them a definition. **Utilities** are commodities or services such as water, electricity, gas, and garbage, provided by a public utility company. If you are in a major city, you may be able to find helpful data at http://www.whitefenceindex.com, which lists average monthly utility prices for 21 U.S. cities. Be sure to note that the total average listed includes internet, TV, etc., which our budget worksheet categorizes separately. Select your city from the list on the right, then use the drop-down menu below the chart to select the utility you want to check. If no nearby city is listed, we suggest estimating based on your own experience. Go to the website that provides your gas, electricity, or water, and show the students what the rates are for that company. Ask around for the different rates based on the size of apartment or house where you live. You can also try an internet search for information about your particular city.

Transportation

http://www.eia.doe.gov/oil_gas/petroleum/data_publications/wrgp/mogas_home_page.html provides up-to-date average gas prices for 10 major cities, nine states, and all regions of the United States. http://www.bankrate.com/calculators/auto/auto-loan-calculator.aspx provides a car loan payment calculator, which will allow you to calculate monthly payments for cars of varying prices. The website for your local transportation authority should provide information on the cost of bus passes and other public transportation options.

Car Insurance

Though a few years out of date (2007), http://www.iii.org/media/facts/statsbyissue/auto/ gives a state-by-state average for car insurance.

Internet, Cable, and/or Home Phone

If you are in a major city, you may be able to find helpful data at http://www.whitefenceindex.com, which lists average monthly utility prices for 21 U.S. cities. Select your city from the list on the right, then use the drop-down menu below the chart to select the utility you want to check (phone, television, and internet are all options). If your city is not listed, we recommend looking up prices on the websites of local providers (cable or dish companies, DSL providers, etc.).

Entertainment

Students will likely have a more realistic idea of the price of movies, clubs, etc., although they may not realize how much they routinely spend in total on these activities. You can do a reality check by asking them to multiply the number of times they want to go out by the average price of a movie ticket or other activity.

Food (in-home/groceries)

There are two ways to calculate a reasonable monthly expenditure on groceries, although both will require some work on your part. However, this is a category that students tend to drastically underestimate, so it is an important one for which to give them a reality check. The first option is to use a local grocery store website (Safeway, Ralph's, Stop 'N' Shop, etc.) to find prices for common grocery items. You will have to create a mock grocery list, and then total the cost of the items to get a realistic monthly figure. Many grocery stores that now offer delivery will allow you to fill a cart online, which will provide a running grocery total.

The second option is to use the prices provided for basic grocery items at http://www.bankrate.com/calculators/savings/moving-cost-of-living-calculator.aspx and add them up to get a reasonable monthly figure. However, the grocery items listed may not give you enough options to create a completely realistic shopping list. Regardless of how you create your list, it is very helpful for students to see a realistic grocery list and the corresponding prices, as most of them have no experience with providing for their food beyond snacks.

Food (dining out)

Pick a couple of popular local restaurants, ranging from fast food to sit-down dining, and locate their menus online. You can use these examples to help students calculate a realistic figure, based on how many times they plan to eat out at different types of dining establishments each month.

Health and Dental Insurance

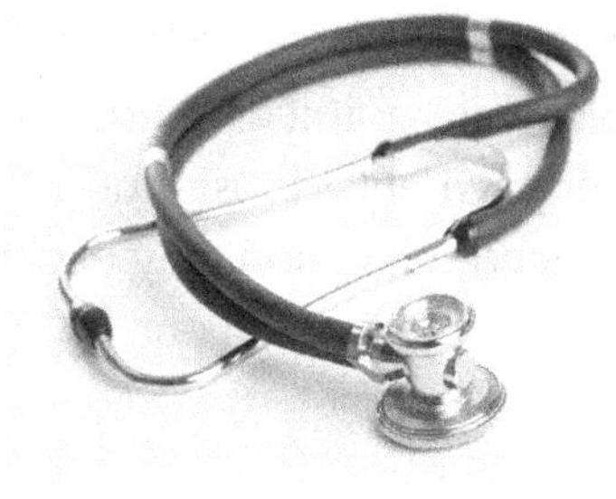

For most students, this is included in their job benefits. For those students whose jobs do not include benefits, they will have to choose whether or not to buy insurance. You can use a website for any insurance provider in your state to get a quote. Blue Cross / Blue Shield® offers coverage in most states, and provides online quotes for a variety of plans. Their website is http://www.bcbs.com/coverage/find/plan.

Medical Expenses

For most students this includes over-the-counter medications and medical supplies, and co-pays for doctors' visits and prescriptions. We estimate this figure to be approximately $20-80 per month, depending on the health of the individual and the details of their insurance plan. For students without health insurance, this figure should be higher.

Clothes, Memberships, Personal Care, and Charitable Donations

Most of these will vary widely, depending on personal choice. Many students may already have a good idea of their spending on clothing, memberships, and personal care.

- For clothing, you can ask your students how often they shop, and how much certain items of clothing cost (shoes, dresses, pants, shirts, outfits, etc.).
- For memberships, tell the students to consider health club memberships (such as 24 Hour Fitness® and YMCA™), along with AAA® memberships. AAA memberships provide towing services in case your car breaks down. Go to www.aaa.com and click on the "Join" link at the top to see the different annual costs of membership, and what each membership level provides. You will need to divide these costs by 12 to determine the monthly cost for the students' budgets.
- For personal care, remind them that this includes hair cuts (discuss the range of costs for hair cuts, color, products, etc.), soap, deodorant, shampoo, conditioner, makeup, feminine products, pedicures, manicures, professional massages, etc. Many students will forget about the many small items they use that are included in this category.
- For charitable donations, tell students that this is when you are able to help the causes that you believe in by donating money. The government even offers tax breaks to those who donate money to charities to encourage giving. This is the area on your budget where you can spend money for other people and organizations, and contribute to their growth.

Student Loans

This figure is specified for some students on their job cards. For everyone else, you can explain that the amount people owe in student loans after they graduate depends on how much money they had to borrow to pay for their education. Students who earn more scholarships will have fewer loans and therefore lower loan payments. Students who choose to work while going to school will also have fewer loans and lower payments. Those students whose careers do not require advanced education may decide to assume that they did not go to college and therefore have no student loan payment.

Savings

A healthy budget puts at least 10 percent of income into savings, but ultimately students can decide how much they want to save. It may be helpful, however, to give an explanation of why savings are important and to discuss how savings fit into the "Needs vs. Wants" discussion. While savings may be identified as a want, families are always only one crisis situation away from it becoming a need. Most financial planning advice recommends having three to six months of income saved in case of emergencies, particularly those emergencies, like unemployment, that result in lost wages. You do not have to drive this point home too forcefully, however, as students will soon experience an emergency in the simulation, and will learn firsthand the necessity of having savings to fall back on.

Note to Teacher

Plant the idea now that students should start thinking about how they will pay for college. By the time students decide to apply for scholarships, many find that they have not prepared appropriately to meet the specific requirements of the scholarships they would like to receive. Though you will not have time to cover this in-depth, introduce the idea and suggest to students to begin thinking now about costs of post-high school education, and refer them to a college or career counselor if one is available at their school.

Here is an online article that encourages 10 percent monthly savings: http://moneyfor20s.about.com/od/savingmoney/f/howmuchsave.htm

FUTUREPROFITS

If a person gets his attitude
toward money straight,
it will help straighten out
almost every other area in his life.
Rev. Billy Graham, Religious Leader

Materials needed:

- In an Instant! ... Or Not Q and A sheet – 2.4.2*
- 3 "Ticket to Success" sheets – 2.4.1 (or the amount for the number of teams you will have – we suggest 3)*
- 3 Golden Door Flashcards – 2.4.3 (or the amount for the number of teams you will have)*
- 12 Door Flashcards – 2.4.3 (6 positive and 6 negative)*
- Whiteboard and pen, or chalkboard and chalk, or poster paper and pen

Key Concepts:

1. The choices you make now affect the choices you will have later.
2. Waiting for and working toward a goal often results in significantly greater rewards, but also requires sacrifice.

Prep Time: 30 minutes

Advance Preparation Tasks:

- Print and prepare materials for game, In an Instant ... or Not

**For all additional resources, including handouts, video links and helpful websites, see www.futureprofitsresources.org*

Keep in Mind

- Poverty can foster feelings of "we deserve this," which fosters an immediate gratification mentality. Often long-range financial planning is not a priority.
- Help students develop a sense of hopefulness about their future and the opportunities they have, especially when making small, wise decisions today.
- Students may not see a correlation between education and the quality of their future life, which helps contribute to high dropout rates in urban areas.
- Students may be under the impression that they will be able to live comfortably without graduating high school or college.

Many of your high school students may have a strong immediate gratification mindset. Because their families are often living paycheck-to-paycheck, teens may not be exposed to good examples of long-range financial planning. As mentioned before, the victim mentality perpetuates the attitude of "we deserve this," and can be common in low-income families. For example, if a family's food stamps are spent on snacks and candy at the beginning of the month, there may be no money left to buy food at the end of the month. Parents often allow for that spending because they feel guilty that food is scarce and want to offer their children a "treat." Parents often feel empowered when they are able to provide "treats" for the children, and children often feel special and happy in those small moments. Within this framework, it is important to understand that long-range financial planning is regarded as a lesser value than providing immediate joy and happiness for their children. From the parents' perspective, much more than snacks or candy may be sacrificed.

Another example is how tax refunds may be viewed. Many will consider it a large check from the government to spend on something extravagant, while at the same time ignoring practical needs, such as past due utility bills, which threaten the utilities being shut off.

Additionally, many teens have experienced so much trauma in their lives, that they do not imagine very far into the future. Life experience has trained them to think more about survival and getting the most out of today than about how to maximize their opportunities in the future. However, without learning to think about the long-term outcomes of their decisions, they will likely perpetuate the cycle of living in survival mode. The goal is to help the students begin to develop a sense of hopefulness about their future opportunities and begin to recognize the connections between their actions now and their success in the future. Students should begin thinking about making decisions based on their future goals vs. immediate gratification.

One of the most significant issues related to delayed gratification is the attitude many students have toward academics. Throughout the nation many low-income students do poorly in school, increasing the dropout rate. A recent study showed the average graduation rate in the nation's 50 largest cities to be only 53 percent, with some cities reporting significantly lower percentages.[1] The reasons students do not graduate vary, but a strong contributing factor is that many do not see a correlation between their effort in school now and their quality of life in the future. Many students believe they can survive comfortably without a high school diploma or college degree. This curriculum continually underscores the importance of education and the relationship between education and future opportunities.

[1]Dillon, Sam. (2009, April 22). Large Urban-Suburban Gap Seen in Graduation Rates. The New York Times, p. A14.

Lesson Snapshot

Review (3 minutes)
- Ask what "cost of living" means
- Ask what surprised them about the cost of living

Introduction (2 minutes)
- The budget simulation is an opportunity to experience the difficult decisions that adults often have to make with their money
- Instant vs. Delayed Gratification influences our decisions

Activity #1: Delayed vs. Instant Gratification Game: In an Instant! … or Not (25 minutes)
- Divide class into 3 groups and give overview of rules
- Each group representative chosen and given a "Ticket to Success" sheet
- Ask questions from Q & A sheet and give points accordingly

Discussion: Delayed vs. Instant Gratification (10 minutes)
- What would you pick: $1,000 today or $1 million in a year?
- What would you pick: $5,000 today or $5 million in five years, with working hard and moving scenario?
- Ask students their reasons for picking each, and draw out different perspectives
- Define and explain instant gratification giving one or two examples
- Define delayed gratification, referring to Golden Door as an example
- Refer back to the $5 million choice in prior discussion and point out the benefits that were not seen by the students before

Activity #2: Budget Adjustment (5 minutes)
- Students can choose to save for an expensive item they might like to buy in the future. If they choose to do so, have them write that item on a blank line at the bottom of their worksheet. Have students readjust their budgets accordingly
- Collect budget simulation worksheets (or have students put them away)

Wrap up (5 minutes)
- Ask students for examples of delayed gratification in real life
- Share examples of making cookies, studying for a test, or practicing for a sport
- Challenge the students to look for examples of delayed gratification this week

Review (suggested time: 3 minutes)

Start off the class by asking one of the students what "cost of living" means. Ask for another student to share something that surprised them about the cost of living in their city or the cost of living for an adult. You may also want to ask if any students talked with their parents/guardians and what they learned from them. After the students share, thank them for sharing.

Introduction (suggested time: 2 minutes)

Ask students how many of them had to make difficult decisions about how to spend their money when they adjusted their budgets last week. Tell students that the reason for doing the budget simulation is for them to experience the difficult decisions that adults often have to make with their money. Last week was about "Needs vs. Wants." This week will introduce the concept: "Instant vs. Delayed Gratification." Both of these ideas influence decisions made about how to prioritize where money goes.

Activity #1: Delayed vs. Instant Gratification Game: In an Instant! ... or Not (suggested time: 25 minutes)

The objective of this interactive game is to introduce students to the risks of instant gratification and the rewards of delayed gratification through a process of trial and error.

Rules:

1. The class will be divided into 3 teams, and a team representative will be given their team's "Ticket to Success." The teacher will ask a question, and the first team to raise their "Ticket to Success" gets the opportunity to answer the question first.
2. If the team answers incorrectly, they lose 100 points from their score. Then, the other teams can raise their "Ticket to Success" and have a chance to guess.
3. When a team answers correctly, they get 100 points added to their score, and they get to choose between receiving a checkmark or opening a door.
4. If they choose to open a door, they will pick Door #1, #2, or #3. Each "door" has a point value. Some are positive and some are negative, so it may add points to their score, but it is also possible to lose points. Because they chose to open a door, they do not get to compete to answer the next question.

5. If they choose to receive a checkmark, the game goes on to the next question and all three teams get to compete. When a team accumulates 5 checkmarks, they automatically receive a Golden Door, which is always worth 1,000 points. If at any time a team chooses to open a door instead of receiving a checkmark, they lose any checkmarks they already have.
6. The team with the most points at the end wins.

Directions For Instructor:

1. Split the class into three groups. (The easiest way to do this is to assign each student a number 1-3. Tell the 1's to go to one side of the room, 2's in the middle, and 3's to the other side of the room.) At this point you should give the students an overview of the game rules. However, the game may seem confusing at first, so you will need to guide students through each stage of the game as you go, until they get the hang of it.
2. Instruct each group to choose a representative who will speak for their team. Give a "Ticket to Success" (the team buzzer sheet) to each representative.
3. Remind the students that the representative who raises their "Ticket to Success" fastest gets to answer the question first. If it is a tie, you can play rock-paper-scissors to decide. Remember scissors beat paper, paper beats rock, and rock beats scissors.
4. Ask the first question on the "In an Instant! ... Or Not Q and A Sheet." If the team answers incorrectly, subtract 100 points from their score. Give the other groups a chance to answer until either a group answers correctly or all three groups have tried to answer, then go to the next question.
5. When a team answers correctly, give them 100 points and remind them that now they have a choice to make. They can choose to open a door, but they don't know whether the points will be positive or negative and they won't be allowed to compete to answer the next question. Or, they can receive a checkmark and start working toward a Golden Door, which is a guaranteed 1,000 points. Each time a student requests to pick from a door, shuffle the door cards and place three of them on a desk. The one on the far left will be Door #1 and so forth. Show the class the point value behind the selected door, and adjust the team's score accordingly. Then show the class what was behind the other two doors as well before moving on to the next question.

Note to Teacher

In this game, teams that choose the Golden Door will usually win. In the rare cases this does not happen, discuss the unusual situations where instant gratification turns out to have a big payoff. For instance, a few people do win the lottery. Reinforce that the number of lottery winners is very tiny compared to the number of people who spend a lot of money on lottery tickets over a lifetime, and never win. In most cases, delayed gratification is a much more reliable path to success.

6. As soon as a team accumulates five checkmarks, give them a Golden Door card, worth 1,000 points. They can start their checkmark count over if they want to work toward another Golden Door.
7. You can decide when the game is over, depending on the amount of time you have and when you think students have begun to realize that the best choice is to take the checkmarks and wait for a Golden Door. You can also end the game when you go through all the questions. (This game usually results with the team who waits for a Golden Door card almost always winning.)

Discussion: Delayed vs. Instant Gratification (suggested time: 10 minutes)

1. What would you pick?

You will help students debrief the game in a moment, but begin the discussion by asking, "If I were to give you a choice between receiving $1,000 today or $1 million in a year, raise your hand if you would pick the $1,000 dollars today? Okay, now who would pick the $1 million next year?" Most likely, the majority of students will pick the $1 million. Follow up with this question, "What if I gave you a choice between $5,000 today or $5 million in 5 years, BUT to get the $5 million you would have to learn how to teach all the FutureProfits lessons, work 12 hours a day, Monday through Friday, and move to a developing country (where working utilities are hard to find) to help people start small businesses. Who would choose the $5,000 today? Who would choose to work for the $5 million in five years?" Most likely, the majority of students will choose the $5,000 at this point. Ask the students to share their reasons for each decision.

After the students have had a chance to respond, analyze each scenario with the students, emphasizing the concepts of instant and delayed gratification. Some suggested comments are: "In the first scenario, I offered you $1,000 today or $1 million in a year. Of course, $1,000 would be great today. You could hit the mall, take your friends out, put some money away for college, maybe help out with bills at home. But, a year seems totally worth it to wait for $1 million instead, especially if you don't have to do anything in between! So it's fairly easy to reject that $1,000 today for a guaranteed $1 million in a year. But let's take a look at the next scenario: $5,000 today for doing nothing, or $5 million in five years if you meet a long list of somewhat complicated requirements. That makes you think twice about the $5 million, doesn't it? Five years is a long time to wait, and it requires a lot of work and sacrifice to get the $5 million. What if you weren't able to meet all the requirements, and you ended up with nothing? On the other hand, you could leave this classroom today with $5,000 without any worry or struggle. $5,000 dollars could buy a lot of things that your family really needs. Taking the easy money now might be very hard to turn down. But what is easiest and fastest is not always best."

2. Define and Explain Instant Gratification

Say to the students, "These scenarios, and the game we played, are all about choosing between **instant gratification** and **delayed gratification**. Let's take a minute to define what those words mean. Does anyone think they know what instant gratification means?" Take a few responses, then write the following definition on the board: *Instant Gratification = fast reward*. Elaborate by saying something like: "Instant gratification happens when we get or do something that gives us an immediate positive feeling. Because we enjoy that feeling, we are often tempted to choose instant gratification. However, the pleasure we get with instant gratification usually ends as quickly as it comes, and it may also have some negative consequences in the longer term."

It is generally helpful to offer students one or two analogies to help them relate to the concept. The following are some possible samples, although you can certainly use a personal story instead.

Clothing Analogy:

How many of you have ever been really excited to buy a new item of clothing, or the latest cool pair of shoes? The excitement of buying it gives you immediate pleasure, and the excited feeling may even last until the first or second time you wear it. But, pretty soon the item isn't new anymore, so it no longer gives you a special feeling, or an even newer and cooler version comes out, and now you want that instead. That's an example of instant gratification. You get an immediate positive feeling from buying the item and wearing it the first time, but there is no lasting satisfaction. You need to keep buying new things to keep recreating that positive feeling. And, because you already spent that money, you won't have the money to buy something else that you want later.

TV vs. Studying Analogy:

I know every one in this class has had to make a decision before about how much time to spend studying for a test. Maybe the new episode of your favorite TV show is on, or your favorite sports team is in the playoffs. Watching TV is so much more relaxing and enjoyable than studying; it gives us that immediate feeling of pleasure. However, what happens when you get to class the next day? The feeling of pleasure is quickly replaced by stress and frustration when you don't do well on the test. This is a good example of how choosing instant gratification can have negative consequences later. What if bombing the test means you fail the class and have to take it again in summer school? When June rolls around, you would much rather be having fun with your friends, but now you have to spend your summer sitting in class to make up for the instant pleasure you chose earlier.

Snacks vs. Car Analogy:

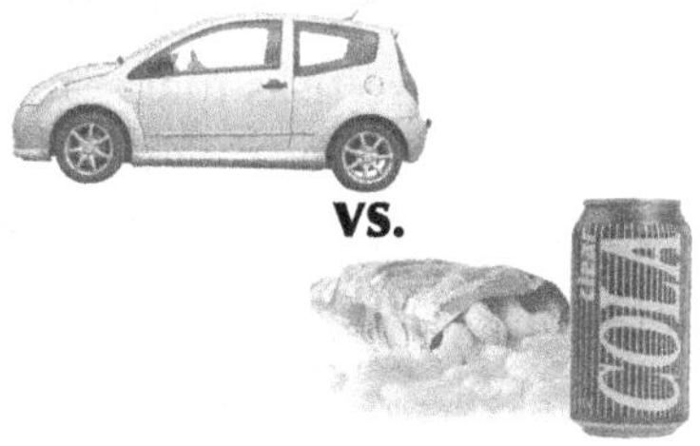

Who wants their own car to drive around during high school? Pretty much everyone wants a car, but not everyone is able to get one because they are expensive. We may think that we'll never have enough money to buy a car, but if we add up all the money we spend on snacks and sodas during the day, it may add up in the long run.

For example, if you bought a soda every day for a year, that's about $365 you spent on soda for the year. Add a snack to that, and you've spent over $700 on sodas and snacks for the year. That money, if saved over the year, could go toward getting a used car to drive around during high school. That's how instant gratification can be most of the time. It deals with the here and now, fulfills your need or desire at the time, and it may not even be a bad decision, but adds up and can leave you without something much more valuable.

3. Define and Explain Delayed Gratification

Once you've given an example of instant gratification, ask the students, "Who has an idea what delayed gratification means?" Take a few responses, then write the following definition on the board: *Delayed gratification = waiting and working for a bigger or better reward.*

Say to the students, "As you could see in the game we played, the team that won was the one that stayed consistent and waited for the golden door. They knew the reward was greater and better if they waited. They didn't get the experience of picking one of the three doors and possibly receiving instant points, but when they eventually did get a door, it brought them much closer to the goal of winning. Waiting and working toward the delayed gratification was a more likely method of succeeding in the game."

Ask the students who did not pick the checks for the Golden Door about their reasons for picking the other doors. This may bring up a myriad of reasons that also connect with why students pick instant gratification over delayed gratification. For some, there may be an element of curiousity and risk. With any risk, there is a possibility of danger or loss. But it can be fun to take a risk and guess what might be behind the doors. Although they have heard of the negative points, the chance they could also get positive points quickly drives them to take that risk. They might think, "Maybe I will be the one who doesn't get stuck with negative points." The main benefit of taking the risk is the allure of getting positive points, and the fun of choosing something unknown. In discussing risk with your students, make sure that risk is seen as being both a positive and negative thing. Although risks are fun to take, and can sometimes bring benefits to us, one of the main elements to consider when taking a risk is what will happen in the long term. When we allow the long-term perspective to guide the risks we choose, we will often take wise risks that lead to greater opportunities.

Return to the scenarios from the beginning of the discussion to draw out the explanation of delayed gratification. A suggested discussion may include:

Looking back at the offer for $5 million, what may have discouraged you from choosing that route is all the hard criteria involved with obtaining the money. Working so many hours a day, moving to a place you don't know and might not like, and doing a lot of studying and memorizing. It may look hard, so you are tempted to stop without trying, especially if you can still get $5,000 right now for doing nothing. During those five years, you would probably struggle, and you would feel frustrated and discouraged at times. But at the end of the five years, you would have earned $5 million. Imagine what you could do with $5 million! The possibilities are endless! You could buy a house or start your own business, which would not only help you to own more things, but it would also help your money grow to more than $5 million over time. You would be able to enjoy the $5 million so much more than the $5,000, which would probably be gone in a couple of weeks or a couple of months. Not only is it a lot more money, but you would also have the satisfaction of succeeding at the challenge, and the benefit of all the experience you gained in the process.

The biggest difference between those who do okay and those who have great success is whether they are willing to wait and work for the bigger and better rewards that come with delayed gratification. Delayed gratification requires patience, hard work, determination, and courage. If you can overcome your fears of failure, while working hard, staying consistent, and staying focused, you will be able to achieve and maintain success. That is the value of delayed gratification.

Activity #2: Budget Adjustment (suggested time: 5 minutes)

Instant vs. Delayed Gratification is a particularly significant concept for budgeting, and students need to have an opportunity to relate what they learned in today's lesson to their experience of creating a budget and making financial decisions in the simulation. The idea of saving for big purchases, instead of buying on credit, should be introduced. Although the topic of credit has not yet been covered, students should be familiar with the idea of saving and working toward a financial goal.

Have students get out their budget simulation worksheets (or pass them out if you have collected them). Ask every student to think of an item that they would really like to buy, but that is expensive enough that it would require them to save money over several months (or years) before they could afford it. It could range from a flat-screen TV or laptop, to a car (or a fancier car if they already have one), or even a down payment for a house. Encourage the students to be creative in dreaming about a big purchase that they might want to make in their imagined 25-year-old lives.

Explain to the students that, as adults, there are big purchases that we want to make. Some are practical, like paying for college or buying a house. Others may not be practical or necessities, like a TV or a luxury car, but we may still decide that we value them enough to spend our money that way. But any big purchase is a good example of why waiting for delayed gratification is so important. We will probably have to sacrifice some of our instant gratification and spend less money now, in order to save up enough money for the big purchase that we really want.

Tell students that they now have the option of adjusting their budgets to start saving for that special big purchase that they just imagined. If they want to work toward it, they should write in the name of the item in one of the blank lines on the bottom of their budget. They should decide how much money they will save for the item each month, and then must adjust their spending in other categories so that the income and expense lines still balance. Generally any adjustments will have to come out of "Wants" categories, not "Needs," unless they make a reasonable adjustment like getting a roommate. They must continue to stick to a realistic cost of living for your local area. If students do not want to save or cannot find the flex room in their budgets, they can decide to keep their budgets as is.

If you are keeping the budget worksheets, collect them again.

Wrap Up (suggested time: 5 minutes)

End with asking the students if they can think of examples of delayed gratification that they have seen or experienced in their lives. If they cannot think of anything, tell them that delayed gratification is all over the place, and give one of the following examples:"

Chocolate Chip Cookie Analogy:

When you are baking chocolate chip cookies, the batter looks and tastes irresistibly good. It tastes so good that you might as well eat all of it. But if you ate all of it, and didn't let it cook for a period of time, you would miss out on what the end product was meant to be – warm chocolatey goodness that can sometimes be gooey, with a nice cold ice cream scoop on top, which would taste much better than the cold cookie batter that isn't actually cooked (and the raw eggs might not actually be the best for you).

Studying for a Test Analogy:

Most people who study for tests end up doing better on their tests. That is because they set aside the time to commit to memory the most important information they need to know for the test. And then the more they study, the more it pays off in the end when they get good grades. And the more they get good grades, the more it pays off (literally) when they want to go to college and can earn scholarships because they were a great student.

Practice for a Sport Analogy:

Ask students to raise their hand if they play a sport. Have you ever wondered why every successful athlete or musician knows the word "practice" very well? It is because the more time and effort they put into their sport or instrument before they actually perform, the better they will be when they do perform. This is another example of delayed gratification. Most people don't like to practice because the most fun and "gratifying" part of the sport is the actual game. But if the practice didn't come before that, the game would not be as gratifying because you would be more likely to lose.

Remind the students that the benefits of delayed gratification are all around them, and challenge the students to look for examples of delayed gratification this week. Thank the students for their participation.

Vocabulary:

- delayed gratification
- instant gratification

In and Instant! ... or not — Question and Answer sheet

1. What are the two main parts of a budget?
   a. Income and expenses

2. Taylor Swift is classified as an artist in what genre of music?
   a. Pop or Country

3. What famous document begins: "When in the course of human events..."?
   a. The Declaration of Independence.

4. Where is the safest place to store your money?
   a. Bank

5. What character is actor Daniel Jacob Radcliffe better known as?
   a. Harry Potter

6. In the movie Forrest Gump, what actor said, "My Mama always said, 'Life was like a box of chocolates; you never know what you're gonna get.'"
   a. Tom Hanks

7. What movie's main character is Lara Croft?
   a. Tomb Raider

8. Name one common bank account that you can have at a bank.
   a. Savings Account or Checking Account

9. What is the closest planet in our solar system to the sun?
   a. Mercury

10. The final dance scene is exactly the same in which two Disney Movies?
    a. Sleeping Beauty and Beauty and the Beast

11. In the Twilight move, how many Cullens are there?
    a. 7

12. How many red stripes are there on the American Flag?
    a. 7

13. How is an NCAA Football different from an NFL Football?
    a. Stripes (an NCAA football has one stripe at each end)

14. Name one place that many people go in order to cash a check.
    a. Check Cashing Outlets or Banks

15. What is Lil Wayne's real name?
    a. Dewayne Carter

16. Singer Alicia Keyes had her acting debut on what sitcom as a child?
    a. The Cosby Show

17. Pop sensation and teen icon Miley Cyrus's Dad is a country singer famous for what hit single?
    a. Achey Breaky Heart (by Billy Rae Cyrus)

18. Give two examples of needs that adults have to pay for.
    a. Food, clothing, shelter, transportation

19. What are the names of both teachers teaching "FutureProfits"?
    a. Subject to class

20. How many American presidents had there been before Theodore Roosevelt?
    a. 25

21. What does the text term smh mean?
    a. shake my head

22. Basketball superstar LeBron James was drafted to the NBA in what year?
    a. 2003

23. Through which Bank account can you receive checks?
    a. Checking account

24. The untimely death of music icon Michael Jackson tragically happened on what date?
    a. June 25, 2009

25. What is the name of the very first American Idol winner?
    a. Kelly Clarkson

26. How is your take home pay different from your annual income?
    a. Take home pay is your income after taxes are taken out.

27. In what year did the Gold Standard end?
    a. 1931

28. What is the middle name of the 44th president of the United States?
    a. Hussein

29. What is California's state animal?
    a. Grizzly Bear

30. What is the state capital of Maine?
    a. Augusta

Note to teacher: We chose to include a mixture of "pop culture" questions and budget questions in order to help the students review but also get students excited to answer questions for the game.

Materials needed:

- Emergency Cards – 2.5.2 (blank) or 2.5.3 (California)*
- Budget Simulation Worksheets With Emergency (new) – 2.5.1*
- Budget Simulation Worksheets (old—without emergency, that students have already been working on)
- Pen or pencil for each student
- Calculator for each student

Money without brains is always dangerous.
–Napoleon Hill, Author

Key Concepts:

1. Emergencies happen in everyday life, and they can cause significant financial hardship.
2. Planning ahead and saving can help prevent getting trapped financially by uncontrollable emergencies.
3. Even having a very high income cannot guarantee protection from the impact of an emergency.

Prep Time: 30 minutes

Advance Preparation Tasks:

This lesson's preparation is similar to the preparation for the lesson, "Life at 25." If you come from a city where the cost of living is similar to San Jose, CA, use the "Emergency Cards for students – California"* and skip down to step #2 below. If you previously created your own job cards, follow step #1 to fill in the blanks for some of your own Emergency Cards (see "Emergency Cards for students – Blank"*).

**For all additional resources, including handouts, video links and helpful websites, see www.futureprofitsresources.org*

Advance Preparation Tasks (cont.)

1. There are only seven emergency cards out of 30 that will need to be filled out.
   a. Use your city/state's minimum wage payment for the following emergency cards: **Professional Basketball Player** and **Actor / Actress**. Multiply the hourly minimum wage by 40 hours per week, then by four weeks per month to get an approximate amount for the monthly job income. There is also a **McD's minimum wage worker** who loses a week's pay along with a **General Emergency** card where the student loses his or her job and now has to work a minimum wage job, but at 30 hours a week. Follow the same equation above, but with 30 hours a week instead of 40 hours a week.
   b. Use the previously created Daycare Center Teacher salary to determine what he or she would make without a week's pay. Subtract (previous monthly salary divided by 4) from the previous monthly salary to get an approximate amount for the new monthly job income.
   c. Divide the previously created **Psychologist** salary by two to determine the approximate amount for his or her new monthly job income.
   d. For the **Software Engineer** getting paid unemployment, you'll need to do some research to determine what the unemployment benefits are in your state. Use the following website to find the unemployment information based on your state: http://www.servicelocator.org/OWSLinks.asp. Look for an "Unemployment Benefits Chart" that could tell you the new unemployment monthly income based on the previous salary for your Software Engineer. The total amount should be slightly higher than the monthly job income for a minimum wage worker. See additional resources for general unemployment facts and information.
2. Print and pre-cut emergency cards for students in class. (Have a few more cards than the amount of students in class in case there is a problem with one of the emergencies.)
3. Take out any emergencies that are specific to jobs that none of your students have. For example, if the emergency card says, "For the Professional Basketball Player" and there is not a Professional Basketball Player in the class, take out that card.
4. Print copies of the new Budget Simulation worksheets. This will help the students to write their emergency on a new worksheet and redo their budgets.

Keep In Mind

- Emergencies in low-income families often result in compounding and reinforcing cycles of debt, crisis, and poverty.
- Emergencies are often seen as family issues vs. individual ones, which can strain students, family relationships, and further the cycle of financial crisis within the family.
- Be sensitive. It's crucial that students understand that their simulated emergency is random and is not a reflection on any actual student.

The students with whom you will be working will most likely be familiar with emergencies. Many of their families have had "emergencies" affect their life when they were not prepared for it. Often this results in compounding and reinforcing cycles of debt, crisis, and poverty. People who are trapped never intend to be in that place, but often find themselves with few choices when faced with an unexpected and difficult situation. Although the students may be familiar with emergencies, they may not know the full extent of how a person can be affected financially, because many times families will not share the details of their financial situation with their teens. In this lesson, students will get an introduction to the realities of how an emergency can dramatically impact an adult's financial stability. Although unexpected situations will always happen in life, there are ways to prepare for them so that the cycle of debt and crisis is not continued.

When a financial emergency happens, it often can become a family concern, rather than just an individual one. Many times people in this situation will look to family members to loan or give them money when they are in need. Although it is a value of families in general to help those closest to you in need, it may end up perpetuating the cycle of poverty within low-income families. If a student is on the giving end of a financial emergency, money is often not available to be returned. This not only strains the student's money situation, but family relationships as well. This may come up in the lesson, or in conversations with students. If a family member is expecting money from the student, encourage students to either make the loan a "gift" and not expect money back in return (as people are often unable to pay the money back) or to offer their help in services rather than money. For example, a student may be able to help with cooking, cleaning, or childcare, and the person in the emergency can use the money they may have spent on those services toward their emergency instead. Although there is a sense of urgency in helping a family member in an emergency, it is important to remember that sometimes the most healthy option for that family member is to not give money directly, but to help in other ways. This is one way to help break the cycle of unhealthy dependency on family members.

Remember that students may have an emotional response to receiving their emergencies. Some of the emergencies are sensitive situations that students or their friends may have actually experienced. Make sure to communicate clearly that everyone is receiving an emergency, and that these emergencies reflect a variety of experiences that any adult might have. Some emergencies are completely beyond the individual's control, while others would occur as the direct consequence of an individual's decision. Because some of the emergencies imply irresponsibility, it is crucial that students understand that the emergency they receive is random and is not a reflection on the actual student.

Lesson Snapshot

Review (5 minutes)
- Instant vs. Delayed Gratification – Definitions and Examples

Introduction (2 minutes)
- Introduce emergencies

Activity #1: Emergencies!! (22 minutes)
- Hand out new budget simulation worksheets, instructing students to write their name and job before emergency
- Hand out emergency cards, starting with most specific to most general, along with the old budget simulation worksheets
- Explain to the students what to fill in on their new budget simulation worksheets (monthly job income, taxes, savings, and additional emergency expenses)

Discussion: Emergencies (5 minutes)
- Ask who thinks they have the worst emergency
- Ask if any students think the emergency will not affect them
- Ask what categories they think they'll need to cut expenses down

Activity #2: Redo Budgets (10 minutes)
- Ask for general questions
- Each student works individually, with teachers assisting where needed

Lecture: Preparing for and Coping with Emergencies (5 minutes)
- Focus on concepts of saving, needs and wants, and how to be creative in spending money

Wrap up (1 minute)
- Next lesson: Budget Simulation debrief

Review (suggested time: 5 minutes)

During the review, follow up with the students to see if they have discovered "new" examples of delayed gratification throughout the week. It may be helpful to review the definitions of instant and delayed gratification first. Ask for student volunteers who remember the definition of each. Then ask the students if anyone saw an example of delayed gratification last week, where the reward after waiting was better than the reward that was offered at the beginning. To encourage more conversation, remind them about the Golden Door from the "In an Instant" game, or review the $5,000 now vs. $5 million in five years scenario.

Introduction (suggested time: 2 minutes)

Today students will learn what it is like for adults when emergencies happen. Some emergencies are uncontrollable, and may even be unfair, but there are often still consequences. Other emergencies happen as a direct result of decisions that we make, without necessarily planning ahead for the financial impact of those decisions. By learning about how emergencies can affect us financially, it can help us to make wise decisions with our money now and prepare us for things that may happen in the future. This is another aspect of understanding delayed gratification. By preparing in advance for emergencies, our delayed gratification reward is being able to avoid some of the painful consequences an emergency could have.

Note to Teacher

If students have a negative reaction to the emergencies, remind them that even though emergencies are hard to deal with, they happen to everyone and can be planned for in their budgeting process.

Ask the students to share a few emergencies they know about from their own experience or an emergency they have heard about from someone else. After the student shares, ask them how they think it would have impacted that family or person financially.

This is a great opportunity to be dramatic in your presentation. Help students to get intrigued and invested in their simulation experience by hyping up what is about to happen. You may want to introduce this lesson by saying, "Unfortunately, there will be times in all of your lives that emergencies will happen. Today, in our simulation, everyone's life will change dramatically. You are all about to receive some bad news, and it is going to affect your finances. After you receive your emergency, you will have to make a new and revised budget based on the specific emergency that happened in your life."

Activity #1: Emergencies!!

(suggested time: 22 minutes)

1. Hand out copies of the new budget simulation worksheet (with emergency). Instruct the students to write their name and their job before emergency on their new worksheets as soon as they have received them. Tell the students that for many of them, their job will not change, but some may lose their job, so that is why this line is included.

2. Give an emergency to each student. Pass them out in the following order:
   a. Hand out cards based on specific jobs.
   b. Hand out cards based on specific circumstances (i.e., someone who has a roommate or a car).
   c. Hand out remaining cards.

Read each aloud so that the whole class hears the different emergencies. This will heighten the expectation for those students who have yet to receive their emergency, and will hopefully encourage the students to continue conversations about their emergencies with their friends outside of class. It also allows students to hear about a wide range of possible situations with which an adult might have to cope.

To save some time, read only the emergency situation rather than reading the details of the emergency (what their new monthly income and taxes are). These are written at the bottom to help students with some of the math of their emergency. As summarized before, some of the emergencies correspond to specific jobs, so it is easiest to distribute those first. If you have the "old" budget worksheets, you can pair them in advance to the matching emergency card and then simply read the emergency and the name of the student before handing both the emergency card and old budget to the student. If the students have kept their "old" budget simulations worksheets, ask, "Which student is the Professional Basketball Player?" When the student raises their hand, read aloud their emergency and give them the card with their emergency written on it.

In addition to job-specific emergencies, there are also emergencies that are specific to certain lifestyle choices a student has made in their original budget (for example, living in an apartment, living with parents/guardians, owning a car, etc.). You will need to distribute those next. Again, pair them with the student's completed budget worksheets in advance (use the notes column to see which students fit each situation) or ask the class, "Who lives with a parent, guardian, or other family member?" and then read the corresponding card and hand it to that student. Move on to the least specific emergencies, until each student has been given an emergency card.

After reading the first emergency card, explain to the whole class what that student will be doing once he or she receives the card. Point out to the class that the new monthly job income, taxes, savings, and additional expenses are listed at the bottom of the card. Show the students where they will fill in this information on their new budget worksheet. Use the following explanations:

- "Emergency" line—The students should write a short description of their emergencies in the "Emergency" line at the top of their new worksheets.

- "Monthly income and monthly taxes"—Each emergency card will explain the situation with that student's monthly income. If the job changed or the student is able to get a second job, they will need to recalculate taxes based on the new annual income. For most students, taxes are already calculated on the emergency card. If they have the same job, they will not need to worry about changing their taxes. They can use the same amount from the monthly tax line on the old budget worksheet.

- "Savings from before emergency"—Some emergencies indicate that the student can use what was saved in the original budget. If that is the case, the student can put that amount in the savings line. They can choose to use their general savings, their "delayed gratification" savings from the previous lesson, or the total amount in both. The emergency card specifies how many months' worth of savings the student can use.

- Additional expense line—Some of the emergencies have an additional expense listed below the Savings line on their emergency card. If an additional expense is listed, tell students to include this expense on one of the blank lines underneath the other expenses on the budget worksheet.

3. After all the emergencies have been disbursed, every student should have three items in front of them: their old budget worksheet, their new budget worksheet with emergency, and their emergency card. Move into a quick discussion before the next activity.

Regarding "Savings from Before Emergency"

There may be students whose original budgets did not include enough savings to cover their emergency, and are now forced to create a budget with an impossibly small amount of money. Borrowing money should be a last resort, so students must first work through all the ways they can reduce their expenses. If they have cut down their expenses, and still can't afford necessities, they are allowed the option of borrowing money, also known as "going into debt." In these cases, students can be allowed to borrow as little as possible solely to pay for needs.

The concept of debt is not taught until Unit 3, and will be too complicated to give a comprehensive lesson of it here. Focus on helping the students make their budgets work, knowing that they probably will not fully grasp the implications of borrowing until later lessons. For now, help them with the necessary math:

Students can borrow money by using a credit card or taking out a loan (teachers pick which would be appropriate). The bank has set the interest rate at 15%, or $15 for every $100 borrowed. Students should add the amount they borrow to whatever they wrote in the line for "Savings" at the top of the budget sheet, so that the borrowed amount becomes a form of income. They will also add the amount of their "monthly debt payment" into their expenses section. This repayment amount should cover at least the monthly interest (15%), plus 5% of the amount originally borrowed (the principal). For example, if the student needs to borrow $300, they add $300 onto their savings, and put the new total amount on the Savings line. They would also add a minimum monthly payment of $60 ($45 for interest and $15 for the principal) to their expenses.

Discussion: Emergencies (suggested time: 5 minutes)

The purpose of this discussion is to help all students with the next step of redoing their budgets to cope with their emergencies.

Ask the following questions:

- Does anyone think they received the worst emergency of the class? Why?
- Tell the students, "Raise your hand if you think this emergency will not significantly affect your budget." Ask the students who raise their hands why they think it will not affect their budget.
- If you now need to spend less money on expenses than before, which items do you think you'll have to cut back on? (If students are quiet and non-responsive to this question, prompt them by asking about specific categories such as, "How many of you think you'll have to cut your budget in the category of "rent," "clothing," etc.?" This is also an opportunity to remind them of "Needs" vs. "Wants." Further the discussion by asking which of those they should cut first.)
- Tell the students that there are certain recurring monthly expenses that cannot be changed without receiving some kind of "penalty" in real life. For example, there are some cell phone contracts that will charge a cancellation fee for ending the contract early. Another example is at the beginning of a rental contract when a security deposit is required, (which is usually an additional month's worth of rent). This money is paid up front, and one can often get the deposit back. But breaking the lease before the time is up (meaning there is a commitment to paying rent for a certain amount of time, often between six months and one year), usually results in the loss of the deposit, or still owing the remaining months' rent. An option the students may want to consider is having someone move in with them to cut the rent in half rather than moving out of their apartment and breaking the lease.

Note to Teacher

If students are emotionally upset about the emergency they received, it may be difficult to guide this discussion. Keep the tone light-hearted and offer perspective that emergencies are often "unfair," but everyone in the class received one. Make sure to validate the students' answers by thanking them for sharing, even if you disagree with their conclusions. Remember, the point of this discussion is to help them begin thinking through how their specific emergency will affect their simulated life, not to debate, or for you to solve their new budget adjustments.

Activity #2: Redo Budgets (suggested time: 10 minutes)

Before the students begin redoing their budgets for their life after their emergency, make sure that each student has written down their new monthly job income, monthly taxes, savings if allowed, and new emergency expense if applicable.

Tell the students that because emergencies have a financial affect, many will need to change their expenses on their budget. They will have 10 minutes to readjust their budget based on the emergency they received. Ask the students if they have any general questions. These questions should NOT be specific to their emergency. Walk around the room and help students with math or any specific questions. Tell the students to work on redoing their new budgets. They can refer to their "old" budget simulation worksheet for budget categories or items they do not want to change, and keep the same amount for those categories.

After students have had a chance to redo their budgets, students can hold onto their old budget simulation worksheet, but collect from them the new budget simulation worksheets with their emergencies explained.

Lecture: Preparing for and Coping with Emergencies (suggested time: 5 minutes)

The purpose of this lecture is to give the students good ideas for how to prepare for emergencies and deal with the repercussions of emergencies that may happen in their future.

The instructor should cover the concepts of saving, needs and wants, and how to be creative in spending money. Here is an example of exact wording the instructor can use: "One of the most important items in a budget is the money that you put into savings. Lots of adults make the mistake of thinking that savings should only be the money that is leftover at the end of the month when they have finished spending for what they need and want. For most people, that leftover money won't be very much. Instead, a wise budget treats savings like a bill that has to be paid every month, the same as rent or electricity. Consider it like paying a monthly bill to guarantee your future financial stability and security. In this approach, money goes into savings before spending on "Wants" items like entertainment. It may mean less instant gratification each month, but it can protect you from some very painful consequences if an emergency catches you unprepared. Many people put a specific percentage of their money into savings in order to save up for either emergencies or for things they want to buy that are more expensive items. Even if you do save, you may go through a certain emergency where you still have to adjust your budget. This may require some creativity in spending your money so that you do not go in debt or so that you can afford to pay for your basic needs. Often, the areas in which you have to spend less are your wants instead of your needs. You can cut down on some spending in the need categories, such as cooking most of your food at home in order to save, using lots of coupons, or deciding to share a room with a friend instead of having your own room. But cutting down in the needs categories usually comes after cutting down in the wants categories, such as entertainment, vacations, furniture, and other miscellaneous items for which you end up paying."

Wrap up (suggested time: 1 minute)
Thank the students for their participation in adjusting their budgets and experiencing the emergencies they received today. Next class will include a discussion about the emergencies and the budget simulation experience as a whole, and students will have an opportunity to learn about each other's experiences with different jobs and different emergencies.

Vocabulary:
None

Additional Resources:
For additional unemployment facts and information, please visit
www.futureprofitsresources.org.

Financial Survival Skills – Budgeting
Budget Simulation Debrief
Lesson 6

Materials needed:

- None

If you would be wealthy,
think of saving as well as getting.
–Benjamin Franklin,
Politician and Founding Father of the USA

Key Concepts:

1. Every student has the opportunity to be successful, and they should be encouraged to begin dreaming about the future careers they might choose.
2. Having a stable financial future as an adult requires planning and careful decision-making, and building toward future success begins with the choices students make right now.
3. There are different challenges that correspond to different careers and income levels, and students should begin to understand these realities now so that they can make informed choices in planning their future goals.

Prep Time: 10 minutes

Advance Preparation Tasks:

Read through the discussion questions and choose the discussion questions that will work best for your students. We provide many questions to ensure that you can have a productive and edifying discussion with your students.

**For all additional resources, including handouts, video links and helpful websites, see www.futureprofitsresources.org*

Keep in Mind

- The budget simulation is intended to counteract the message students may have received that limited opportunities are available to them.
- Allow sudents to learn from each other through the discussion.
- Your students' parents may hold lower paying or minimum wage jobs, so it is important that they don't feel embarrassed about what their parents do.
- Encourage students toward a higher level of education, and inspire them to want more than minimum wage incomes for themselves.

This lesson is all about processing the students' experiences and feelings from the budget simulation. Students will have lots of opportunities to share about their individual experiences. Since each student had a different career, different salary, and different emergency, this discussion provides a great opportunity for students to learn by comparing the different experiences of their classmates. Many of the discussion questions have been written to draw out these comparisons and to guide students toward certain realizations about the realities of the economic system in the United States. During this lesson, students are encouraged to realize how difficult it is to live comfortably on a minimum wage income. By contrasting the two extremes of jobs, and discussing some of the challenges that may still exist with a middle-class income, students will hopefully be inspired to continue their education in order to increase the opportunities available to them when they are adults. Many of these students will have received negative messages about the opportunities available to them throughout their lives, or may have had authority figures in their lives make assumptions about their lack of ability to succeed; this simulation is intended to counteract these discouraging messages. Be deliberate about conveying that every student has tremendous potential to be successful in any career they choose, but that success does require planning and hard work has to begin now.

Students may have parents that earn minimum wage or very low wages, so be careful to never demean these types of jobs. Students should not be made to feel bad or embarrassed about the types of work their parents do. Instead, the goal is to encourage students toward a higher level of education, and inspire them to want more than minimum wage incomes for themselves. Students are encouraged to recognize that they can earn more money by investing more in their education. It is important for students to realize that education is one of the key systems in which they need to be successful, in order for them to begin breaking the cycles of poverty.

This lesson is very heavy on discussion, so it is important to create an environment or culture where all students are expected to participate and be engaged. This may mean you direct questions to specific students in order to help them engage, or take a few minutes at the beginning of class to set some "ground rules" for discussion that you can point students back to if necessary over the course of the class time. You know your students the best, so do what you think would be best for them to engage and participate in this discussion.

Lesson Snapshot

Review (none)

Introduction (2 minutes)
- Wrapping up the Budget Simulation
- Set up discussion: We will share and learn from each other through discussion

Discussion: Step 1 (3 minutes)
- Split class into 3 groups based on tax bracket percentage

Discussion: Step 2 — Real Life vs. Simulated Life (15 minutes)
- Start with some questions to get the students sharing with each other about their jobs and situations in life so they are thinking of the simulation as a real life situation:
  - Jobs they would consider doing or not consider doing
  - Describe some lifestyle choices, specifically wants based on salary
- Target some questions based on the students' salaries
  - Greatest difficulty with making a budget?
  - Creativity in spending? Use charity giving as an example.
  - Housing situations
  - Health insurance (benefits in jobs)

Discussion: Step 3 — Emergencies (10 minutes)
- Have students share what their emergencies were, any significant lifestyle changes they made, and what specific expenses they had to cut out of their previous budget

Discussion: Step 4 — Budgeting Process (5 minutes)
- Describe your experience making a budget
- Something you plan to do when you create a budget for yourself in the future?
- Anything you would do differently in your original budget?

Discussion: Step 5 — Overall Experience (10 minutes)

- One new thing you learned?
- What kind of job would you like to have in the future? Do you think you would pick a job based on salary, passion, or a mix of both?
- What decisions would you need to make in order to obtain your dreams in the future?

Wrap Up (5 minutes)

- Purpose of the Budget Simulation: to give students a realistic picture of what life could look like for them as adults

Introduction (suggested time: 2 minutes)

Use the introduction time to set the tone for a day of active discussion. Tell the students that we are wrapping up the budget simulation, and encourage them to share what they learned from and felt about the experience. An introductory comment may be: "Today is the final day for the budget simulation. We are going to be spending the majority of time in discussion today about what you thought and learned from the budget simulation. Everyone will have a chance to share so we can learn from each other."

Discussion (suggested time: 43 minutes — see specific breakdown in Lesson Snapshot)

Because today's class is heavy on discussion, it is important to set up the class so all of the students will have an opportunity to share. There is a tendency in discussions for the more vocal students to dominate the discussion, while the quieter students feel like trying to give their opinion is pointless. Part of the point of today's discussion is to hear from everyone.

1. Split the class into three groups based on their tax bracket percentage. Those who were making less than $33,950 are in group 1; those who were making between $33,950-$82,250 in group 2; and those making more than $82,250 in group 3. They will still be engaging in the discussion as a whole class, but some questions will be directed toward the different groups and some questions can be open for the whole class to answer. This will help to compare and contrast the three groups and the different decisions they had to make.
2. Start with some questions to get the students sharing with each other about their jobs and situations in life so that they are thinking of the simulation as a real life situation:

- Tell the students: "Raise your hand if you got a job that you actually would consider doing when you are an adult." After students raise their hands, ask a few of them: "What was your career and salary? Why is this a job you might actually want to do as an adult?" (Either have every student share or ask two students from each section to volunteer to share.)
- Next tell the students: "Raise your hand if you got a job that you would never consider doing

> **Note to Teacher**
>
> *This discussion should engage all students, so you may want to create some unique questions that will encourage all students to be involved. For smaller classes, choose from the following questions and direct them to students who tend to be reserved. Remember, calling specific names and asking open-ended questions will help students share more. When they answer questions, be sure to thank each student for sharing.*

as an adult." After students raise their hands, ask a few of them: "What was your career and salary? Why is this a job that you would not want to do as an adult?" (Either have every student share or ask two students from each section to volunteer to share.)

- Pick two students from each group and ask them to describe some lifestyle choices they were able to make based on their salary. If they need some help with describing their lifestyle choices, ask them specific questions about what their social life was like. Ask them if they were able to do everything they wanted to do. Ask them if there was anything they had to say no to because they didn't have enough money to do or buy what they would have liked. This description may lead to being able to ask the following question:
  - How is money related to the opportunities they had in life?
- Target some questions based on the students' salaries:

  - Ask the students who had made less than $33,950 what their greatest difficulty was with making a budget for themselves. Ask how the process of making a budget felt for them.
  - Ask the actor/actress or the Professional Basketball player how realistic they think it would be to actually have this job in real life at 25. After their response, remind them that there are only about 200 players in the NBA, so there is a very small percentage that actually makes it big. The figures may be better for actors and actresses, or musicians, but the entertainment industry is very difficult to get into. Then ask if there is anyone in the class who has a dream of making it in the entertainment industry. Ask them what they think would be good steps to take in order to position themselves to make it?
  - Ask the students in Group 3, "What is one way that you were able to express creativity in how you spent your money?" Or ask, "What is an opportunity you had to spend your money that you would never think of in your life as a teenager now?" You may want to prompt the students by asking about whether or not they decided to give to charities and which charity they decided to give to. If they haven't decided yet, ask them where they think they would give their money and why. Some students may not see the importance of giving money to a charity, especially if they don't have much money now. Encourage students to think about why it is important to give. Ask students about the

Note to Teacher

In recognizing how difficult it is to be successful as an athlete or entertainer, students should never be discouraged from the big dreams they may have for themselves. It is important for students to have accurate information about the challenges they may face in pursuing these paths, but whether to pursue these paths should be completely their decision. Ask the students what a back-up plan might involve to help sustain them while they pursue their dreams.

issues in the world for which they are concerned. Tell them how giving to a charity can make a difference through helping people and organizations financially.

- Ask the students in Group 3 if they were able to own a house. What kind of costs came with a house about which they were surprised? Students may not recognize that owning a home requires additional expenses, such as home upkeep, furniture, higher utility payments, and property taxes.
- Ask students if they know the difference between rent and a mortgage. Some may have seen renting as a way to save money during this simulation, even if they had the money in their budget to buy a house. In this case, you can explain that in the long run, owning a house will likely save you money in the long term. This will lay a good foundation for a lesson about beneficial loans covered Unit 3, Lesson 4.
- Ask the students in Group 1 if anyone was able to own a house. Then you can ask follow-up questions to this such as: What was your housing situation like? If this were real life at age 25, would you be comfortable with this housing situation? Is it different from what you initially imagined for yourself at age 25 before we started the simulation?
- Ask the students in Group 2 to raise their hand if they lived in a two-bedroom apartment. Then ask the students to raise their hand if they bought a house. You can go through different housing situations to determine what the majority of students chose. Once you see what the majority of students chose for their housing, feel free to point out any patterns that you see, if there was a majority that picked a certain kind of living situation. If there are any students who stand out as making a different decision, ask them what they decided to spend their money on that was different from the rest of their classmates
- Ask the students whose jobs didn't provide health benefits (the house cleaner, the SAT tutor, the psychologist, the co-founder of a rising social networking site, the actress, the barber/ hair dresser, the rising musician/valet parker, the McDonald's worker) if they were surprised at the cost of health insurance. Ask them if they considered going without health care, and if they chose to do so, what they would do if a big emergency came up in life. Mention to the students that many people who are unable to pay for health insurance end up in poverty because of health emergencies that come up in life. A recent study found that 60 percent of bankruptcy claims were filed because of medical bills.[1]

Note to Teacher

This discussion may open up opportunities to inform students on looking at benefits when looking for a job. It would be a good idea to show students that it's important to not only look at the salary of a job, but the benefits as well.

[1]Tamkins, Theresa. (2009, June 5). Medical bills prompt more than 60 percent of U.S. bankruptcies. Retrieved from http://www.cnn.com/2009/HEALTH/06/05/bankruptcy.medical.bills/ on Mar 3, 2010.

- Remind the students of the way the simulation began. A comment may be, "At the beginning of this simulation, you were asked to imagine what your life would be like at age 25. You imagined where you would live, whether or not you would be married, if you would have any pets, if you would still be in school, etc. How was your life in the simulation different than how you originally pictured your life at age 25?" As different students answer, ask them why those conditions were different in the simulation (was it because of budget constraints, personal choice, something they learned that made them make a different decision, etc.)? Further the discussion with questions such as, "What surprised you during the simulation?"

3. Move on to specific questions about their emergencies and the impact of the emergencies on their monthly budgets.

- What emergency occurred in your life? (Either have every student share or ask two students from each section to volunteer to share.)
- Did you have to make any significant lifestyle changes due to the emergency card you received?
- What specific expenses did you have to cut out of your previous budget?
- Ask all of the students if anyone received an emergency that affected them even though they had been saving and spending money wisely. Affirm the students by saying that there are some emergencies that no one can expect or plan for. Ask the students what they think they might do in that situation to cover their expenses and plan for the future after the emergency.

- Ask all of the students if anyone received an emergency that affected them even though they had been saving and spending money wisely. Affirm the students by saying that there are some emergencies that no one can expect or plan for. Ask the students what they think they might do in that situation to cover their expenses and plan for the future after the emergency.
- You may want to preface the next question by saying that there are many emergencies that happen in life that are out of our control. Some are natural disasters or unexpected deaths in the family, or car accidents. Ask students to raise their hand if they had an emergency that upon happening in real life, it would be unexpected or outside of their control.
(This would not apply to the students who had a problem with gambling, or lost a job because of something they did.) Then ask a couple of students: How often do you think emergencies happen in life? What are some actual steps you can take to plan financially for the different emergencies that could happen in real life?

- How did you see an example of instant gratification in the budget simulation? Now that you have learned about delayed gratification, is there anything you plan to do differently in the future when you decide how to spend your money?

4. Move on to some questions about the actual budgeting process.
   - Ask the students to describe their experience with making a budget. Was it easy or difficult? Was it complicated? Was there anything that surprised them? Is there anything they learned about why it's important to make a budget?
   - Based on this simulation, what is something you plan to do when you create a budget for yourself in the future?
   - If you had to start over today, is there anything you would do differently in designing your original budget?

5. Conclude the discussion with specific questions that help the students reflect on their overall experience. If you think it would be beneficial for your students, use these questions to guide a time of reflective writing or journaling, then ask students to share from what they wrote. If discussion works well for your students, you can continue processing together as a group.
   - What was at least one new thing you learned from participating in this budget simulation?
   - Based on this simulation, what kind of job would you like to have in the future? Do you think you would pick a job based on salary, passion, or a mix of both? If you had to choose one or the other, which would you choose?
   - What do you want your life to look like financially when you graduate from high school? What do you want your life to look like financially when you have a consistent income?
   - What decisions would you need to make in order to obtain the career you want? What are some short-term goals that you could work toward now in order to meet the long-term goals in your future?

Note to Teacher

Consider sharing a personal emergency that happened in your life. Hearing about your real-life situation may give your students a better picture of the reality of emergencies in daily life. By sharing a personal experience, it will help to build deeper connections with your class.

Wrap-up (suggested time: 5 minutes)
This lesson should end on a positive note. Tell the students that the purpose of the budget simulation was to give them a realistic picture of what life could look like for a variety of adults in different situations. Lots of us know that we want our lives to be comfortable and happy in the future, but most of us don't think about what it takes to actually obtain that comfortable lifestyle. Encourage your students to think about the small steps they can take now in order to live the lifestyle they dream about for their futures. Remind them that thinking about how they can profit both educationally and financially in the future depends on the choices they make today. Ask the class to think about how much education they want to obtain. Tell the class that what they do in school today will have an effect on what they do after high school. Encourage students to have educational and professional goals and to pursue them the best they can.

Thank the class for their attentiveness and participation.

Vocabulary:
None

This unit centers on the analogy of "The Game" to capture students' interest and to help them understand why they should care about financial concepts that can seem fairly dry (e.g. banking, interest, and loans). Success in the financial world often requires that an individual understand the system and be able to use this knowledge to make the system work in his or her favor. This curriculum is intended to prepare students for financial success by giving them the knowledge to game the system instead of being gamed.

When the unit discusses "gaming" or "being gamed," these are slang terms meaning, "taking advantage of" or "being taken advantage of." If your students are unfamiliar with these terms, please use terms that would best help them understand these concepts of taking advantage and being taken advantage of.

Knowing and understanding how the financial world works will allow students to "game" the system by making wise choices with their money. When students understand how to manage their money well (covered in Unit 2), how to save their money in a safe place that accrues interest and avoids debt (covered in this unit), and how to position themselves to have a consistent income (covered in Unit 4), they will be better equipped to choose and work toward a secure financial future.

While students do need to know how to game the financial world, understanding how they can be gamed is even more essential. This unit addresses the following as ways students can be gamed: being subject to avoidable bank fees, high interest rates, cycles of recurring debt, and predatory loans. Predatory lending institutions often place themselves strategically to thrive in low-income communities. Their abundance and consequent familiarity may cause students to feel comfortable with their services, particularly when alternatives like mainstream banks, which offer better terms, tend to be less familiar and may seem inaccessible. This unit is intended to help students understand how predatory lending institutions work so they will avoid being lured into debt through the advertising from predatory lending institutions.

Lesson Plans:

Lesson 1 explains the banking practices most commonly associated with avoidable fees, and then Lesson 2 covers the advantages of bank accounts. Many students in low-income neighborhoods have a negative perception of banks, learned from their community, culture, and/or parents. This curriculum addresses these perceptions and misperceptions, providing information to establish banks as a positive option. The goal is to help students understand (although they may be wary of "trusting" a bank with their hard-earned money) that mainstream banks offer benefits and can actually be the safest place to keep their money. This is intended to help students avoid being gamed by fees at check cashing outlets and avoid being vulnerable to having large amounts of cash lost or stolen.

Lesson 3 introduces the concept of interest. The core idea of this lesson is that interest can be both positive and negative. The financial world can game people by charging interest, but people can game the financial world by earning interest. The key is to understand when interest is positive and to make interest work in our favor.

Once students understand the concept of interest, they will learn about "good" loans versus "bad" loans in Lesson 4. If students see all loans as "negative interest" it may prevent them from seeking loans for positive means, such as going to college and buying a home. Therefore, students must see that there are few instances where loans can be "good." The details of predatory lending are discussed in Lesson 5. It is crucial for students to be aware of predatory lenders in order to avoid getting stuck in a cycle of debt. Lesson 6, entitled "Slaves to Debt," addresses the potentially severe long-term impact of debt. This lesson returns to some of the themes about power from Unit 1, and emphasizes that the choices students make about borrowing money will determine whether they control their own financial futures, or whether they are controlled by their debts.

Optional Activities

This unit has a lot of potentially new vocabulary. It is important to stress the idea of being gamed by or gaming the financial system so students understand why it is important to learn these terms. Any visuals or personal stories added to make the vocabulary and concepts seem more real will greatly enrich this unit.

- **Optional Unit 3 Review Game — 3.0.1*:** This additional game can be used to review new vocabulary terms. If you would like to include the game, you will need to allow additional time after the unit, or replace it with one of the lesson activities.
- **Optional Activity: Fear of Banks — 3.0.2*:** This optional activity is meant to help relieve fear associated with going to a bank. It requires an additional day to take the students on a field trip, so please plan ahead if you choose to include this option.
- **Lesson 6 Guest Speaker:** It is suggested in Lesson 6 that a guest speaker share his or her personal story of debt, so please plan ahead and extend the necessary invitations in advance.

Outline:
Lesson 1 – The Rules of the Bank
Lesson 2 – How to Game the Bank
Lesson 3 – The Interest Game
Lesson 4 – How You Game Interest
Lesson 5 – How Interest Games You
Lesson 6 – Slaves to Debt / Review

Vocabulary:
- profit
- monthly fee/charge
- direct deposit
- ATM fees
- overdraft fees
- check cashing outlet
- percentage
- FDIC
- checking account
- savings account
- debit card
- ATM card
- interest
- positive interest
- negative interest
- loan
- debt
- student loans
- student loans
- home loans (a.k.a. mortgages)
- business loans
- car loans
- consumer loans
- predatory loans
- predator
- predatory lender
- payday loan
- rent-to-own store
- loan shark
- credit cards
- minimum payment
- slavery
- bankruptcy
- credit score

* *For optional activities, go to www.futureprofitsresources.org*

It's not wise to violate rules
until you know how to observe them.
–T. S. Eliot, Author

Materials needed:

- 1 beanbag
- Story #1 – Karen and the Bank's Monthly Fees – 3.1.1*
- Story #2 – Jimmy and the ATM Fees – 3.1.2*
- Story #3 – Trudy and the Overdraft Fees – 3.1.3*
- "The Game" Video #1*
- Whiteboard and pen, or chalkboard and chalk, or poster paper and pen
- Computer with internet connection, projector, and speakers

Key Concepts:

1. Some people have negative perceptions of banks, but banks are the best option for saving money if people understand and follow the rules.
2. Banks are businesses that need to make a profit.
3. Knowing terms like monthly fee, direct deposit, ATM fees, and overdraft fees will help avoid unnecessary and expensive charges.

Prep Time: 5 minutes

Advance Preparation Tasks:

- Make enough copies of each script so that each of the volunteer student readers and actors can read from separate scripts
- Bookmark "The Game" Video #1 and set up a computer with internet connection to the projector and speakers so the video is ready to show

**For all additional resources, including handouts, video links and helpful websites, see www.futureprofitsresources.org*

Keep in Mind

- Banks may seem untrustworthy to students because they have seen others struggle with the consequences that come from intentionally or unintentionally breaking the rules of a bank.
- Banks may seem untrustworthy to students from Latino households due to the history of financial crises and failed banking systems in many Latin American countries.
- Students must understand how to use mainstream financial institutions to their advantage, and avoid traps that perpetuate cycles of poverty.
- Avoid getting caught in the details of bank accounts and interest, as this information can be dry, complicated, and often lose the students' interests.

Many students from low-income communities don't trust banks for one of two main reasons. First, they may have seen others, including their parents, struggle with overdraft fees and bounced check penalties. Because many low-income families are not necessarily familiar with standard banking practices and may not read the fine print on their accounts, these fees come as a surprise and are perceived as taking advantage of the customer. Even families who are aware of the fees may find themselves in a position where they feel it is essential to write a bad check. As fees build up, individuals may end up owing a significant amount they are unable to pay back. In fact, they might pay more in fees to the bank than they would have paid to a check cashing outlet. As the fees start piling up, people often feel overwhelmed and try to run away to avoid dealing with the pressure to pay the cash back. If they didn't understand how they accumulated the charges in the first place, they may consider banks as tricky and unfair. If they close an account with a negative balance, they also will have trouble opening new accounts in the future, even if the account is at a different bank. Additionally, any time a person closes an account with a negative balance, his or her name is entered into "chex systems," which all banks check when someone tries to open a new account to make sure this person is responsible enough to open an account.

The second reason is that many Latin American countries have experienced financial crises and failed banking systems, particularly during the 1980s and '90s. During this time, some banks closed overnight, leaving customers with no way of recovering their money, and instilling a deep distrust of financial institutions. Therefore, many students of Latino households may have grown up believing that banking institutions are untrustworthy.

The purpose of this unit is to help students gain enough knowledge to: (1) use mainstream financial institutions to their advantage, and (2) avoid traps that perpetuate cycles of poverty. It is important to be financially literate in order to make the most of your money. Lesson 1 explains some standard banking practices that often trap the uninformed. Though students may feel that banks are trying to game them, mainstream financial institutions are still the best option. When teaching this lesson, try to avoid getting caught in the details of bank accounts and interest, as this information is dry, complicated, and can often lose the students and take away from the bigger point. The students need to know some details, but may feel overwhelmed and then shut down if they perceive banks as too complicated to understand. The goal is to give students a basic understanding of banks, particularly bank fees, and how to avoid additional fees by being aware and informed.

Lesson Snapshot

Review (none)

Introduction (5 minutes)
- Explain purpose of unit and what to expect

"The Game" Video #1 (3 minutes)
- Show video clip

Discussion (7 minutes)
- Brainstorm terms associated with a bank
- Explain what gaming/being gamed means in the financial world

Activity #1: Stand Up / Sit Down (13 minutes)
- Instruct students to stand up or sit down through reading each statement, and then ask students to share more

Lecture: Profit (5 minutes)
- Define profit
- Explain that companies need to make a profit
- Explain that a bank is a company; therefore, it sets out to make a profit, not to take advantage of people

Activity #2: Story Skits (15 minutes)
- Story #1
  - Ask for six volunteers to act out the script
  - Explain direct deposit and monthly charge
  - Suggest simple things Karen could have done differently
- Story #2
  - Ask for two volunteers to act out the script
  - Explain ATM fees
  - Suggest simple things Jimmy could have done differently
  - What would you do with $150 if you didn't have to pay it toward fees?

- Story #3
  - Ask for three volunteers to act out the script
  - Explain overdraft fees
  - Suggest simple things Trudy could have done differently

Wrap Up (2 minutes)

- Understand the rules and avoid fees because the bank is still the best possible option

Review

No review for the first lesson.

Introduction (suggested time: 5 minutes)

Introduce the unit by giving an overview of the different concepts the students will be learning over the next six lessons. This unit covers banks and other kinds of financial businesses, interest, and loans. Explain that there are financial survival skills that are essential to making the most of our money. Understanding these topics will help to manage money well and avoid being taken advantage of.

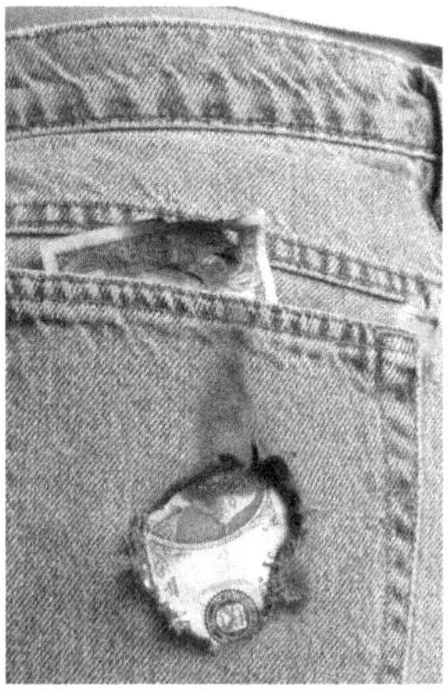

These lessons will use the idea of a game to explain financial concepts. Video clips will introduce each lesson and expand this game concept. Explain that this unit is designed to discuss what "being gamed" or "gaming" the financial world means. This means that students can either be taken advantage of by the financial world, or take advantage of the financial world. Ask the students, "Who wants to be gamed by the financial world? Who wants to game the financial world?"

State that the purpose of this unit is to help students learn how our financial system works. They can use this knowledge to make the most of their money and make sure money is not "burning a hole in your pocket." The goal is to teach students information and strategies they can use to win "the game."

"The Game" Video #1 (suggested time: 3 minutes)

Go to www.futureprofitsresources.org and find the link to "The Game" Video #1. Show the video to the students and move on to the following discussion.

Discussion (suggested time: 7 minutes)

Tell the class, "Today our team is playing against Team Bank, and we're going to concentrate on how to build a strong defense." Ask the class to raise their hands and name a banking term that they've heard before. This can include anything they associate with banks, such as names of particular banks, fees (ask if they know specific types), ATM, types of accounts, etc. As students call out answers, write every term on the board. Ask the student who named the term if they know what it means. Many may have heard terms without knowing what they mean. If they do know the definition, ask them to explain it for the class. If a student gives an incorrect explanation, give the class the correct definition of the term so there is no confusion. If the student does not know the meaning, write the term on the board and tell the class that we'll be explaining it later.

> **Note to Teacher**
>
> *This lesson is heavy on classroom participation. If your class has a tendency to be less involved, you many need to ask more questions to help engage them.*

Some basic terms you should suggest, if students do not mention them, are the following vocabulary: deposit and withdrawal, accounts, checks, ATM, and fees. To help draw out these terms, prompt students with questions like, "What is it called when you add money into your account at a bank?" "What is it called when you take money out of your bank account?" or "What is the name of one type of account that I can have?" Thank each student for sharing and affirm their knowledge, however little or great it may be, of banks.

> **Note to Teacher**
>
> *There is a list of vocabulary terms in the unit description that will be explained during this unit. Please take some time to review the terms and definitions (found in the vocabulary appendix). Some of the terms your students mention will not be explained during this unit. If you decide it is important that these terms are explained, please explain them now, but be careful not to get too caught up in details and lose the students' interest.*

Tell the students that the financial world works like a game. The people are competing to score money instead of points. Either game or be gamed. In the financial world, this means either be in control of your money, keeping it where it can grow and making the most of it, or let others control your money so you end up giving away money you could have kept for yourself. People or companies will try to get your money, but if you make smart choices, you can make or keep more money for yourself instead.

Activity #1: Stand Up / Sit Down

(suggested time: 13 minutes)

The purpose of this activity is to give students an opportunity to recognize and express their existing perceptions of mainstream banking institutions. The purpose is to hear from the students.

Use a beanbag during discussion to give the students clear opportunities to share their thoughts. As you call on them to share, toss them the beanbag. When they are done sharing, have them toss it back to you.

Note to Teacher

Some students may have negative perceptions of banks, and this discussion is not the time to try to correct their impressions. We will provide a lot of information about banks later in this lesson and the next. Thank students for sharing their thoughts and perceptions.

1. Have all the students stand up.
2. Tell the students that you will be reading a series of statements, each statement telling them either to stand up or to sit down. State that after each statement, you will ask follow-up questions. Tell them that you will toss a beanbag to a student, and it will be that person's turn to share, and he or she will need to toss the beanbag back after they are done sharing.
3. Read these statements to the students:
   - Sit down if you would never put your money in a bank. *(Toss the beanbag to a couple of students who sat down and ask them why.)*
   - Stand up if you have already used a bank. Sit down if you have never used a bank. *(Toss the beanbag to a couple of students who are standing and ask them what they used it for and why they chose to use a bank. You may also want to ask whether they had a positive or negative experience.)*
   - Stand up if you think there are a lot of banks in your city. Sit down if you think there are not a lot of banks in your city. *(Toss the beanbag to a couple of students who are standing and ask them to name some banks. You can also ask a couple of students who are sitting why there aren't that many banks in their city.)*
   - Sit down if you would use check cashing outlets. Stand up if you would not use check cashing outlets. *(Toss the beanbag to a couple of students who are sitting down and ask them what they know about check cashing outlets. Also toss the beanbag to a couple of students who are standing up and ask them why they would not use check cashing outlets.)*
   - Stand up if you think there are many check cashing outlets in your city. Sit down if you think there are not that many. *(Toss the beanbag to a couple of students who are standing and ask them to name a couple of places where they see check cashing outlets.)*

- Sit down if you have never thought about where you want to keep your money some day. Stand up if you have thought about where you might keep your money. (*Toss the beanbag to a couple of students who are standing up and ask them where they have thought about keeping their money.)*
- Stand up if you know someone who keeps more than $50 cash anywhere besides a bank. Sit down if you know people who keep cash only in a bank. *(Toss the beanbag to a couple of students and ask them to share one place they think people might keep their cash, if not at a bank.)*

Lecture: Profit (suggested time: 5 minutes)

The purpose of this lecture is to help students understand banks. Students should realize that banks do not set out to take advantage of people, but rather to make a profit, and they operate according to certain standard business procedures. The following activity will then break down a few specific practices and help students learn how to avoid negative consequences resulting from banking rules.

Here is an example of exact wording you can use:
"I'll let you in on a little secret: A bank is the best possible option for your financial success, and we'll talk a lot more about some of those reasons next class. But we also have to know that the bank is a business. The purpose of all businesses is to make some kind of profit. **Profit** is all about making money. If you buy a candy bar for 50 cents and sell it to a friend for 75 cents, you have 25 cents profit, which is money you get to keep. Companies have to make a profit in order to keep running, or lack of money would cause them to shut down. If companies shut down, there would be no jobs and no one to make or sell products we need and want. This situation is the same for a bank. A bank's purpose is not to take advantage of you, but they do have to make a profit. It may seem like banks are trying to game you with fees and charges. Today we'll explore some of the ways the bank will try to make money from you as a customer, and how you can actually game the bank by avoiding these fees and charges."

Activity #2: Story Skits (suggested time: 15 minutes)

This activity has students act out sample situations in which individuals are gamed by the bank and owe money for fees. During the discussion after each skit, students will learn how they can avoid being gamed in the same way.

Introduce this activity by asking the students if any of them have had a bad experience with a bank, or if any will share an experience someone they know has had. Acknowledge that many people don't trust banks due to negative experiences. Emphasize that one of the reasons people have negative experiences is because they may not understand all the rules governing their accounts. If we make sure to understand and follow all the rules, we can avoid fees and charges.

Tell the class that we will be looking at three stories of people who feel like they have been gamed by the bank. Explain that you will ask for volunteers for each story — one to read the story out loud, and others to act out the story as it is read. Tell the students that after each story, you will ask them to identify how the bank gamed that person and what are some simple ways to avoid being gamed that way.

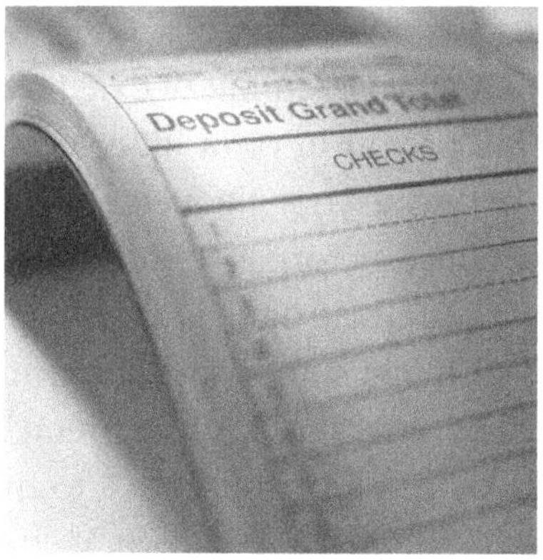

1. Story #1 – Karen and the Bank's Monthly Fees*

Ask for six volunteers:

- A narrator
- Karen
- Two of Karen's friends
- Karen's mom
- Company Manager (who also plays the Bank Manager)

Give a script to each volunteer, except Karen's two friends. Tell Karen's friends to act out their part when they are mentioned in the story. When the narrator reads actions for a character, that actor should perform them.

Have students act out the script. Thank the volunteer students for their acting and have the class give them a round of applause.

Then ask, "What were some of the terms that Karen needed to know in order not to be gamed by the bank?"

*Script can be found at www.futureprofitsresources.org

- **Direct deposit** — when the employer electronically sends the employee's paychecks to his or her bank account instead of giving the employee a paycheck to deposit.
- **Monthly charge** — a charge that a bank sets up for the customer to pay every month in order to keep that account at a bank. Some bank accounts do not have a monthly charge, but many accounts do have monthly charges, or they have requirements that a customer has to meet in order to get the account without the monthly fee.

Note to Teacher

Here are the basic elements of this story:

- *Karen liked to be first at everything, and got a job before her friends.*
- *She opened an account that was connected with a* **monthly fee/charge** *if she did not set up* **direct deposit** *with her account.*
- *She lost $7.50 each month, for a total of $45.00, because she didn't pay attention to the monthly fees.*

Ask the students, "What are some simple ways to avoid being gamed?" or "What should Karen have done differently?"

Highlight these points for your students:
- Stay alert when setting up your account.
- Be aware of the requirements to get a monthly charge waived if possible.
- Some accounts do not have monthly fees; look for these.

2. Story #2 – Jimmy and the ATM Fees*

Ask for two volunteers:
- A narrator
- Jimmy

Give each volunteer student the script, and tell the actors to perform their actions as the narrator reads.
Have students act out the script. Thank the volunteer students for their acting and have the class give them a round of applause.
Then ask, "What term from this story did we need to know to avoid being gamed by the bank?"

- **ATM fees** — ATM stands for Automated Teller Machine, which gives you cash when you need it. All banks have ATMs and most ATMs will work for anyone, but they usually charge customers from other banks a fee to use their ATM.

**Script can be found at* www.futureprofitsresources.org

Note to Teacher

Here are the basic elements of this story:

- *Jimmy doesn't carry usually cash on him, but on his way to any event, he'll stop by the closest ATM to get cash for the night.*
- *ATM fees were what stopped him from making the most of his money. Over a year, the $2 to $5 charges added up, and he spent a total of $150 in ATM fees.*

Ask students, "What are some simple ways to avoid being gamed?" or "What should Jimmy have done differently?"

- Use your own bank's ATM
- Remember that small fees add up over time

Before moving on to Story #3, ask the students, "What would you do with $150 if you didn't have to pay that in fees?"

3. Story #3 – Trudy and the Overdraft Fees*

Ask for three volunteers:

- A narrator
- Trudy
- Trudy's father

Give each volunteer student the script, and tell the actors to perform their actions as the narrator reads.

Have students act out the script. Thank the volunteer students for their acting and have the class give them a round of applause.

Then ask, "What term from this story did we need to know to avoid being gamed by the bank?"

- **Overdraft fees** — Overdraft fees are charged <u>each time</u> you spend more money than what is available in your account. No matter how small the overdraft, the fee is usually the same.

Ask students, "What are some simple ways to avoid being gamed?" or "What should Trudy have done differently?"

- Get an account inquiry: a report from your bank that you can get from an ATM or a teller inside the bank. It shows how much money is left in your account so you don't spend more than you have. Sometimes banks charge a fee if you print this report at an ATM, but you can view it on the ATM screen for free.

**Script can be found at www.futureprofitsresources.org*

- Keep track of how much money is in your account. Use a check register or something similar that helps you keep track of how much money you are spending and receiving without having to stop by a bank. Online banking is common now, so you can look at the purchases you've made and the amount of money in your account by logging into the bank's website.
- When you make a deposit to your account, it can take one to two business days before that money is available to spend. It is important to make new deposits to your account before you run out of money.

Note to Teacher

Here are the basic elements of this story:

- *Trudy opened a bank account with her father to help pay for her needs while she was away at school.*
- *Overdraft fees were charged every time she spent more than what was in her account. She spent only $20 more than what she had, but there was a $30 overdraft fee for every time she used her debit card after her account was empty. She owed a total of $90 in overdraft fees.*

- Prepare a budget to make sure you don't spend more money than you have. (Refer back to Unit 2. If you have not yet taught Unit 2, explain what a budget is. The definition for "budget" can be found in Unit 2, Lesson 1 or in the vocabulary appendix.)
- If you accidentally received multiple overdraft fees for small purchases without realizing it, you may be able to get a fee or two waived. When a fee is waived, that means that it is dismissed, and you won't have to pay it. Call your bank immediately and explain the situation, then ask if they might waive one or two of your fees.

Wrap Up (suggested time: 2 minutes)

Remind the students that many people have not trusted banks in the past because of fees they were charged when they didn't expect it. Remember that the bank is a business that wants to make a profit, but they can't charge you fees unless it is part of the rules for your account. If we understand those rules, we can avoid the fees and avoid getting gamed by the bank. Tell the students that next class will explain why the bank is still your best possible option. Thank the class for their participation.

Vocabulary:
- profit
- monthly fee/charge
- direct deposit
- ATM fees
- overdraft fees

Additional Resources:
For an article on the Latino culture and how it relates to banks, go to www.futureprofitsresources.org.

FutureProfits

Financial Survival Skills – Understanding "The Game"
How You Game The Bank
Lesson 2

The number one problem in today's generation and economy is the lack of financial literacy.
–Alan Greenspan,
Former Federal Reserve Chairman

Materials needed:

- Four Corners cards – 3.2.1*
- "The Game" Video #2*
- Whiteboard and pen, or chalkboard and chalk, or poster paper and pen
- Computer with internet connection, projector, and speakers

Key Concepts:

1. Cashing checks can happen for a fee at a check cashing outlet, or for free at a bank if you have an account.
2. Because the Federal Deposit Insurance Corporation (FDIC) insures money kept in bank accounts, the bank is the safest place to keep money.
3. The two basic types of bank accounts are savings and checking, and each has benefits.

Prep Time: 30 minutes

Advance Preparation Tasks:

- Fold the full sheet of Four Corners cards in half to make cards for the Four Corners activity
- Bookmark "The Game" Video #2 and set up a computer with internet connection to the projector and speakers so the video is ready to show

**For all additional resources, including handouts, video links and helpful websites, see www.futureprofitsresources.org*

Keep in Mind

- Many students avoid banks because they are more familiar and comfortable with check cashing outlets.
- For some students, there may be a language barrier associated with mainstream banking institutions.

The students with whom we work are generally more familiar and comfortable with check cashing outlets than with banks. In fact, having a bank account may be a foreign concept to most of them. Some 28 million Americans are without a bank account.[1] There is often an absence of mainstream banking institutions in lower-income communities, and distrust of banks leads many to avoid banks even when they are available. The language barrier may also keep some students' parents from opening bank accounts. They prefer to go to the local check cashing outlet where their primary language is spoken. As a result, many students may be accustomed to using check cashing outlets and may not be aware of alternatives. However, fees charged by check cashing outlets quickly add up, and keeping the bulk of one's money in cash is unsafe.

This lesson gives students an overview of savings and checking accounts, and contrasts the benefits of such accounts with the drawbacks of check cashing outlets. This lesson also explains that the FDIC insures and guarantees deposits, to allay the fear that money in banks can disappear overnight. The goal is to help students understand why banks are the best option, and to equip them to use banking services to their advantage.

[1]Check Cashers, Redeemed. 2008. Retrieved Apr 16, 2010 from http://www.nytimes.com/2008/11/09/magazine/09nix-t.html?_r=2.

Lesson Snapshot

Review (3 minutes)
- Review the bank terms from the previous lesson

Introduction (2 minutes)
- Benefits of banks

Discussion #1: Benefits of Banking / Check Cashing (5 minutes)
- Brainstorm benefits to putting money in a bank
- One benefit of using a bank: cashing checks for free
- Define check cashing outlet and define percentage

"The Game" Video #2 (5 minutes)
- After showing video, ask if there are additional benefits to keeping money in a bank
- Explain FDIC

Discussion #2: Why *our* community? (5 minutes)
- Why check cashing outlets are common in low-income communities

Activity: Four Corners (10 minutes)
- Students go to the corner which represents where they would put their money
- Create discussion with students by asking them why

Lecture: Bank Accounts (10 minutes)
- Define interest and explain how you gain interest and pay interest
- Go over checking accounts and savings accounts

Discussion #3: Return to Four Corners Activity (5 minutes)
- Pros and cons of each corner
- Would anyone choose differently after learning about bank accounts?

Wrap Up (5 minutes)
- Restate the different ways students can game the bank

Review (suggested time: 3 minutes)

Recap what was discussed last class and ask students to name the main terms discussed that refer to ways the bank makes a profit and can potentially game you. Write down the main terms on the board. Be sure to review these four ideas:

- Monthly fee/charge
- Direct deposit
- ATM fees
- Overdraft fees

Here is an example of exact wording you can use:
"Last class, we looked at some of the ways banks can game us. There are a lot of fees and details that can get us in trouble if we don't pay attention. We can end up owing the bank money we didn't expect to pay. But if we know about these fees and are careful, we can avoid being gamed by the bank. It's all about a good defense — being informed and paying attention. What are some of the terms we discussed last class that refer to ways the bank tries to make a profit and game you?"

Introduction (suggested time: 2 minutes)

Today is about how we can game the bank. There are many benefits to putting your money in a bank. Although we have to be careful about fees and rules like we discussed last class, keeping money in a bank also gives a lot of benefits that are not available anywhere else. Some of these benefits will be discussed today.

Discussion #1: Benefits of Banking / Check Cashing (suggested time: 5 minutes)

Begin by asking the class what are some benefits to putting money in a bank. As students brainstorm ideas, write them on the board.

One important benefit that should be covered in this discussion is the benefit of cashing checks for free. Ask students what a check cashing store or outlet is. After taking answers, inform the class that a **check cashing outlet** is a place that will take your check and give you cash for a fee. This includes liquor stores, local supermarkets, and any other stores that will cash checks. The fee varies depending on the store, but the average check cashing outlet charges from one to three percent. Write "1%-3% fee" on the board so that students can see the amount. This means the check cashing outlet keeps between one to three dollars for every $100 from the check cashed.

Understanding the concept of percentages in money will help students see the practicality of understanding math in regard to everyday life. Define **percentage**. The definition is "a rate, number or amount in each hundred" or in plain terms, "a smaller amount taken from the whole amount."

Ask how much it costs to cash a check at a bank. Allow for responses, then tell the students that if you have a bank account, cashing your check at that bank is free. There is no fee. One of the ways to game the bank is by taking advantage of their free-of-charge services such as cashing checks.

The following video explains this benefit more.

"The Game" Video #2 (suggested time: 5 minutes)

The purpose of this video is to help students understand how much money they will lose by using a check cashing outlet instead of a bank. Because our students tend to be more familiar and comfortable with check cashing outlets, we want them to understand why the free check cashing services offered by banks are such an important benefit.

Go to www.futureprofitsresources.org and find the link to "The Game" Video #2.

After the video, ask students if they heard any additional benefits for keeping money in a bank. Add them to the list that was previously brainstormed on the board. They will hopefully add FDIC (the Federal Deposit Insurance Corporation, which guarantees money deposited in banks up to $250,000). Ask students why it's important to know about the FDIC. Responses should include that the United States government guarantees money deposited in banks so it won't just disappear.

Students may also need to review how $900 could be lost by using check cashing outlets. If necessary, you can show them how to figure out how much of money is lost to fees. Use the example of $30,000 in income, and show the following equation on the board: $30,000 x .03 (3% fee) = $900. Ask students how many of them would rather be able to spend the $900 some other way. Ask a couple of students to share something they would buy with $900.

The hope is that students will not let people take their hard-earned money simply for cashing a check. If they open bank accounts, they can cash checks for free.

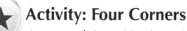

Discussion #2: Why *our* community? (suggested time: 5 minutes)

Ask students if there are more check cashing outlets than banks in their neighborhood. This may not be the case for some cities, especially if low-income areas are not far from tourist and business locations that do have banks. If this is not the case in your students' community, ask them why they think people would want to cash their checks at a check cashing outlet instead of a bank.

If students answer that there are more check cashing outlets than banks, ask why they think there are so many more check cashing outlets in their community than banks. After taking answers, offer the following perspective:

"In low-income communities, there are usually more check cashing outlets than banks. Banks often stay out of lower-income neighborhoods because they believe they won't make a big enough profit in lower-income areas.[2] Check cashing outlets take advantage of this. They know that people have to cash their checks, and they know that there aren't many options available to do it. They can charge high fees, and people still use their services, because there's not enough competition to cash the checks for a cheaper rate. In higher-income communities, this is not the case. There are usually no check cashing outlets in those areas, and there are usually several banks from which to choose."

Activity: Four Corners

(suggested time: 10 minutes)

The objective of this activity is to show students the value of bank accounts and to introduce the concept of interest.

1. Place the Four Corner cards (3.2.1) in the four corners of the room. Each card has one of the following on it: Checking Account, Savings Account, In Closet At Home, or Spend It As Fast As You Can.

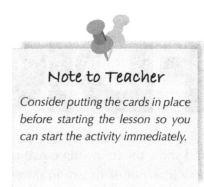

Note to Teacher

Consider putting the cards in place before starting the lesson so you can start the activity immediately.

[2]Check Cashers, Redeemed. 2008. Retrieved Apr 16, 2010 from http://www.nytimes.com/2008/11/09/magazine/09nix-t.html?_r=2.

2. Introduce this activity by instructing students that they are receiving a fictitious $900 (the money they would save from not using check cashing outlets). You could say, "Now that we've saved $900 by cashing our checks at a bank instead of a check cashing outlet, we have to decide what to do with that money. You have four choices, one in each corner of the room:
   - Savings account
   - Checking account
   - In closet at home
   - Spend it as fast as you can

   Ask students to stand up and go to the card showing where they want to put their $900.

3. When students are at their corners, call on a few from each of the four groups and ask why they chose that particular corner. After a few students have shared from each corner, have them return to their seats.

Lecture: Bank Accounts (suggested time: 10 minutes)

There are two basic types of bank accounts:

- Checking accounts
- Savings accounts

You can lead into the topic by saying, "Now that we know banks are a safe place for money, and that there are benefits to keeping your money there, we'll talk about the two main types of accounts: savings accounts and checking accounts. But first, we have to understand the definition of interest."

Begin by defining interest. Then explain the concept of interest being positive or negative depending on the context. These terms will be defined in the following lesson, but it is important to introduce the concept now. Contrast the interest associated with bank accounts to the negative fees associated with check cashing outlets.

You can say, "In order to understand the benefits of keeping your money in a bank, you need to understand interest. We'll talk about interest in greater depth next class, but for now, let's begin with a basic idea of what interest means. **Interest** is a percentage of money either paid or received on a repeating set schedule. When banks gives you interest, they are giving you "free" money just for keeping your money at their bank. Some accounts pay up to three percent interest over a year. This means that for every $1,000, you get $30 extra dollars. This is the opposite of what a check cashing outlet does. A bank can give you three percent of your money as opposed to taking three percent of your money."

Note to Teacher

Students may not fully grasp the concept of interest. This concept will be covered in detail in Lesson 3 of this unit, so for now, students should understand that banks will add to the money they keep in their accounts, while check cashing outlets will take away part of their money.

Write the words "giving you interest: checking account and savings account" on the board. Then write the words "negative fees: check cashing outlets." Students may express confusion since we talked about banks charging fees last class. Make sure to explain that check cashing outlets charge a fee every time you use their services. It is impossible to avoid this charge. In general, banks only charge fees when people break the rules for their accounts. If people are careful about knowing the rules and smart about how they use their account, it is possible never to pay a bank fee. So people can get free services like check cashing, earn money from interest on their accounts, and never pay the bank any of their money.

Go on to explain how each type of account works and how much interest they typically yield.

Checking accounts pay the lowest amount of interest — usually none or a very low percentage rate. The advantage is that you can spend the money anytime and almost anywhere using checks or a debit card. A debit card is a card the bank gives you that allows you to transfer money electronically from your bank account to make purchases. This means you don't have to carry much cash. You can also write checks and mail payments for expenses like rent and utilities. It is important to know the rules connected with a checking account because some will provide checks to the customer free of charge, and others may charge a small fee to print checks.

Write these bullet points on the board for students to see and remember:

- Lowest amount of interest (little to none)
- Debit card
- Write checks

Savings accounts usually yield more interest than checking accounts. These accounts come with an ATM card, but you can only use this card at your bank (and sometimes other banks, but usually for a fee). ATM cards allows you to deposit and withdraw money from your account without going inside the bank. Your ATM card cannot withdraw money from your account when you make purchases at stores, only at the ATM Machine. If you are trying to save money for a big purchase or an emergency fund, having less access to your money can make it easier to save.

- Gives more interest
- ATM card
- Helps you save

Bring it back to interest again, so students can see how interest relates to these accounts. Explain how interest works in their favor and how, over time, they can make money for keeping their money in a bank account. You can use an example of how much money they would get back if they invested $1,000 into a savings account at 1% interest over a year. (Equation: .01 x $1;000 = $10) It may not seem like a lot, but it is still free money, and over time the money adds up.

Note to Teacher

If you have a debit card and a separate ATM card, bring both in to show them to the students and explain the differences of each. Because cards all look the same (credit, debit, and ATM), the differences can get confusing.

If you have extra time, you can ask students what they know about credit cards, and how credit cards differ from ATM or debit cards. Make sure to point out that debit cards are connected to a bank account and that credit cards are like borrowing money and paying it back later. Credit cards are covered in a later lesson, but it may be helpful to introduce it now.

Discussion #3: Return to Four Corners Activity (suggested time: 5 minutes)

Return to the Four Corners Activity and brainstorm the pros and cons of each option. Write pros and cons of each on the board. Some examples are provided.

Then ask, "If I asked you to pick one of the four corners now, how many of you would change where you put your money?"

After some students share, encourage them to think about the option that would most likely help them win the financial game. The options of leaving their money in their closet at home or spending it as fast as they can do have some pros, but these pros tend to be short-term, while their long-term implications are cons.

Savings Account

PROS	CONS
Helps you make more money (interest)	You don't have quick access to your cash
Helps you save more money	You trust an institution with your money (which may be a new risk) instead of keeping it yourself (which "feels" safer)
Keeps your money in a safe place	You have to spend time finding the right bank, choosing an account with good terms, keep on top of your statements and other paperwork, and remember your online log-in and password

Checking Account

PROS	CONS
Access to checks and making purchases with a debit card	You may need to pay a monthly fee but it will often include other benefits
Quick and easy access to money	You may need to pay to order checks
Helps you not to spend all the cash in your pockets	Easy access to money may mean you spend more than if you had to get cash from an ATM
Keeps your money in a safe place	You don't receive as high an interest rate as with savings accounts

In Closet At Home

PROS	CONS
You know exactly where your money is	Easily stolen
Easy access	Not insured in case of a natural disaster
	Easily spent and not saved
	Doesn't earn interest
	You have to carry enough money for your purchases to the store, for rent, etc.

Spend It As Fast As You Can

PROS	CONS
Instant gratification of purchasing something you want or need	Easy to run out of money to spend on needs
	Easily lost
	Easily spent and not saved
	Doesn't earn interest

Then ask, "If I asked you to pick one of the four corners now, how many of you would change where you put your money?"

After some students share, encourage them to think about the option that would most likely help them win the financial game. The options of leaving their money in their closet at home or spending it as fast as they can do have some pros, but these pros tend to be short-term, while their long-term implications are cons.

Wrap Up (suggested time: 5 minutes)

Have the class repeat the two main types of bank accounts. Ask which of the accounts usually has the higher interest rate.

Conclude the class by restating the main ways we can game the bank and how that helps us win the financial game:

1. Take advantage of the bank's free-of-charge services such as cashing checks. This saves us from paying fees at check cashing outlets.
2. Know the rules for your account so you can avoid paying bank fees.
3. Keep your money safe by being aware of FDIC and the protection banks offer. Keeping money in a bank, where it is insured, is safer than keeping cash at home, because cash can be stolen or destroyed in a fire, and then it's gone forever. If a bank gets robbed or destroyed by fire, or just goes out of business, the government guarantees everyone's money.
4. Choose an account with a high interest rate so the bank gives you money for having an account.

Preview next class by saying, "Next class, we're going to talk some more about interest. Interest can work for us or against us in the financial game, and we'll learn how to make it work for us."

Thank the class for their attention and participation.

Vocabulary:

- check cashing outlet
- percentage
- FDIC
- interest
- checking account
- savings account
- debit card
- ATM card

Additional Resources:

For articles about pros and cons of check cashing companies and moving from using check cashing to using credit unions, go to www.futureprofitsresources.org. Additionally, to see the effect that check cashing outlets have on communities, visit www.predatorylendingassociation.com.

This website helps show how check cashing outlets are placed strategically in low-income communities. ***We highly recommend that you visit this site before class if you would like to use it.*** *The predatory lending association site was created for satirical purposes to try to illustrate the dangers of predatory lending. We use it to point out how blatant predatory lending can be. If you want to use this site, we suggest visiting it in advance to see what it offers and prepare for any questions students may have.*

Use the "Poor Finder" tab to show students what locations are targets for predatory lending services.
Scroll down to "Predatory Lending Tools" section.
Click on "Poor Finder" tab.
Type in your city's zip code.
Note: Different symbols on the map represent different things:
Bottle: Liquor Store
Diamond: Pawn Shop
Money Symbol: Payday Loan Services

The single biggest difference between financial success and financial failure is how well you manage your money. It's simple: to master money, you must manage money.
–T. Harv Eker, Author

Materials needed:

- 2 signs: "Positive Interest" and "Negative Interest" – 3.3.3*
- About 55 M&M's® (or other kind of candy that you choose)
- Picture of Interest Worksheet – 3.3.1*
- The Interest Game Plan Worksheet – 3.3.2*
- "The Game" Video #3*
- Whiteboard and pen, or chalkboard and chalk, or poster paper and pen
- Computer with internet connection, projector, and speakers

Key Concepts:

1. Interest can be either positive or negative, and it is important to know the difference in order to make the most of your money and avoid being taken advantage of by companies.
2. Positive interest means earning more money. Negative interest means paying more money.
3. When dealing with positive interest, we want the interest rate to be high. When dealing with negative interest, we want the interest rate to be low.

Prep Time: 20 minutes

Advance Preparation Tasks:

- Buy a pack of regular M&M's (which should contain 50-55 M&M's) or two packs of peanut M&M's (which contain about 20-25 each).
- Print the Interest Signs document (3.3.3) and cut through the middle to have two separate signs. Punch holes in the top corners of the signs. Take a string and tie it through the holes so it can hang around a student's neck.

**For all additional resources, including handouts, video links and helpful websites, see www.futureprofitsresources.org*

Advance Preparation Tasks (cont.)

- Make double-sided worksheets with the Picture of Interest Worksheet (3.3.1) on one side and The Interest Game Plan Worksheet (3.3.2) on the other. Make a copy for each student.
- Bookmark "The Game" Video #3 and set up a computer with internet connection to the projector and speakers so the video is ready to show.

Keep in Mind

- Students may have a negative connotation associated with the word "interest."
- It is important for students to understand both the positive and negative elements of interest.
- Students must understand that when they receive interest they want the highest interest rate possible, and when they pay interest they want the lowest interest rate possible.

Interest can be a complicated subject to understand. Many students in low-income situations have already had owing interest impact their lives or their families in a negative way. They may assume all interest is negative, leading them to assume that interest-bearing accounts should be avoided. To make the most of their money, students need to be informed about the ways interest can work in their favor so they can take advantage of their financial options.

At the same time, it is critical that students do not assume that all interest is positive, so they continue to be wary of how high interest rates can lead to mounting debt. Students need to understand negative interest (interest owed on borrowed money), so they won't get talked into something they do not understand by predatory lenders.

Building this basic understanding of interest will prepare the subsequent lessons on loans and predatory lending. Bottom line: the lesson is a success if students walk away understanding that when they receive interest (through bank accounts and investment options) they want the highest interest possible, and when they pay interest (on loans and other means of borrowing money) they want the lowest interest rate possible.

Lesson Snapshot

Review (3 minutes)
- Recap last class by discussing the different ways students can game the bank

Introduction (2 minutes)
- Explain how interest can be used to game you, and the importance of understanding positive and negative interest

Activity#1: The Interest Game (10 minutes)
- Give two student volunteers 25 M&M's each
- Explain the rules
- *Make Activity #1 SOUND*

"The Game" Video #3 (3 minutes)
- Show video clip
- *Make Activity #1 SOUND*

Lecture #1: Positive and Negative Interest (10 minutes)
- Hand out the double-sided worksheets
- *Make Activity #1 SOUND*
- Explain the Picture of Interest
- *Make Activity #1 SOUND*

Activity #2: The Interest Game Plan (7 minutes)
- Explain the Interest Game Plan
- *Make Activity #1 SOUND*

Lecture #2: Interest Growth (5 minutes)
- Explain interest growth using the analogy of trees vs. weeds

Discussion: Return to Activity #1 (5 minutes)
- *Make Activity #1 SOUND*
- Ask about the number of M&M's left and explain the correlation to real life

Wrap up (5 minutes)
- Two kinds of interest
- When we want high or low interest rates
- Next lesson: How you game interest

Review (suggested time: 3 minutes)

Ask a couple of students to share one way to game the bank. Students should mention one of the following:

- The bank is safe and insured through FDIC
- The bank offers free services to cash checks
- The bank gives you money (interest) for keeping money in an account
- It is possible to avoid bank fees if you follow the rules for your account

Make sure to review any of these four methods of gaming the bank that the students do not mention.

Introduction (suggested time: 2 minutes)

Transition by saying, "Last class we began talking about the interest we can earn with savings and checking accounts. Today we're going to talk a lot more about interest. Many people out there will try to use interest to game you. They want to get you trapped in debt by paying them lots of money for their services. But you can game interest if you have the right information and are smart with your money. You can be the one getting paid and watching your money grow. What you need to learn is how to tell the difference between positive and negative interest."

Begin by defining interest again. You can say, "Since we're going to spend all of this lesson talking about interest, let's begin by remembering the definition of interest. **Interest** is a percentage of money that is either paid or received on a repeating set schedule. Remember, we talked about how a savings account with a 1% interest rate would give us $10 back if we deposited $1,000? (Put the equation on the board again: $1000 x .01 = $10.) Usually savings accounts are on a yearly interest schedule. So using this example, this means the bank would pay you $10 every year, as long you keep the account. The percentage is 1%, and the schedule is yearly. (If you want, you can explain that banks actually give you a portion of that $10 every month, for a total of slightly over $10 a year.)

Activity #1: The Interest Game (suggested time: 10 minutes)

The purpose of this activity is to give students a concrete, interactive example of how positive and negative interest work. This activity will continue through the entire class so students can see the effects of interest over time.

1. Pick a predetermined sound that you will make every few minutes throughout this lesson. This can be ringing a bell, making a call ("Hey-oh!" or "Ding! Ding! Ding!"), or any other noise that will stand out as the marker for this activity. You will see reminders to make the sound throughout the lesson. Each time you make the sound, you will collect M&M's from the negative interest student, and give M&M's to the positive interest student. (For specific amount of M&M's to give or take away, see the Note to Teacher on page 190.)

2. Ask for two student volunteers. When you ask for the first volunteer, representing negative interest, ask for or pick a student you know won't mind doing silly things in front of the class. Give that student a sign that says "negative interest." Give the second volunteer the sign that says "positive interest."

3. Give each student 25 M&M's.
   You don't need to tell students the following, but just be aware as you play: the students are welcome to eat the M&M's if they so desire, but the amount they eat will change their situation in the game. You will continue to take M&M's from the negative interest student, and give M&M's to the positive interest student. If the positive interest student eats all of his or her M&M's you can stop giving him or her more M&M's, since we don't earn interest on money that we've already "spent."

Note to Teacher

You are welcome to choose another small candy to hand out (such as Skittles® or jelly beans). Just pick a candy that is enticing, so they may decide to eat some of it.

4. Explain the game to the student volunteers:
- Tell the student with the positive interest sign that whenever you make the predetermined sound, he/she will tell you how many M&M's are in his/her hand, and then will receive anywhere from 0-5 M&M's from you.
- Tell the student with the negative interest sign that whenever you make the predetermined sound, he or she will owe you 5 M&M's. Tell the student also that if he or she does not have the M&M's to give you, you will require him or her to do whatever you ask to continue paying off the debt he or she owes you.

After explaining the game, make your predetermined sound for the first time, collect 5 M&M's from the negative interest student and give 2 M&M's to the positive interest student, then move on to the video.

Note to Teacher

The first time you make the predetermined sound, you should give the positive interest student 2 M&M's. If the student does not eat any M&M's and saves them, you should give him or her one more M&M each time the sound is made (so 3 the next time, then 4, then 5 and so on). If the student eats any of the M&M's, then give him or her 1 additional M&M for every 10 M&M's he or she still has. The student must have all 10 M&M's to receive the extra 1, so if a student has 18 M&M's, the "interest" payment is only 1 extra M&M.

When the negative interest person runs out of M&M's to pay you back, make that student do something silly, such as jumping jacks or push-ups in order to "pay back" everything he or she "owes." The intention is to demonstrate that negative interest causes us to pay more than the initial amount we borrow.

"The Game" Video #3 (suggested time: 3 minutes)

The purpose of this video is to introduce students to positive and negative interest.

Go to www.futureprofitsresources.org and find the link to "The Game" Video #3. During the video, **debt** is defined as when one owes money to a company or person.

**Make the predetermined sound. Give 0-3 M&M's to the positive interest student, based on how many he/she has in hand. Collect 5 M&M's from the negative interest student. If he/she does not have 5 to give to you, instruct the student to do something silly, such as push-ups or jumping jacks.*

Lecture #1: Positive and Negative Interest (suggested time: 10 minutes)

The purpose of this activity is for students to understand that interest can be either positive or negative and to see when interest works for or against them.

1. Hand out the double-sided worksheets.

**Make the predetermined sound. Give 0-4 M&M's to the positive interest student, based on how many he/she has in hand. Collect 5 M&M's from the negative interest student. If he/she does not have 5 to give to you, instruct the student to do something silly, such as push-ups or jumping jacks.*

2. Show the "Picture of Interest," and explain how interest can work for or against us. It may help the students to follow if you draw this on the board as you explain.

Your explanation should be similar to the following:

"Interest is one of the terms we need to know when dealing with money, because it comes up all the time. It's important to know that there can be positive benefits with some kinds of interest and negative consequences with other kinds. We'll call one side "**positive interest**," because it helps your money work for you, and you receive extra money over time. The other side will be called, "**negative interest,**" because it can work against you, and you'll pay extra money in the long run. In the financial world, banks and people do not use the terms positive and negative interest, but it is helpful for us to use them right now so we know when interest is good for us, and when we should stay away from it."

3. Discuss and explain the positive interest side, where it reads, "You receive interest."
   - Ask students if they have any ideas how someone might gain "positive interest." Because of the previous lesson, students should be able to mention bank accounts, specifically savings and sometimes checking.
   - Then explain the picture like this:

"When you give money to the bank, they will give you positive interest for keeping your money there. Remember, since banks are businesses, they need customers, so banks give benefits so you'll become a customer."

4. Discuss and explain the negative interest side, where it reads, "You pay interest."
   - Ask students how they think banks get the money they use to give out positive interest. Because of the previous lesson (Unit 3, Lesson 1), students should be able to mention bank fees (such as monthly fees, overdraft fees, or ATM fees). Some students may guess about loans from looking at the picture.

   Then explain the other side of the picture:
   - "A bank lets people borrow money to buy things like cars, education, and houses. Whenever banks let people borrow money, they will charge interest. This makes it possible for people to make big purchases and pay the bank back a little bit every month. In exchange for using the bank's money, people pay interest on the money they borrowed. This is the primary reason that the bank is in business, and also the way they make money. They are not taking advantage of the customers, because the customers agree beforehand to pay the extra money when they get the loan from the bank. We're calling this 'negative interest,' because we are the ones who have to pay back what we borrowed plus extra money for interest."

**Make the predetermined sound. Give 0-5 M&M's to the positive interest student, based on how many he/she has in hand. Collect 5 M&M's from the negative interest student. If he/she does not have 5 to give to you, instruct the student to do something silly, such as push-ups or jumping jacks.*

Activity #2: The Interest Game Plan (suggested time: 7 minutes)

The purpose of this activity is to help students understand when they would want high or low interest. We won't go into much depth here on various forms of negative interest, since the next lesson is devoted to different forms of negative interest.

1. Continuing from the previous activity, ask students if they can think of instances where they have seen negative interest. Negative interest hasn't been covered, so students' answers may be limited. Have the students flip the worksheet over to the other side.

2. Discuss and explain "The Interest Game Plan." You can say something like the following: "We see negative interest in many situations. We pay interest whenever we borrow money. The official term for the money borrowed is a "loan", which will be discussed in detail next class. The worksheet shows many of the forms of negative interest that are on Team Debt. It includes Predatory Lending, Rent-to-own Stores, different forms of borrowing money,

Car Loans, Credit Cards, and Check Cashing Outlets. Many forms of positive interest are on Team Success. They include interest-bearing accounts from banks (such as savings and sometimes checking) and other forms of investments. We'll be discussing investments in a later lesson."

3. Ask students what kind of interest is connected with Team Success, where we get more money. They should respond with positive interest, so have them write "positive" on the blank under Team Success.

4. Remind the students that interest is a percentage of money. Then ask, "Since positive interest gives us money, would we want the interest rate to be HIGH or LOW?" They should respond with HIGH. Explain that the higher the interest rate, the more money we will receive. So if we are deciding between different savings accounts, which will pay us positive interest, we want to look for the highest interest rate possible. It is beneficial to "shop around" to see which bank will offer the highest interest rate.

5. Ask the students, "If Team Debt makes us pay money, what kind of interest would we be dealing with?" They should respond with "negative interest," so have them write "negative" on the blank under Team Debt.

6. Remind students that there may be times in life where it is necessary to borrow money and pay negative interest. Ask the students, "Since negative interest means we pay more money, would we want the interest rate to be HIGH or LOW?" They should respond with LOW. Explain that the lower the interest rate, the less money we will have to pay. So if borrowing money is absolutely necessary, look for the lowest interest rate possible. As with bank accounts, "shop around" at different banks or credit cards to see which offers the lowest interest rate for borrowing money.

7. Explain that even on Team Success, we need to be really diligent with saving money and not borrowing more than we can repay. Interest rates on the negative interest side tend to be higher than interest rates on the positive interest side, since the bank survives on the difference. Ultimately, we want to save more money than we borrow. If possible, it is better to stay away from borrowing money.

**Make the predetermined sound. At this time, assuming the negative interest student did not eat any M&M's, he / she will owe you 5 M&M's, but will not have them to give to you. Instruct the student to do something silly, such as push-ups or jumping jacks. Give 0-6 M&M's to the positive interest student, based on how many he / she has in hand.*

Lecture #2: Interest Growth (suggested time: 5 minutes)

The purpose of this lecture is to use the analogy of trees and weeds to further explain positive and negative interest growth.

You can explain it like this:
"Interest can be complicated, so it's helpful to compare it to something familiar. Most of us are familiar with how trees and weeds grow. Let's talk about a tree. When a tree grows, it needs sunlight and water. These things help it grow faster and stronger. Just like trees, in order to make money grow, you need to make sure it is getting positive interest (either through a bank account or investment) and that you are adding more saved money to it. The more money you put into the account, the faster the money grows. Negative interest is like weeds. Weeds will grow and grow very quickly, and if you don't do anything to get rid of them, they just take over your yard. Just like with weeds, the more money you borrow, the harder it is to pay that borrowed money back and get rid of your debt. So when you take advantage of positive interest, you grow your money and make it work for you. When you are careful to avoid negative interest, you are staying away from borrowing money and owing a larger amount."

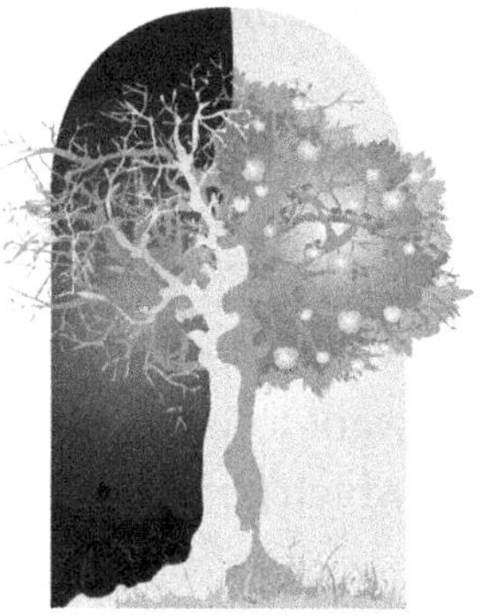

Discussion: Return to Activity #1 (suggested time: 5 minutes)

**For the final time, make the predetermined sound. Again, the negative interest student will owe you 5 M&M's, but will not have them to give you. You should instruct the student again to do something silly, such as push-ups or jumping jacks. Give 0-7 M&M's to the positive interest student, depending on how much he or she has already eaten.*

1. Tell students that the Interest Game has now ended.
2. Ask the two students how many M&M's they were left with.
3. Point out that the 25 M&M's you gave the negative interest student were like a loan that the student had to pay back, plus interest. However, since negative interest means we have to pay back more money than we borrowed, the student ran out of M&M's and couldn't pay you the interest he/she owed. Doing push-ups or jumping jacks is like the work we have to do to earn the money to pay negative interest. The result is owing more than what we originally received.
4. Ask the two students if they ate any M&M's, and how many were eaten.
5. Explain that if the positive interest student ate any or all of his or her M&M's, it is like what happens when we spend money. The more we spend, the less interest we receive, and

therefore the less our money grows.

6. Explain that if the negative interest student ate any or all of his or her M&M's, it is also like spending money. The difference is that the negative interest student already owed someone else his / her M&M's. Therefore, the more he / she "spent" on other things besides the debt, the less money he / she had to pay the interest when the sound was made. So he / she ran out of M&M's more quickly and had to start working to pay off what was owed.

7. Ask the class, "What do you think happens in real life when people owe something to someone else and cannot pay it back?" Tell students that often, what they bought with the borrowed money gets taken away, whether it was a home, a car, or something else. Also, when people are unable to make a payment, it gets recorded and makes it very difficult for them to borrow money again in the future.

Wrap Up: Lesson Review Questions (suggested time: 5 minutes)

The main things students should understand after this lesson are there are different kinds of interest, and when they receive interest, they want the highest interest rate possible, but when they pay interest, they want the lowest interest rate possible.

Wrap up this lesson by asking students this series of questions to make sure they understand the main concepts:

- Question: What are the two types of interest discussed during this lesson?
  - Answer: positive interest and negative interest
- Question: Why is it important to know that interest can be either positive or negative?
  - Answer: We need to know about both types of interest so we don't assume interest is always good or bad. Sometimes we can game interest, and sometimes interest can game us. It's important to know the two different kinds of interest so we can tell the difference and make interest work in our favor. We cannot be gamed by interest when we know what to look for — whether we want a high interest rate when we invest or a low interest rate when we borrow.
- Question: When we are receiving interest, do we want a high rate or a low rate?
  - Answer: a high interest rate
- Question: When we are paying interest, do we want a high rate or a low rate?
  - Answer: a low interest rate

Conclude by telling the students that negative interest is a major reason many people end up in debt and can't pay back everything they owe. Once someone gets deeply into debt, it's very hard to take back control of his or her financial life. Ask students if they have any questions about the things discussed today.

The next lesson is about some of the biggest traps to avoid so students won't let interest game them. Thank the class for their attention and participation.

Vocabulary:
- interest
- positive interest
- negative interest
- loan
- debt

Additional Resources:
For additional resources on interest for teens and for interest and debt calculators for teens, go to www.futureprofitsresources.org.

Financial literacy is an issue that should command our attention because many Americans are not adequately organizing finances for their education, health care and retirement.
–Ron Lewis, Former U.S. Congressman

Materials needed:

- Charade Cards – 3.4.1*
- Loan Charts – 3.4.2*
- "The Game" Video #4*
- Whiteboard and pen, or chalkboard and chalk, or poster paper and pen
- Computer with internet connection, projector, and speakers

Key Concepts:

1. Certain large purchases, such as college tuition or buying a home, will likely require a loan.
2. Loans can be part of a sound financial plan, if the value of the object purchased will increase more than the cost of the negative interest paid.
3. When the value of the object purchased is less than the cost of the negative interest, the loan should be avoided.

Prep Time: 10 minutes

Advance Preparation Tasks:

- Print the charade cards in the attachment, and cut them so they are separate cards.
- Either make copies of the loan charts for each student, copy the loan charts onto transparencies to project them, or draw your own version on the board. (See Loan Charades Activity below for explanation.)
- Bookmark "The Game" Video #4 and set up a computer with internet connection to the projector and speakers so the video is ready to show.

**For all additional resources, including handouts, video links and helpful websites, see www.futureprofitsresources.org*

Keep in Mind

- Keep information about loans simple so you don't lose the students' interests. The basic idea is that certain types of loans can be part of a sound financial plan.
- Most financial institutions in low-income communities that offer immediate access to funds are predatory, and many residents may see no other alternative.
- Discussing the benefits of student loans, home loans, and business loans will help students to dream about opportunities for their futures.

When teaching about loans, the subject can either be highly oversimplified or covered in a way that would take weeks to explain. This curriculum takes the simple approach because it is crucial that students grasp the most basic idea — only a few types of loans can work in their favor. The goal of this lesson is to convey why these loans can be beneficial, while other loans should be avoided. When more specific details about loans are given, it can be confusing and cause students to disengage. Most of the students are at least several years away from even considering a loan, so the nuts and bolts of loan terms will likely seem irrelevant. Instead, this curriculum intentionally prioritizes the clarity of the larger concept — understanding which types of loans can be part of a sound financial plan.

In general, teens from lower-income backgrounds do not have many examples of people using loans effectively to maximize their own advantage. Financial institutions that offer loans most readily in lower-income communities are usually predatory, offering borrowers money at extremely high interest rates, or at rates that are initially favorable but balloon rapidly. Because of cultural and language barriers and the absence of mainstream financial institutions, individuals may see no alternative to predatory loans. Lower-income families generally borrow money in urgent situations, when they may feel unable to turn down whatever terms will provide immediate access to funds. These loans tend to perpetuate cycles of mounting debt and poverty. For these reasons, this curriculum attempts to guide students away from borrowing money by teaching the general principle that loans are to be avoided.

However, there are a few situations in which obtaining a loan is part of a sound financial plan. These circumstances include student loans, home loans, and business loans. Understanding that these types of loans are available and can be leveraged to their advantage is critical, so students are able to identify the occasions when borrowing money is in their best interests. For example, many students think college is so expensive they cannot even consider it a possibility for their futures. This curriculum does not want to further discourage students from attending college by giving the impression that student loans should be lumped in with all other forms of borrowing money. The potential to own a home or start a business also provides hope along with a vehicle for building wealth and breaking cyclical poverty. This curriculum encourages loans that might make these dreams a reality.

Although the details of loans can be complicated, the goal of this lesson is to clearly establish the basic idea that a few specific types of loans can significantly benefit an individual's future. Bottom line: this lesson is a success if students walk away from this lesson with the hope that they might be able to obtain something they once thought was unattainable through beneficial loans.

Lesson Snapshot

Review (5 minutes)
- Positive and negative interest
- Low or high rates when dealing with interest?

Introduction (7 minutes)
- Borrowing money is usually understood as a loan
- Loans can be either good or bad
- This lesson is about how loans can be good

"The Game" Video #4 (5 minutes)
- Show video clip

Discussion: Loans (3 minutes)
- Define "loan"
- Where do people go to borrow money?
- What objects do people borrow money to buy?

Lecture: "Good" Loans (5 minutes)
- Two main questions to ask to evaluate if a loan is good or bad:
  - Is the interest attached to the loan LOW?
  - Does the value of what you are buying go up over time?

Activity: Loan Charades (20 minutes)
- Play charades with the six different types of loans
- Pause after each charade is guessed to discuss the loan:
  - Is it a "good" loan or a "bad" loan?
  - Show/draw the diagram of the term showing the value of the object over time compared to the money spent over time
  - Define and explain the term

Wrap Up (5 minutes)
- What determines a "good" loan, and which loans are considered "good"?

Review (suggested time: 5 minutes)

The two main topics to review are:

1. Positive and negative interest, and how to differentiate between the two, and
2. When we should look for a high versus low interest rate.

Ask a couple students what they remember learning the previous class. As students respond, follow up on the topics they say, asking questions to draw out the details you want to emphasize. For example, if a student says, "positive and negative interest," ask him or her to share an example of a situation in which interest is positive. Then ask another student to share an example of a situation in which interest is negative. Ask students why it's important to understand interest, or how interest might impact their lives today and / or in the future. Students should remember interest can either give them more money or cause them to pay more money, so being able to identify when it is helpful or harmful is critical.

Ask the students to raise their hands if they would want a high interest rate with a credit card. Then ask the students to raise their hands if they would want a high interest rate with a bank account. This will help to reinforce that there are ways to avoid being gamed by interest and to make it work in your favor.

Introduction (suggested time: 7 minutes)

Tell students that we'll be focusing on negative interest for the next two lessons.

- Ask students again why we call it negative interest.
- They should respond with, "Because you pay interest, so it costs you more money." Remind students that negative interest is almost always associated with borrowing money.
- Ask students if they have ever let a friend borrow money. If so, what was it for?
- Explain to the students: "If you lend your friend $20 dollars, you are giving him or her a loan. You probably won't charge interest, but if you expect your friend to pay you back, that's a loan."
- Ask students if they think that borrowing money is good or bad, and why.

There should be many different reactions. Some may think borrowing money is fine, and some may think it is bad. Affirm each of them for sharing.

Explain that borrowing money can often be bad. It is important to avoid negative interest in order not to pay extra money. However, there are a couple of situations when paying negative interest on borrowed money can actually help, if we are getting enough value out of what we buy with the loan.

- Ask the students if they know anyone who has obtained a loan and what the person did with it.

After a few students answer, explain that, even though debt should be avoided, it may be necessary for people to borrow money for certain large purchases. For example, buying a home usually requires getting a loan, because very few people have enough cash saved to pay the full price of a home.

This lesson looks at a few situations in which borrowing money has positive benefits. Knowing when it is smart to borrow money is another way to game the financial system.

"The Game" Video #4 (suggested time: 5 minutes)

Go to www.futureprofitsresources.org and find the link to "The Game" Video #4. Show the video to the students and move on to the following discussion.

Discussion: Loans (suggested time: 3 minutes)

- Ask the students: "So from watching the video and considering our conversations so far, who can tell me what a loan is?"

After students give answers, write on the board this basic definition, so that all can see:

Loan = Borrowed money, paid back with interest

The formal definition is here for reference: Loan — When a lender gives money or property to a borrower, and the borrower agrees to return the property or repay the borrowed money along with interest, at a predetermined date in the future.

Note to Teacher

Some students may mention they can borrow money from a family member and not have to pay interest. This can be true, but if for some reason, the money is not paid back, it can cause strain or hardship in the relationship. This is one reason to encourage students to be very careful with borrowing money from, or lending money to, friends or family members. In formal loans, there is a written agreement. This not only protects the person lending the money, but it can also protect the person receiving the money from being taken advantage of by the lender.

- Ask the students where people go in order to borrow money.
- Ask the students what kinds of things people borrow money to buy. Write students' answers on the board.

Lecture: "Good" Loans (suggested time: 5 minutes)

Once students mention a few things for which people borrow money, clarify that there are a couple of situations in which borrowing money can actually help make more money in the future. It will usually take at least five years or more for the benefits of the loan to outweigh the cost of interest, so these loans are only good in the long term.

Go on to tell students that when you get a loan and have to pay negative interest, there are two questions to ask yourself to determine if the loan is a good idea:

1. Is the interest rate attached to the loan LOW? The interest rate is the percentage individuals have to pay each year on top of the money being borrowed. For example: If someone takes out a loan for \$150 with a 10% interest rate, he would pay back the \$150 plus an extra \$15 each year until the full amount was paid off.

   Equation: \$150 x .10 = \$15; \$150 + \$15 = \$165

   The higher the interest rate, the more extra money you will have to pay over time. In order to keep our money, we should look for a low interest rate that will charge less extra money.

Note to Teacher

This is an overly simplified calculation of yearly interest, but it will give students a sufficient basic understanding without complex calculations or explanations.

2. Does the value of the object purchased with the loan go up or down over time? The next activity will explain this concept.

Activity: Loan Charades (suggested time: 20 minutes)

The purpose of this activity is to demonstrate why a few types of loans are beneficial, even though they charge negative interest, while most types of loans should be avoided. The goal is to introduce the concepts of appreciation and depreciation, though the curriculum avoids those terms for the sake of simplicity. The activity focuses on three positive loans and three negative loans:

- *Student Loan*
- *Home Loan (Mortgage)*
- *Business Loan*

Vs.

- *Car Loan*
- *Consumer Loan (typically credit cards)*
- *Predatory Loan / Payday Loan* (students can say either)*

**Payday Loan will be defined next lesson, but students may already be familiar with this as a predatory loan.*

1. The following game of charades will help teach about specific loans. There will be six charades and each of them will be a type of loan.
2. Split the class into two teams, and ask for a volunteer from Team 1 for the first charade.
3. Explain the rules:
   a. One student will have a minute to act out his/her charade for his/her team without using words. Team members can guess as many times as they want until the minute is over.
   b. If the team members answer correctly, they will be awarded two points.
   c. If they have not guessed the correct term before the minute is over, the other team gets one guess. If the other team answers correctly, they will be awarded one point.
   d. The team with the most points at the end wins.
4. Give the first student the first charade. After each charade is guessed correctly, stop to discuss that term by asking the discussion question about whether or not it is a good situation for borrowing money, showing the chart, and explaining the term before moving on to the other team. Specific discussion questions and explanations are below. Once the term is discussed, move on to the next charade for the next team.

After each term is guessed correctly, ask the following discussion question before continuing to the next charade:

- Do you think this is a good situation for borrowing money? Why or why not?

The Loan Charts (3.4.2)* are provided to help illustrate why some loans can be positive, while others are always negative. As you can see from the charts, the horizontal axis is "Time" and the vertical axis is "Money." There are two lines on each graph. One line shows the amount of money paid for the object over time (borrowed amount plus interest). The second line shows the value of the object over time, which is the amount of money for which a person would likely be able to sell the object. The decision to get a loan is considered a sound financial decision when the value of the item purchased is likely to increase more than the interest on the loan, so that the net financial impact is positive. The line representing the cost of the loan

*Loan Charts found at www.futureprofitsresources.org

will always increase over time. In each case, we need to carefully examine the line representing the value of the object purchased with the borrowed money. If that line goes up over time over the cost of the loan, it is a "good" loan. If that line goes down over time or remains under the cost of the loan, the loan should be avoided. No actual numbers have been provided because the actual amount of money for loans will change depending on the situation. The main idea to communicate to the students is that with a "bad" loan, the money paid goes up, as the value of the object goes down.

Make copies of the charts to pass around, copy them onto transparencies and project them, or draw your own version on the board. A brief explanation for each type of loan is provided below.

- **Student Loans:** An individual borrows money, usually from the government or a bank, to pay for college tuition and other school expenses. In explaining the "resale" value of a student loan, it can be difficult to explain the "object" that one is selling over time. Explain that looking for a job is like selling individual skills to potential employers. Having a college degree makes a person more valuable in the workplace. Getting a college education makes job skills worth more money. The value of the education increases because having a college degree means receiving higher wages over a lifetime. There will be more money earned in salary than what was spent on interest for the loan. Mention that student loans usually have very low interest rates, around 2% to 8%, to help people go to college.

- **Home Loans (Mortgages):** An individual borrows money, usually from a bank, to purchase a house, condo, mobile home, or other type of residence. In general, the value of real estate increases over time, so it can make up for the negative interest paid on the home loan. However, this is not a guarantee, so buying real estate can be a gamble. There are times when people are suddenly much less willing to spend money on homes, housing prices fall dramatically, and homeowners who want to make a profit may have to wait indefinitely until prices go back up. Keeping a home for a long time (at least 5-10 years) can provide more assurance that the value will increase over that time. Buying a home is also smart because it replaces paying rent for an apartment. Rent is money that is paid to someone else for the use of their property that you

will never get back. Money paid toward a home loan can be recovered when you sell the home. Interest rates on home loans vary over time, but usually range from 5% to 8%.

- **Business Loans:** An individual borrows money to start a new business or to make an existing business bigger. Let students know the growth of the value of a business depends on how successful the business is. With a well thought-out business plan, getting a business loan will often end up paying off in the long run, because the profit will be more than the negative interest paid. If the business does not do as well as planned, the owner may end up owing more money than what was earned. The average interest rate for a business loan should be around 5%.

- **Car Loans:** An individual borrows money to purchase a car or other vehicle. When buying a new car, it loses 20% of its value as soon as it is driven off the lot, and it continues to lose resale value the longer you own it and the more you drive it. Because of this, you cannot get back all the money spent on the car loan, and since you are paying for the cost of the car plus negative interest, you will end up paying more for the car than it was ever worth. Although cars typically decrease in value, that doesn't mean a person should not buy them. It just means that it is important to be strategic in which vehicle to buy and how to pay for it. If you are using a loan to buy a less expensive car to get to work so you can make more money, a car loan can actually be a good loan. If you are using a loan to buy a car to show off the rims, stereo, etc., it will end up being a bad loan. For a great video on the financial benefit of buying a used car instead of getting a loan for a new car, see the additional resources for this lesson. Car loans tend to have somewhat higher interest rates, around 5% to 25%, depending on your credit score.

- **Consumer Loans:** An individual borrows money to purchase an item that is often expensive, like a big screen TV, laptop computer, furniture, etc. A consumer loan is usually obtained by using a credit card, although it is possible to get a consumer loan from a bank. Ask students if they have seen commercials that say they can buy a TV or mattress and pay nothing for a year. These stores are actually offering consumer loans and will usually require an individual to apply for a store credit card. Explain that consumer purchases will almost always go down in value. A used TV, laptop, or couch is not worth as much money as a new one. As with cars, the negative interest added to the loan means you will end up paying more than the item was ever worth. Consumer loans, particularly credit cards, often have very high interest rates — as much as 30%. The next lesson explains credit cards in greater depth.

Additionally, these loans often have a negative impact on your credit score, which will be discussed at the end of this lesson.

- **Predatory Loans:** Predatory loans involve borrowing money for urgent or emergency circumstances such as medical expenses, rent, utility bills, or food after the monthly paycheck runs out. These loans are not provided by banks or credit card companies, but are offered by businesses willing to take advantage of people with no other choices. Generally, individuals who borrow money from these lenders are desperate and willing to agree to pay extremely high fees or interest rates in order to obtain immediately-needed money. The value of the loan will never go up in value. The fees and interest are so high that one will always pay more for the loan than whatever the loan was used for, and the money is usually spent immediately on something with no resale value. These loans should be heavily discouraged, and will be discussed more in depth in the next lesson.

The main message students should walk away with is that the items bought with money from home loans, student loans, and business loans will often go up in value over time, so there will be more money back than the negative interest paid. Although there is negative interest, more money and value is earned than spent. We are gaming interest, and making loans work for us. Obtaining these "good loans" and paying them off on time will also help us build up our credit scores. (Credit scores will be discussed in detail in Lesson 6 of this unit.) New car loans, consumer loans, and predatory loans will always end up costing more money than the items purchased are actually worth, so they are gaming us and should be avoided. We cannot win with these types of loans.

Wrap Up (suggested time: 5 minutes)

Ask the class what determines if a loan is considered a "good" loan. *(The value of the object goes up over time)*

Then ask the class which loans are considered "good." *(Home loans, business loans, and student loans)*

Finally, tell the class that although there are some loans that can be good or necessary, most loans are very dangerous and can make us lose control of our financial situations if we are not careful. Next class we will look in greater depth at the ways loans can game us.

Vocabulary:
- loan
- interest rate
- student loan
- home loan / mortgage
- business loan
- car loan
- consumer loan
- predatory loan

Additional Resources:
For a great video on the financial benefit of buying a used car instead of getting a loan for a new car, go to www.futureprofitsresources.org and watch the "Drive Free, Retire Rich" video by Dave Ramsey. Also provided online is more information on student loan interest rates.

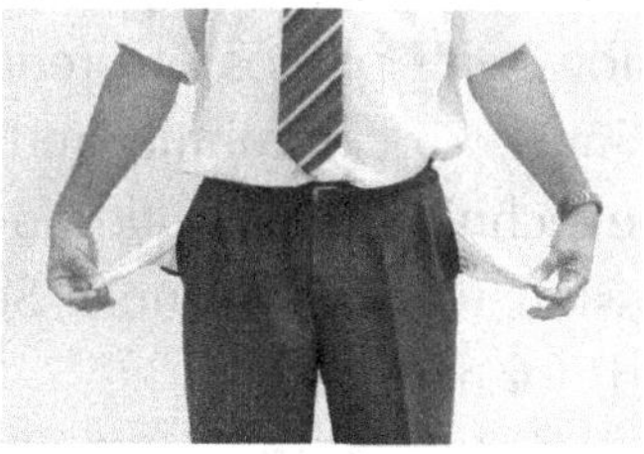

Some debts are fun
when you are acquiring them,
but none are fun when you set about
retiring them.
–Ogden Nash, Poet

Materials needed:

- 4 Predatory Lending Activity Signs – 3.5.1*
- 3 copies of a picture of a car – 3.5.2*
- "The Game" Video #5*
- Optional: Slide show of predatory lending locations in your community (see Advance Preparation Tasks)
- A "Resources for Debt Counseling" handout (see Advance Preparation Tasks)
- Whiteboard and pen, or chalkboard and chalk, or poster paper and pen
- Computer with internet connection, projector, and speakers

Key Concepts:

1. Predatory lending seems reasonable at first, especially when it feels like the only option in an emergency. Therefore, it is critical to understand how the costs can build up over time.
2. Predatory lenders deliberately do business in low-income communities where they can take advantage of people who need access to money and have few other options.
3. Knowing your options when you have to borrow money gives you the power to choose the type of loan least likely to trap you in long-term debt.

Prep Time: 30 minutes (Allow an additional 40 minutes if you plan to include the optional slide show.)

**For all additional resources, including handouts, video links and helpful websites, see www.futureprofitsresources.org*

Advance Preparation Tasks:

- Print the Predatory Lending Activity Signs and cut in the middle to have four signs. Punch holes in the top corners of each, and take string and tie through each so one can hang around each student's neck.
- Make three copies of the car picture.
- If you are planning to include the optional discussion, "Predatory Lending in Our Neighborhood," you will need to create a slide show with photos of predatory lending locations in your community. Prior to this lesson, go into your community and take pictures of those locations. Alternatively, if you don't have the technical capabilities to take pictures and create a slide show, lead students in a discussion without pictures. See "Optional Discussion: Predatory Lending in Our Neighborhood" for more details.
- If the time or resources permit, take the students on a field trip around the community to point out and discuss predatory lending services in their community. This option eliminates the need for the optional discussion.
- Research local options for debt counseling and create a handout entitled "Resources for Debt Counseling." Preferably, this handout should include non-profit resources with phone numbers and addresses.
- Bookmark "The Game" Video #5 and set up a computer with internet connection to the projector and speakers so the video is ready to show.

Keep in Mind

- Many families in low-income communities see predatory lending as the only option for borrowing money.
- Many students may assume predatory lending companies are reasonable.
- Use facts to reveal the predatory nature of these businesses.
- Be careful not to criticize people who use predatory lending.

Many students' families live from paycheck to paycheck, with no savings or long-term financial planning. Therefore, when there is an unexpected expense, they turn to family members, payday loan stores, or in extreme circumstances, loan sharks. Many students know people who use these services on a regular basis, so they become comfortable with them, and assume they are reasonable options. However, students and families tend to be unaware of the outrageous interest rates that accompany these loans. Even students that realize payday lenders and loan sharks are expensive may not realize that less expensive alternatives exist or that careful financial planning can help one avoid turning to them in the first place.

Because students may see these services used regularly, they may someday use the same services simply because they have not been exposed to alternatives, and consequently repeating the patterns and practices they saw in their families. However, the high interest rates charged by these lenders are a major reason why families perpetually stay in debt. Students need to be equipped with the appropriate knowledge to make informed and careful decisions about whether or not these lenders are actually the best option for them in the future. At the same time, it is essential to be considerate about the fact that many of the students' families use these services. Students may take offense if they perceive you as criticizing their families, especially if their parents or other family members are working very hard to make ends meet and feel they have no alternatives. Also be aware that, for those families already deeply into the cycle of recurring debt, getting free of debt would be extremely difficult, and this realization may cause students to despair. One way to relieve students from this burden is to provide them with a handout of resources for debt counseling, which is explained in greater depth in the Advance Preparation Tasks and Wrap Up sections.

In addition to payday loans and loan sharks, this lesson also discusses rent-to-own stores and high-interest credit cards. This curriculum will not teach all the details of various predatory loans. However, students should walk away with the understanding that: (1) the high fees and interest rates charged by these types of financial "services" will cost them a lot of money and create debt that is difficult to pay off, and (2) these places are set up to take as much money from people as possible.

Lesson Snapshot:

Review (3 minutes)
- Two main questions to evaluate if a loan is good or bad:
  - Is the interest attached to the loan LOW?
  - Does the value of what you are buying go up over time?

Introduction (2 minutes)
- Dangerous loans

"The Game" Video #5 (5 minutes)
- Show video clip
- Give definition of "predator"

Discussion #1: Predators (5 minutes)
- Discuss the predators in the film and how they relate to the financial world

Activity: Joe's Options (20-25 minutes)
- Introduce scenario and hand out signs to four volunteers
- Explain each option and ask students to guess how much they would pay for the car repairs using that option
- Write final estimated amounts on the board

Discussion #2: Predatory Lending (5 minutes)
- Discuss activity — Which option would you choose?
- Discuss predatory lending on a personal level

Optional Discussion: Predatory Lending in Our Neighborhood (5 minutes)
- Predatory lending in the community

Wrap Up (5 minutes)
- Return to analogy of predators
- Emphasize refraining from using predatory lending services
- Hand out Resources for Debt Counseling
- Next lesson: more about the cycle of debt

Review (suggested time: 3 minutes)

- Ask students to name the two main questions they should ask themselves to evaluate if a loan is good or bad. The questions are as follows:
  - Is the interest attached to the loan LOW?
  - Does the value of the purchase go up over time?
- Ask the students to name the three types of loans that can be good
  - Student loans
  - Home loans
  - Business loans
- Ask the students to explain why these loans can be good even when one is paying negative interest.

After some students answer, recap the reason by explaining it's because the value of the item for which you are paying is expected to be higher than the amount you are paying in interest.

Introduction (suggested time: 2 minutes)

The previous lesson focused on how some loans can be good. Today's lesson is about some of the most dangerous loans to obtain. Many loans are dangerous because they cause people to get caught in a cycle where the amount they can afford to pay back each month is less than the extra interest added, so they owe more and more money. There are even companies that intentionally charge high interest rates to people living in low-income communities. These companies want their customers to get stuck so the company can make a huge profit off of the interest people pay.

"The Game" Video #5 (suggested time: 5 minutes)

Go to www.futureprofitsresources.org and find the link to "The Game" Video #5. This video explains different kinds of animal predators to communicate an analogy of predators in the financial world. The video explains what a predator is, but it is important to define predator with your students after watching the video. Ask students what a **predator** is, and then give the definition: an organism that lives by preying on other organisms.

Discussion #1: Predators (suggested time: 5 minutes)

The following questions are somewhat rhetorical and most students will know they don't want to be taken advantage of by these predators. Ask the questions quickly, knowing that some "jokers" in the class will probably raise their hands anyway:

- How many of you would walk up to any of these creatures and reason with them?
- How many of you would put your hand in their mouths, giving them an easy opportunity to bite?
- How many of you would you want to live in the same environment with these animals?

Ask students to give their best guesses to the following question:

- If these animals are examples of predators, how do you think predators might act in the financial world?

After a few students answer, tell them that, similar to predatory animals, predatory lenders are really dangerous. They make themselves look like a normal part of their surroundings, and they may even make people believe they are benefiting from the predator's services. They sneak up on the prey and make the prey feel safe before they pounce. But unlike the predatory animals, predatory lenders will often feed on their prey without the prey knowing it. Because predatory lenders are so good at making their prey feel comfortable and safe, those who borrow money from them still sometimes believe that theirs is the best and safest option.

Predatory lenders are companies or people who lend money with such excessively high interest rates or fees that it is nearly impossible to pay the money back in the time required. This time can be a week instead of a month, but at a lower rate, which causes the person borrowing money to feel they are getting a good deal. The shorter time will actually cause the money owed to build quicker than a month's time. Predatory lenders will make borrowing money from them look like the best option, but in reality, their fees will usually create a cycle of debt that the borrower will have a very difficult time breaking. These companies intentionally target people in low-income communities, because the companies know these people have few other options.

- Finally, ask students to give examples of predators in the financial world. If they don't have ideas, tell them they will be able to identify several financial predators by the end of this lesson.

Activity: Joe's Options (suggested time: 20-25 minutes)

The purpose of this activity is to provide a concrete example of how different predatory lenders work, and how expensive it really is to use their services.

1. Start by explaining the scenario to students: Joe's car breaks down and it's going to cost $300 to fix. The car is critical for Joe to get back and forth to work.

2. Call four volunteers. Give each student one of the following signs to hold or wear.
   - Payday loan
   - Loan shark
   - Credit card
   - Save money

Note to Teacher

Volunteers will be in front of the class for a while, so you may have them move their chairs or desks in a row facing the rest of the class, so they can sit down.

3. Give three pictures of a car to the volunteers with the three predatory lending signs so the class can see these volunteers represent Joe paying for his car to be fixed immediately.

4. Tell the class that each volunteer represents a different way Joe can get his car fixed. These options all require interest or high payments, so volunteers will end up paying the $300 plus much more money in interest over time. Ask the class to guess how much Joe ends up paying in total, using each of these services. Write their guesses on the board behind each volunteer.

5. Give students a brief explanation of how the financial service named on each sign works. After each description, tell the class the actual amount Joe would pay in total for the car repairs using that option (repairs plus interest). Write the amount on the white board. First explain saving money so you can use it as a comparison to the other options.

Brief explanation of each of Joe's options:

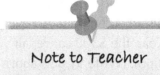

> **Note to Teacher**
>
> *This activity is heavy on lecture and much preparation is necessary. Familiarize yourself with each option so the activity runs smoothly. You may want to prepare some sort of slide show to help with remembering the details of each option.*

- **Save Money:** One option is for Joe to ride the bus and save enough money until he has the cash to pay for the repairs. Unfortunately, Joe will have to be patient and live with the inconvenience of public transportation. Because Joe hasn't saved money yet, he won't be able to pay for the repairs immediately. But over time, he'll be able to acquire enough money to make his car run again.

If Joe saves $20 every week for a year, he would have $1,040 ($20 x 52 = $1,040). That's enough to fix the car as well as take a six-hour road trip to see his cousin. (Write "$300 plus road trip" above the student who saves money.) This number will actually be higher if Joe decides to save his money in a savings account at a bank, gaining interest on the money he is saving.

- **Payday Loans:** Ask students if they know how a "payday loan" works. If they do not know, provide the correct answer. Tell them that a payday loan is when a person borrows money between paychecks and agrees to pay it back as soon as he/she gets paid from their job...on "pay day." It's like getting the money from the paycheck early, and then paying it back from the actual paycheck. This may seem like a fair deal, however, there is a high fee charged for the amount borrowed. Payday loans are usually used for emergencies, such as surprise medical bills or Joe's current car problems.

Look at Joe's situation, and assume that his payday lender charges a fee of 20% of the amount borrowed. If he gets a payday loan for $300, the loan will be due in two weeks, and he will owe $360. But it's very unlikely Joe will be able to get that much money in two weeks, so he'll have to renew the loan. At the time of the loan renewal the interest for the first two weeks is due...that's $60. At the end of four weeks, he'll have paid $120 in interest and still owe the original $300. If Joe does this every two weeks for a year, he'll have paid $1,560 in interest and still owe the original $300! Point out that 20% interest adds up very quickly because it is compounded every two weeks. If Joe finds a way to pay the initial $300 at the end of a year, the $300 car repair would have cost him $1860 ($60 x 26 = $1560; $1560 + $300 = $1860). (Write $1,860 above the volunteer with a payday loan.)

- **Loan Sharks**: A loan shark may be the worst predatory lending service out there. A loan shark is someone who is willing to lend money to a person in dire need, charging extreme amounts. For example, to borrow $300, the loan shark may require $450 be paid back. That's 50% interest! Loan sharks can do this type of transaction because they usually lend money without any kind of written agreement to people in desperate situations. Their desperation is why most people who turn to loan sharks go along with the lender's outrageous demands. Because there is no written agreement, the person who borrowed the money is often scared to report the loan shark to any authorities, even if the demands are illegal. This situation can worsen if the person is unable to pay back the money because the loan shark may inflict harm on that person or his or her family.

Look at Joe's situation. He borrows $300 from a loan shark, who gives him one month to pay it back and charges 50% interest. That means Joe will owe $450 in one month. Joe can't get that much money that quickly, so he renews the loan. The loan shark agrees to give him another month if he pays last month's interest upfront. Joe pays $150 and still owes the initial $300. The loan shark charges 50% interest again. If Joe is unable to pay the original loan back over a year's time, he would pay $1,800 in interest plus the original $300 loan. At the end of a year, the original car repair will cost $2,100 ($150 x 12 = $1800; $1800 + $300 = $2100)! (Write $2,100 on the board above the student who uses a loan shark.) Eventually, the loan sharks may use illegal methods to pressure Joe into paying the money back, even threatening harm, and Joe will most likely have a different kind of emergency situation for which he never accounted.

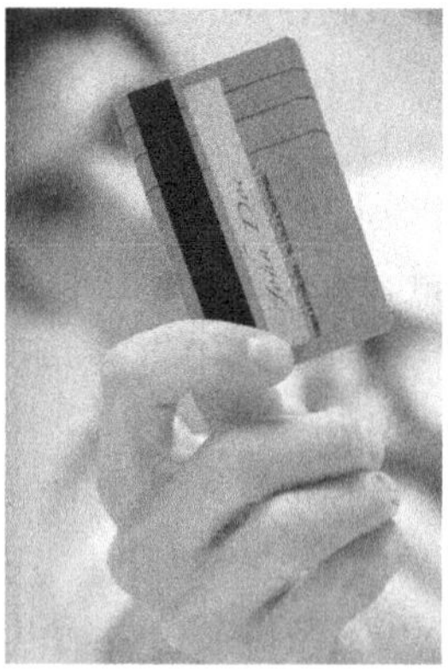

- **Credit Cards:** Credit cards can be the most dangerous loan because of how easily students can fall into this type of debt. It is critical to emphasize how dangerous credit cards are and how they should only be used for emergencies. People who are very careful about how they use their credit cards can avoid being gamed by the credit card companies. The only way to do this is to pay back the entire amount borrowed before the end of every month. But most people spend more money using their credit cards than they can afford to pay back that month. If you aren't sure you can stop yourself from spending more than you can pay back right away, it is better to avoid credit cards completely. Credit cards often charge very high interest rates, and require the consumer to pay back only a minimum monthly payment. This **minimum payment** is a small percentage of the total balance owed. A cardholder can make a payment that is in excess of the minimum payment due. However, a payment cannot be for less than the minimum payment due without incurring additional fees. If only the minimum payment is made month after month, the cardholder may be paying only enough money to cover the interest and a little bit more. It can take decades to pay off the original amount, creating a trap that can only be escaped by paying more than the minimum payment. Meanwhile, people usually keep charging new purchases to their credit cards each month, increasing the amount they owe. Often this amount gets so high they have no way to pay it back, and must declare bankruptcy. Some credit cards charge up to 34% interest.

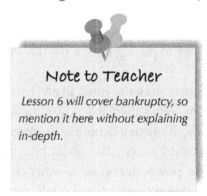

Note to Teacher

Lesson 6 will cover bankruptcy, so mention it here without explaining in-depth.

Consider how much Joe will pay with 25% interest. If Joe paid for just the repairs on his car, never used his credit card again, and he made just a minimum payment of $28.51 each month, he will end up owing $42.12 in interest during one year. In total, his car repairs would cost him $342.12. (Write $342.12 on the board above the student who used a credit card.) **Point out to students that many people misuse their credit cards by continuing to make charges, and end up in a deep cycle of debt.** If Joe continues to make charges on his credit card, it will take him a much longer time to pay off the original $300 car repair. Therefore Joe should only use his credit card to pay for his current emergency situation. If he only used his credit card for his current emergency, this is a good example of credit card use.

Discussion #2: Predatory Lending (suggested time: 5 minutes)

Give students a chance to respond to the activity.

- After learning about each option, where would you go to get money?
- Do you think Joe may have had other options?
- What would you have done in Joe's place?

Move on to discuss the deeper question of how people can get stuck in cycles of predatory lending.

- How many of you have seen someone you know who goes to a predatory lending location every week or month?

Once an individual gets in a cycle of owing money to predatory lenders, it is extremely difficult to get out. If someone gets a payday loan, then spends half of his or her paycheck to pay back the loan, he or she is likely to run out of money for food before the next paycheck comes. He or she might get another payday loan in order to buy food, and then the next paycheck also goes to paying back a payday loan, and this creates a cycle that is very hard to break.

Since students most likely have not started borrowing money yet, encourage them that now is the best time to make an informed decision about whether or not they want to avoid that cycle of debt in their futures. Having information about how these predatory loans work gives them the power to choose whether or not they will allow predatory lenders to game them. Many people get trapped in the cycle because they do not realize how much money they will end up owing.

Many people who use predatory lenders feel like they are in a desperate situation with no other choice. Families often use these services when they need to pay for food, rent, taking care of kids, etc., but then they end up caught in a trap they can't escape. Saving money for emergencies, as shown in the budget simulation, can help us avoid a situation with no other options, and allow us to stay in control of our financial futures. Knowing all of our options is also important in making an informed decision about the least expensive loan to pursue in an emergency when borrowing cannot be avoided.

Ask the students which lenders they would avoid. They should answer payday loans and loan sharks. Then ask what Joe's best option would be. They should answer that he could use a credit card, but should pay more than the minimum payment every month so that he pays it off as quickly as possible. Another option for Joe is to cut down on expenses like cable or entertainment, which are "wants." Joe could go to public places (sports bar or library) to watch TV. Sacrificing some other expense for a short time is always a better option than a predatory loan.

Optional Discussion: Predatory Lending in Our Neighborhood

(suggested time: 5 minutes)

This discussion is optional as the activity may run 20-25 minutes. The purpose is to help students apply their learning about predatory lenders by analyzing their own communities. Before the lesson (see Advance Preparation Tasks), create a slide show of pictures taken locally that show predatory lenders or signs that advertise predatory lending. If you want to incorporate local community analysis into the previous activity ("Joe's Options"), show local pictures of each type of predatory lender at the end of each explanation of Joe's Options.

Show the slide show to students. After each picture, ask students the following:

- Where was this picture taken?
- Are you surprised that this place or service is predatory?
- Did it seem predatory to you before today?

If you don't have the technical capabilities to take pictures and create a slide show, one alternative is to lead the students in a discussion. Ask students the following questions:

- Have you seen signs around your community advertising that you can get money fast? Where are these signs? What do different signs say?
- Where are there predatory lenders in your community?
- Are you surprised that many of the signs and places you see every day are predatory?
- Did they seem predatory to you before today?

Wrap Up (suggested time: 5 minutes)

Return to the predator analogy. Just as predators survive on prey, predatory lending companies survive by taking advantage of the poor. These companies place themselves in low-income communities because they know that the people living in these communities are more likely to have emergencies where they need to borrow money quickly and will not have many other options.

Emphasize to your students the importance of avoiding loans from predatory lenders. There may be times in their lives when they will have to borrow money, but the point of this curriculum is to prevent students from being taken advantage of, or to avoid being gamed. The information they have learned will equip them to choose cheaper and safer loans.

Although this lesson was about how to avoid predatory lending and getting caught in cycles of debt, the reality is that students may know someone who may already be trapped. Provide a handout with places that are trusted resources to help people understand the options that are

available for their particular circumstances. It is important not to put any students or their families on the spot by making them feel embarrassed about admitting their families are in the position of needing help. In order to be sensitive to their personal situations, give the handout to all students.

Finally, in the next class students will learn more about the danger of getting stuck in a cycle of debt.

Vocabulary:

- predator
- predatory lenders
- payday loan
- rent-to-own store
- loan shark
- credit cards
- minimum payment

Additional Resources:

For additional resources on consumer protection for predatory lending, payday lending, rent-to-own centers, and credit card calculators, go to www.futureprofitsresources.org

Chains of habit are too light to be felt
until they are too heavy to be broken.
–Warren Buffett, Investor and Philanthropist

Materials needed:

- "The Game" Video #6*
- Whiteboard and pen, or chalkboard and chalk, or poster paper and pen
- Computer with internet connection, projector, and speakers

Key Concepts:

1. Borrowing money with high interest rates or fees creates cycles of debt that can be nearly impossible to escape.
2. Debt can become so big that it controls our lives, costing us the freedom to make choices about how to use our money.
3. Borrowing and repaying money affects our credit scores, which affect whether or not people will loan us money in the future and on what terms.

Prep Time: 15 minutes

Advance Preparation Tasks:

- Bookmark "The Game" Video #6 and set up a computer with internet connection to the projector and speakers so the video is ready to show.

For the main activity in this lesson, you have a choice between inviting a guest speaker and a lecture/video activity entitled "Riches to Rags."

*For all additional resources, including handouts, video links and helpful websites, see www.futureprofitsresources.org

Advance Preparation Tasks (cont.)

- Guest Speaker option:
  - Find a guest speaker who can share his/her story for 20 minutes
  - Prepare guest speaker with guidelines specified in the activity description
- "Riches to Rags" option:
  - Look through the stories in the additional information to familiarize yourself with one to two stories you want to briefly share with students
  - Bookmark the Antoine Walker clip so it is ready to show

Keep in Mind

- Some students may react strongly if they perceive the term "slave" as directed personally. Be careful to apply the term "slave to debt" broadly.
- A slave to debt loses the freedom to make his or her own choices and becomes controlled by the debt until it is repaid.
- Some students may view debt as an unavoidable part of life.

The term "slave" may trigger strong reactions from some students. Many African-American students may trace their heritage to slaves brought to the United States against their will. In addition to the issues raised by human trafficking, the ongoing ramifications of slavery are still recognizable today in the ways that de facto segregation and racial disparities continue to plague our society. Some students may react strongly if they perceive the term "slave" as directed at them, their family members, or a group of people with whom they identify. This curriculum does not imply that debt slavery is directly related to coming from a certain racial or ethnic background. All people are equally susceptible to debt and can become enslaved by borrowing large sums of money. Be careful to apply the term "slave to debt" broadly and only to hypothetical situations, so students do not perceive it as a personal affront.

The term "slave" is used to communicate the severe impact debt can have on a person's life, and to reflect the dynamics of control that can be at play in borrower/lender relationships. The roots of almost all forms of slavery are financial. Those who enslave others do so for profit, by selling people for cheap labor or sexual acts. Slavery to debt is similar in that the slave "owners," in this case predatory lenders, operate in search of the highest possible profits without regard for the detrimental impact on the "enslaved" borrowers. The impact on the "slave" is similar as well, in that the individual loses the freedom to make his or her own choices and becomes controlled by the debt until it is repaid.

Many students know people who are in debt, and the concept of debt will be familiar to them. They may even be so used to people they know owing money that they view debt as an unavoidable part of life, assuming that they too will eventually live with debt. This is a dangerous assumption if it leads students to have a casual attitude about borrowing money. Though students may be familiar with the concept of debt, they may not know the reasons why people are in debt, how debt can build, or the severity of the possible repercussions of debt. Students must understand the process of "falling into" debt, the choices they can make to avoid it, and the extremely difficult consequences it brings. This curriculum is designed to help prevent as many students as possible from becoming trapped by unmanageable debt, so they can maintain control of their own financial and life choices.

Lesson Snapshot

Review (2 minutes)
- Predatory lending institutions and why they are predatory

Introduction (3 minutes)
- Review definition of debt and the difficulty of paying for basic necessities while repaying a large debt
- Introduce the concept "slaves to debt"

"The Game" Video #6 (5 minutes)
- Show video clip

Discussion: Slaves to Debt (10 minutes)
- Explain reasons people go into debt
- Explain cycle of debt: how it builds and why it's dangerous
- Define slavery, then relate it back to being a slave to debt

Lecture: Credit Scores and Bankruptcy (8 minutes)
- Explain how credit scores and bankruptcy negatively impact one's life

Activity: Guest Speaker OR Riches to Rags (20 minutes)
- Have a person share their real life story about how debt affects individuals and families, OR...
- Riches to Rags
  - Money doesn't solve all problems
  - Show Antoine Walker video and discuss

Wrap Up (2 minutes)
- Know your options and stay away from debt

Review (suggested time: 2 minutes)

Lead students through a quick discussion about the previous class.

- Ask students to list the different predatory lending institutions we discussed last class. They should name payday loans, rent-to-own stores, loan sharks, and credit cards.
- Ask students why these places or things are considered predatory. They should mention something about high interest rates and fees that create a cycle of debt, and deliberately target lower-income communities where people have few alternatives.

Introduction (suggested time: 3 minutes)

Remind students that learning about predatory lending equips them with information so they can make smart decisions and protect their financial futures. If they know how predatory lenders work and the availability of other borrowing options, they can't be gamed. Having knowledge about financial options and their long-term effects gives us the power to choose what is best and positions us to take control of our choices before ever starting a cycle of debt.

- Ask students what debt means. After they share some answers, remind them that debt is when one owes money to a company or person.
- Ask students if they remember from the budget simulation what was difficult for people with low incomes, such as the minimum wage workers. They should remember these individuals had trouble paying for all of the basic necessities, especially after emergencies.

Remind students that paying for our needs requires a lot of smart and careful money management. It is even harder if we need to pay back borrowed money every month. Getting caught in this kind of cycle is the ultimate way of getting gamed. It is so hard to break out of this cycle that we can become "slaves to debt." Today's lesson focuses on what becoming slaves to debt looks like and how it happens.

"The Game" Video #6 (suggested time: 5 minutes)

Go to www.futureprofitsresources.org and find the link to "The Game" Video #6. Show the video to the students and move on to the following discussion.

Discussion: Slaves to Debt (suggested time: 10 minutes)

- Ask students why they think people go into debt. Allow for responses, then explain there are usually three main reasons:
  1. We make unwise choices by buying things we want when we do not have enough cash to pay for them.

2. We may lose our jobs or be unable to get a job, and then go into debt just paying for personal or family needs. If we are unemployed long enough, just paying for rent and food can create a lot of debt.
3. We borrow money from predatory lenders, and then cannot afford to pay back the high interest or fees without borrowing more money to help pay off what we already borrowed before.

- Ask students, generally speaking, what it means to be a slave. After some answers, tell them a slave is someone who is the legal property of another person and is forced to obey the owner. In **slavery**, a person's freedom is taken away, and that person lacks options and choices. Slaves have no power or control to decide what happens to them.
- Ask the students, "After talking about debt, what do you think it would mean to be a slave to debt?"

Allow for responses, and then explain what it might look like. Draw from the following:

Because of interest, especially high interest from predatory loans, debt is always growing. If we cannot pay back money faster than the interest grows, we end up owing more and more. Debt can build up and become a cycle that looks like this:

In January, you don't have enough money to pay for 'need' items or you decide to spend money you don't have on a 'want' item, so you borrow money. But in February you don't have enough money to pay back the loan as well as pay for your needs, so you borrow money again. This time you borrow enough to pay back your debt plus extra to help pay for your needs, so now you owe more...plus you've added more interest or an extra fee. In March you have the same problem — not enough money to pay back the loan and pay for your needs — so you borrow again. That means more interest or another extra fee, so the debt grows.

Every dollar you have to pay back your debt is money that can't be used to cover your needs that month, which makes it more likely you will run out and have to borrow even more. Every dollar you owe to someone else is also money over which you no longer have control, because you don't get to decide how to spend it. At some point, debt can become big enough, or so difficult to pay back, that you'll have no options or choices left.

We call this being a "slave to debt" because you have to work and work to pay off the money you owe, but you have no power to decide what to do with the money you earn. All the money has to go to the company or person you owe. If you owe money on a car or house, and you're unable to make your payments, the person or company who gave you that loan will take the car or house away. Until you completely pay the lender back, the items you "own" are legally the property of the person or company who loaned you the money. If you stop paying back the money you borrowed, the company who lent you the money can also go to court and get an order to have your wages garnished. This means your employer will give your paycheck directly to the lender instead of you. If debt gets big enough, you may lose control over what happens to you or your property. Sounds a lot like being a slave, doesn't it?

- Ask students if anyone has a reaction that he or she would like to share, or has any questions.

Lecture: Credit Scores and Bankruptcy (suggested time: 8 minutes)

Another way that debt can control your life is called a credit score. Ask students if any of them know what a credit score is. If no one knows, ask if they have seen commercials that say "Bad Credit? No problem!" This phrasing is usually used in car commercials. Explain that every person who borrows money in America has a **credit score.** A credit score is a number assigned to a person to indicate to lenders how likely that individual is to repay a loan on time. It is determined by how much money you have borrowed, on what kinds of loans, and how often you have repaid the loan on time. Your credit score may seem like a random number that does not mean much, but it can have a huge impact on your life. The score ranges from approximately 300-850 points. A high number indicates good credit.

Ask students if they can guess how someone would get good credit (a high credit score). They may not know, so make sure to mention the following:

- Borrow less money
- Borrow money for "good" loans like student loans and home loans
- Pay money back on time

Each year you do these things, you add to a positive credit history, and having a long history of good financial decisions makes your credit score even higher. With good credit, it is much easier to get loans when you need them, like home or business loans, and you will often be able to borrow money at a lower interest rate. If you show you are trustworthy and responsible by paying off borrowed money regularly, companies will be more likely to let you borrow additional money at affordable rate.

If your credit score is low, you have bad credit.

Ask students if they can guess how someone would get a low credit score. Make sure to mention the following:

- Borrow lots of money
- Get "bad" loans like consumer loans
- Pay money back late or not at all

With bad credit, it is difficult to get new loans, and you will usually be charged higher interest rates. Having a low credit score can make you look irresponsible, which can also make it more difficult to do things like rent an apartment, since landlords want to know you'll pay rent on time. Even when you sign up for a cell phone plan, the cell phone company will check your credit score. Many employers now check an individual's credit score to see if that person is responsible with his or her money, so having a bad credit score can also impact your ability to get a job.

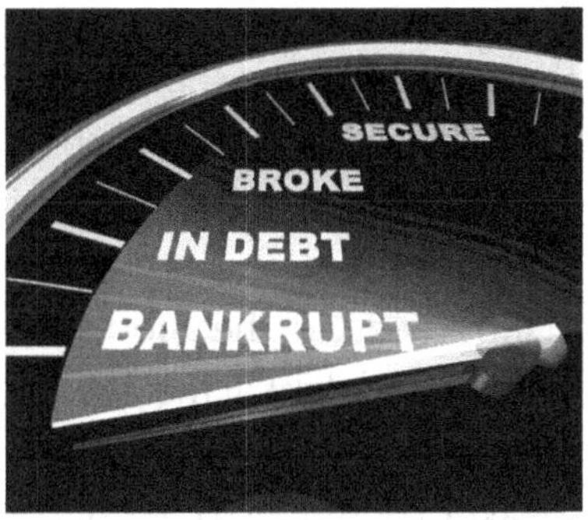

If someone has borrowed too much money and is incapable of paying it back, he or she may have to claim bankruptcy. Ask the students what they think bankruptcy is. Also ask them to share any stories of people they know who have dealt with bankruptcy. Allow for responses, and then explain that bankruptcy is when a person goes to court and asks the court to declare that it is impossible for him or her to pay back what he or she owes. The court will sell off most of the person's property and give that money to the lenders, and then the person's debts are erased. Usually people declare bankruptcy because they don't have any other choices. Bankruptcy stays on a person's credit report for seven years and makes their credit score very low. Declaring bankruptcy has a long-lasting impact even beyond the seven years. With such a low credit score, it is almost impossible to rent an apartment, borrow even small amounts of money, or get a job, so it leaves a person with almost no choices and no control.

Activity: Guest Speaker OR Riches to Rags (suggested time: 20 minutes)

This activity gives the option of inviting a guest speaker or leading the students through an activity titled "Riches to Rags." It is important for students to hear a real and personal story from someone who has been deeply impacted by debt, especially if the speaker is someone who the students will perceive as being like them. If you are unable to find such a speaker, another option is to lead students through the Riches to Rags Activity described below. This activity basically communicates to students that money doesn't solve all their problems. Choose what you think will work best for your class.

Guest Speaker Guidelines:

The ideal guest speaker is someone who can communicate what it was or is like for him or her to feel like a slave to debt. It is helpful to expose students to people in their community who have experienced serious debt to reinforce that the experience is real and very difficult. It can be easy to dismiss the cycle of debt as something that happens to other people, so personalize the experience by having a real person share how it happened to him or her. If students are able to relate to the experience of someone like them, they will hopefully be deterred from getting into debt.

The guest speaker should share his or personal story, focusing on the reason he/she fell into debt, the drawbacks of debt (specifically how it impacted daily life), how being in debt felt, and how he or she dealt with it or is trying to move forward now.

Make sure to let the guest speaker know what the students have learned in regard to predatory lending and debt. If the guest speaker can speak from personal experience about the dangers of predatory lending institutions, it will reinforce the message of avoiding all predatory loans. The speaker should also clearly communicate some alternatives to using these types of businesses, or what he or she could have done differently to avoid being trapped by debt. It is extremely important for the speaker to emphasize any choices he or she could have made differently so students can see that it is possible to avoid getting trapped by debt. Give the guest speaker as much time as needed, allowing enough time to wrap up the lesson. Be sure to encourage students to ask questions.

Riches to Rags:

Ask students if they think it would be easy to stay out of debt if they made more than a certain amount of money. Have several volunteers name a number for what salary they think is enough. If they answer something like, "more than minimum wage," affirm that it is true that making a higher salary makes it easier for an individual to pay for all of his or her needs without borrowing money. Then remind them that you are asking how much it would take to make staying out of debt easy.

Note to Teacher

Many low-income students believe the best way to avoid struggling with money is simply to get a very high-paying job. They know from experience that having a low income makes managing money difficult, but they assume that having a higher income is an instant fix for all financial problems. They do not realize that how an individual manages money is ultimately more important than how much money the individual earns.

After several students answer, ask if anyone can name a famous person who had a lot of money and lost it. If the students don't name anyone, you can use a couple of names from the list in the additional resources at the end of this lesson and ask, "Who's heard of Nicolas Cage?" or "What about Mike Tyson?" Try to pick people your students will be familiar with, and briefly describe the debt situations that have trapped them.

Tell students one of the most important things to remember is that having a lot of money does not automatically solve all your problems. It is easy to get stuck in a cycle of debt, no matter how much money you have. Many famous actors, athletes, and entertainers have claimed bankruptcy. According to Sports Illustrated, almost 80 percent of National Football League players are close to bankruptcy only two years after they retire.[1]

Without knowing how to manage money well, it is easy for people to get so used to spending money that they can't stop, and end up owing more than they can afford. When it comes to avoiding debt, how you manage your money is much more important than how much money you make. No amount of money, however large, can keep you from spending everything you have, unless you make smart decisions about how to spend it. Rich people can get gamed just like everyone else.

Next watch a short 11:18-minute video from ESPN's Outside the Lines about Antoine Walker and how he went from "riches to rags." Go to www.futureprofitsresources.org and find the link to "OTL: Antoine Walker."

After the video, ask students the following questions. There are some "sub-questions" to help discussion continue.

- What was Antoine Walker's perception of money?
    - Do you think Antoine was greedy for money? Why or why not? Remind students what Antoine's coach said about Antoine being set for life because of the kind of money he was making. He believed Antoine was both book smart and street smart, but Antoine still fell into debt because of his greed.
- How did Antoine go from riches to rags?
    - What were some of the ways he lost money?
    - He said he was in debt because he led an expensive life. Do you agree with this statement? Why or why not?

[1]Seven Costly Pro Athlete Screw-ups. Mark Riddix. Mar 10, 2010. Retrieved article Apr 17, 2010 from http://sports.yahoo.com/top/news?slug=ys-investopediamoneyloss031010.

   - If the students did not mention the following reason, you should tell the students that one of the reasons Antoine fell into debt is because he purchased a bunch of houses and made a bunch of investment deals, but did not have the time, the right people, or the money to maintain them.
- From watching this video, is it fairly easy or difficult for someone with a large income to go bankrupt? Why?
- After this video, do you think the amount of money you have determines whether or not you will be stuck in a cycle of debt? Why or why not?

Wrap Up (suggested time: 2 minutes)

Remind the class that the goal of the Future Profits classes is to help them be able to keep as much of their hard-earned money as possible. There are people and companies that want to game them and get their money. Knowing how different financial companies work can help students avoid these traps and game the system so it helps them get the most out of their money. When you make wise decisions with your money and stay away from predators, you can instead use your money to invest in your future and your community. Keep in mind that every time you get a check or need some fast money, you have choices. The choices you make will determine whether you keep control over your money, or whether the money will control you, causing you to become a slave to debt.

Vocabulary:
- debt
- slavery
- bankruptcy
- credit score

Additional Resources:
For more information on credit scores and links to stories about well-known or recent stars who went from "riches to rags," go to www.futureprofitsresources.org.

Additional Information for Riches to Rags

The following are stories about well-known or recent stars who had millions but lost it all, or had to claim bankruptcy or lose something they "owned."

- Heavyweight boxing champion, Joe Louis, also known as the "Brown Bomber," owed hundreds of millions: http://en.wikipedia.org/wiki/Joe_Louis
- Popular rapper, MC Hammer, is known as going from rags to riches back to rags again: http://en.wikipedia.org/wiki/MC_Hammer
- Famous actor, Nicolas Cage, lost his home in foreclosure in November 2009: http://money.cnn.com/2009/11/13/real_estate/Nicolas_Cage/
- See the following article for bankruptcy stories on Scottie Pippen, Evander Holyfield Lenny Dykstra, Latrell Sprewell, John Daly, Jack Clark, and Mike Tyson: http://sports.yahoo.com/top/news?slug=ys-investopediamoneyloss031010
    - Star basketball player, Scottie Pippen, lost $120 million because of poor financial planning and bad business ideas.
    - Boxing champ Evander "The Real Deal" Holyfield made over $250 million but is now broke due to buying a house that was too large to maintain financially. It had 11 bedrooms, 17 bathrooms, a movie theater, a bowling alley and an Olympic-size swimming pool.
    - John Daly lost millions through gambling.
    - Pro-baseball player, Jack Clark, went bankrupt because he couldn't stop buying luxury cars. Whenever he got bored with one, he would get rid of it and buy another.
    - Mike Tyson spent his money on everything he laid his eyes on, and filed for bankruptcy in 2003.

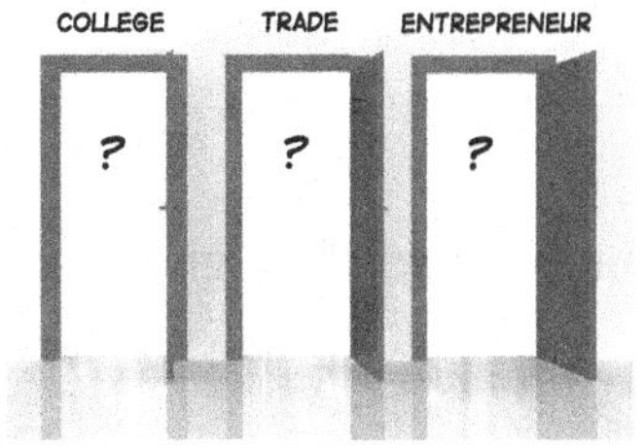

Throughout the *FutureProfits* curriculum, and especially in this unit, the concept that decisions students make today will impact their life in the future is continually emphasized. This is important for students to grasp because it will help prepare them for success.

Students from low-income communities often become stuck in the trap of making unhealthy decisions, which keep them in recurring cycles of debt and poverty. This often comes from a lack of vision for the future, and is fueled by a sense of despair from living in poverty. These cycles can severely limit their choices for their future. An example of this can be seen in the exceedingly high dropout rates in low-income communities. In this cycle, youth enter the work force sooner rather than later, and struggle financially because of an underdeveloped understanding of finances, and a lack of skills required to pay for the standard living expenses of an adult. As Unit 2 communicated the reality of paying for these expenses, this unit gives students a perspective on how education and training relates to their future income.

In America, college is the most secure path to follow in order to have a successful future. While it is the intention of this curriculum to encourage all students to stay in school and go to college, it is also important to address the reality of the high dropout rates that exist in low-income communities. Success must be seen as an attainable and desirable option for students. Therefore, in this unit students will not only learn about making college attainable, but also learn about the different types of career paths outside of college that can set them on a path of success.

Through inspirational, real-life success stories, students are shown relatable examples of how others gained the tools for wise decision making and goal setting, which led to a successful life. They will recognize that others have been through similarly difficult experiences in life and succeeded. The lessons throughout this unit return to the message that the students' choices today — both big and small — impact their future, giving them the tools they need to succeed.

Lesson Plans:

For teachers to be adequately prepared, it is important to read through the materials fully before teaching the unit.

The unit starts off with a video that gives a clear description of what life might be like on a minimum wage income. The reality is that minimum wage may be the alternative for students if they drop out of high school now. Because the drop out rate is so high in low-income communities, it is important for students to realize what living on a minimum wage income really looks like.

Lesson 2 moves on to describe the statistical nature of how education is related to income. Most students who drop out of high school end up making around minimum wage. Although these statistics only consider formal schooling, education and life-long learning in general are often what make the difference for those who fall into poverty. No one ever sets out to fail financially; they often don't realize the impact that their choices now will have on their future, especially when entering the work force. Therefore in Lesson 3, three stories of people who have succeeded in the midst of great pressure and struggle are presented. This will help students to see and be inspired by the mindset of determination and perseverance that leads to success.

Lesson 4 defines success and outlines multiple paths to becoming successful, including college, and alternative paths such as apprenticeship and entrepreneurship. Although college is one of the most successful paths that students can take, some may never be able or have the desire to go to college. It is the intention of this curriculum to provide a picture of college as being attainable for all, and to make students aware of non-academic alternative paths toward success.

To further sharpen the students' critical thinking skills, Lesson 5 focuses on the process of decision making. It teaches students to slow down and make wise choices now. Even the seemingly minor decisions made now have the potential for positively impacting students' futures. As one of the steps to decision making is to decide and act, Lesson 6 brings the students through a process of creating a "Life Map." This allows students to start making the plan that they want to follow that will lead to success. Good intentions are not enough to obtain success; sound decisions and an action plan must be implemented in order for students to arrive at their desired goal.

Outline:

Lesson 1 – Only the Minimum
Lesson 2 – Education vs. Income
Lesson 3 – Stories of Success
Lesson 4 – So I Finally Graduated High School ... Now What?
Lesson 5 – Decision Making
Lesson 6 – Life Maps

Vocabulary:

- profit
- minimum wage
- documentary
- inflation
- sweat shops
- *optional: transition to independence expenses*
- *optional: contracts*
- *optional: deposits*
- *optional: fees*
- education
- success
- resume
- trade
- apprenticeship
- entrepreneurship
- start-up capital
- entrepreneurial mindset
- wisdom

Materials needed:

- Video: "30 Days – Minimum Wage," Disc 1, by Morgan Spurlock
- Computer with internet connection, projector, and speakers, OR DVD Player with TV
- Whiteboard and pen, or chalkboard and chalk, or poster paper and pen

People who work sitting down get paid more than people who work standing up.
–Ogden Nash, Poet

Key Concepts:

1. Living on a minimum wage income may get you enough to survive, but it will be difficult for that to be your only income.
2. Living on a minimum wage income not only affects you financially, but is also difficult to deal with emotionally and sometimes physically.
3. As a student, you must be intentional about your choices regarding life, career, and education in order to have options other than minimum wage jobs when you enter the workforce.

Prep Time: 30 minutes

**For all additional resources, including handouts, video links and helpful websites, see www.futureprofitsresources.org*

Advance Preparation Tasks:

- Buy a copy of the "30 Days – Minimum Wage" DVD or find the video online. It can be found online at www.amazon.com. Search the "Video On Demand" section for "30 Days – Minimum Wage." It will be from Season 1, Episode 1, with an original airdate of June 15, 2005. The cost is $1.99. You can also search www.hulu.com for a free version of the film, as it is occasionally aired on that site. It is also available in the "Watch Instantly" section on www.netflix.com.
- Watch the video and be familiar with where to stop and fast-forward so that the clips fit into the 50-minute lesson.
- If using the online version, set up a computer with internet connection, projector, and speakers so the film is ready to show.
- Go to the website referred to in the "Additional Resources" of this lesson to find out what the current minimum wage is in your state, and federally, so you can tell the students the accurate numbers during the introduction.

Keep in Mind

- It is important that students do not feel bad or embarrassed about the types of work their parents may do, especially if they are working minimum wage jobs.

The video used in this lesson is intended to give the students a visual image of how hard it can be for a person to live on a minimum wage income. Many students in low-income neighborhoods have parents who either have minimum wage jobs or have very low paying hourly jobs. The instructor should never demean these types of jobs. It is important that students do not feel bad or embarrassed about the types of work their parents do. Making ends meet on a minimum wage income is very difficult and shows an element of courageous perseverance for a parent to strive to live and provide for children on a minimum wage income. The ultimate goal in learning about the difficulty of minimum wage is to encourage students toward a higher level of education, which is a focus of future lessons. The relationship of education to income in our society is one of the systems in which students need to be successful in order to begin breaking the cycles of poverty.

Lesson Snapshot

Introduction (8 minutes)

- Meaning of minimum wage
- Current minimum wage amount where you live and in the nation
- Why it varies state to state
- Share a personal story about your experience with minimum wage

Activity: "30 Days – Minimum Wage" Video (27 minutes)

- Show sections of the video
  - Show Chapter 1
  - Show Chapters 3 through the beginning of Chapter 8
  - Show beginning of Chapter 9
  - Show Chapter 11 through the end

Discussion: Minimum Wage (10 minutes)

- Discuss students' reactions to the video
- Discuss elements of the video students didn't understand
- Discuss different areas of life affected by a minimum wage job
- Ask students to share their personal experience with minimum wage, if any

Wrap Up (5 minutes)

- Produces a feeling of being overwhelmed and trapped
- Introduce the unit, "What You Need to Succeed," and preview what the unit is about

Introduction (suggested time: 8 minutes)

1. Begin the class by asking students if they know the meaning of "minimum wage." After taking answers, tell the class that **minimum wage** is the amount of money per hour that employers are required by federal law to pay employees.
2. Ask the class what they think the minimum wage is in the state in which you live. After receiving answers, inform the class what the minimum wage is, both in your state and in the nation as a whole.
3. After telling the students that the minimum wage varies from state to state, ask students why they think the amounts are different. Explain how the wage range is based on the cost of living in that state. If you have already taught Unit 2 of the curriculum, they will already be familiar with the cost of living. If not, please explain that the cost of living is the amount that a person pays for their basic needs, and it is greater in some areas, and lesser in other areas.
4. Finally, share a personal story about your experience with minimum wage. Be sure to mention how much it was when you were growing up, what kind of job you had, and what you liked or didn't like about it.

Activity: "30 Days – Minimum Wage" Video

(suggested time: 27 minutes)

The purpose of this video is to have students understand how difficult it can be to survive on minimum wage.

- Introduce the video by asking students what a **documentary** is. Then explain that a documentary is a film in which people involved in real events are observed in order to create a factual report. Ask the students if they have seen the documentary, *Supersize Me*. *Supersize Me* is by Morgan Spurlock, who decided to see what would happen if he ate only McDonald's for 30 days. Because of *Supersize Me's* popularity, most students have seen or have at least heard of this film.

Note to Teacher

The entire video will not be shown in order to fit into a 50-minute lesson. The following outline provides the clips that would be best to show, with explanation on what was skipped. If you have more time, feel free to show the whole video. There are a few parts of the film where expletives are used. Be cautious in showing the film to a younger audience.

- Go on to tell the students that he then started a documentary series called, "30 Days," in which he did a documentary about minimum wage.
- The video is about how two people, Morgan and his fiancé Alex, attempt to survive for 30 days living on a minimum wage income. This video was made in 2004. After this video was made, in 2007, the government decided to raise the minimum wage amount. Although the wage is lower in the video than it is today, the concepts are still very much the same.

Begin at Chapter 1, Fast-forward to 2:23
Show 2:23 - 3:30 *(1 minute)*

Now skip to Chapter 3 to show Chapters 3-7, and beginning of Chapter 8 up through 28:02, stopping at Day 18
9:55 - 28:02 *(18 minutes)*
Skipped chapter details: Day 1, Morgan and his girlfriend found a place to live in a rougher area of town because it was the only place they could afford. During Day 2, Morgan got a job at a temp agency and Alex got a job at a coffee shop downtown.

Skip to Chapter 9 to show the beginning minute
30:56-32:09 *(1 minute)*
Skipped chapter details: Day 18, Morgan talked to his brother and his brother had him take his kids to see how difficult it would be to live on minimum wage with kids. During Day 23 and 24, Morgan's niece and nephew come and they spend more money to have a good time with the kids. Alex gets mad at Morgan for spending so much money.

Skip to Chapter 11 to show the end of the film
39:28 - 44:18 *(5 minutes)*
Skipped chapter details: Day 25-26, Alex didn't get to do anything special for her 30th birthday. Morgan decided to take her out to the park and dinner. But they missed the bus and had to take a cab home, which ruined their day.

Discussion: Minimum Wage

(suggested time: 10 minutes)

After all video segments are shown to the class, choose from the following questions to spark conversation with the class:

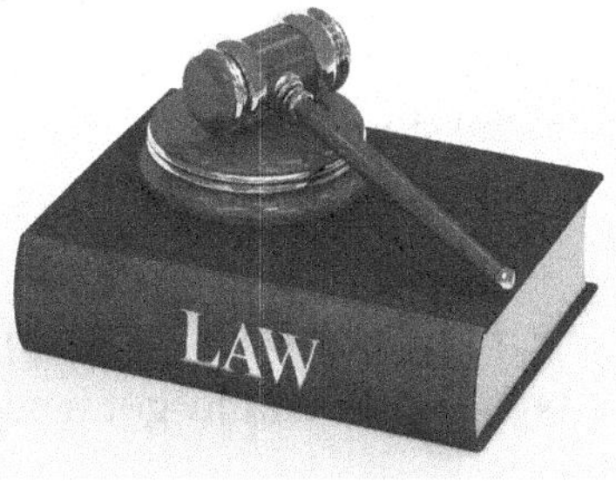

- Morgan said he made less than the minimum wage. Instead of earning $7 an hour, he received $4.20 an hour. Why do you think that is? (If students don't know, explain that after taxes he really was only making $4.20 and that sometimes when one works with a "temp" agency, they charge a fee for their assistance in helping you find a job.)

- In the video, the minimum wage hadn't been raised for a long time. What do you think is one of the reasons why the government doesn't raise minimum wage very often?
- How do you think health care impacts those working on minimum wage? Do you agree with the statement Morgan made that there isn't "health care" in America, just "sick care?" Why or why not?
- In the film, they had to pay a deposit for electricity. What are some of the other expenses that come up that we don't expect?
- Other than lacking in money, what else do you think you would lack if you had a job that made minimum wage as your only source of income? (If students need some help thinking of other things they may lack, you can ask the questions below to help spark their thoughts.)
    - Do you think you would have a lot of time to spend with your family?
    - What do you think your stress level would be like?
    - How much energy do you think you would be able to give after work?
    - How do you think it would impact you emotionally?

Note to Teacher

This can be a good time to introduce expenses people pay as they transition to independence, such as rent deposits, cell phone deposits, start-up costs, school fees, parking fees depending on where you live, etc. Lesson 2 outlines an optional discussion to cover this topic in greater depth.

- What would be the hardest part about living paycheck-to-paycheck for you?
- Emergencies have deep financial impact. Were you surprised at the amount for medical bills? What do you think you would have done when those unexpected payments came up?

- Ask students what they thought about Morgan's quote: "If I stopped eating, I could save so much money." Remind the students that this may seem like a simple solution, but would still impact him financially. Once he stopped eating, or even if he ate less, his body would react in unhealthy ways and he would need to go to the doctor again.
- How do you think taking care of kids affects your ability to live on minimum wage?
- Morgan had to get a second job to afford living expenses. Would you work a second

job if you needed to? How do you think a second job would impact you? (This question brings up a lot of the emotional aspects of living paycheck to paycheck. It is important to talk through feeling tired, but more importantly, how it would affect your family or those around you.)

- How would you try to stay away from having to work two jobs?
- Why do you think Morgan Spurlock made this documentary?

Finally, ask the students about any personal experiences they may have with minimum wage. Use your discretion on the sensitivity of this topic based on your class.

Wrap Up (suggested time: 5 minutes)

Ask the students what the difference is between this couple and real life. After some answers, tell the students that the couple ended up owing money, but their situation only lasted for 30 days, which means they were able to pay back the money they owed and go back to their previous lives as they were. Many people who work and live off of minimum wage do not have the ability to do the same. They often feel overwhelmed and trapped in their situation.

Throughout this upcoming unit, we will be learning more about what you need to succeed. Your future, and what you want your future to look like, depends fully on the choices you make today. There are choices that you can make to avoid working a minimum wage job, or working multiple jobs, in order to make a living. The following lessons focus on how choices affect our life path.

Thank the class for their attentiveness and participation.

Vocabulary:

- minimum wage
- documentary

Additional Resources:

For additional resources on current minimum wage and an article about the pros and cons of the minimum wage rising, go to www.futureprofitsresources.org.

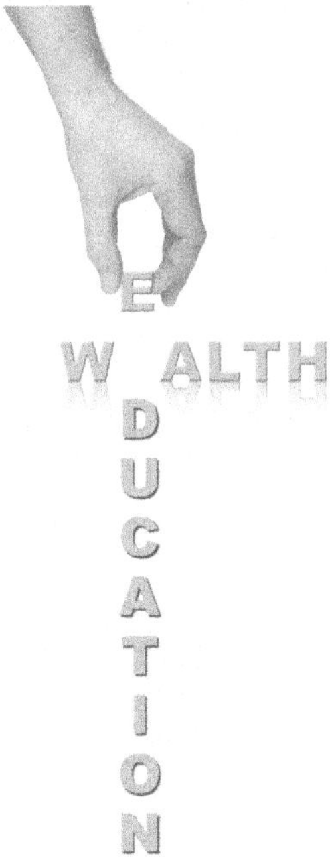

Materials needed:

- Computer with a PowerPoint program, internet connection, and a projector (speakers are optional)
- Questions for "Who Wants Future Profits?" PPT template – 4.2.1*
- Who Wants Future Profits? (PowerPoint Presentation) – 4.2.2*
- "Education Pays" Chart – 4.2.3*
- Prize for the final contestant for the "Who Wants Future Profits?" game
- Whiteboard and pen, or chalkboard and chalk, or poster paper and pen

A man who has never gone to school
may steal from a freight car;
but if he has a university education,
he may steal the whole railroad.
–Theodore Roosevelt, Former U.S. President

Key Concepts:

1. Education is not only a degree one receives, but it includes the skills and abilities one gains while learning and pursuing a professional goal.
2. The more education an individual receives usually helps him or her attain a higher income level and decreases the likelihood of being unemployed.

Prep Time: 30-60 minutes

**For all additional resources, including handouts, video links and helpful websites, see www.futureprofitsresources.org*

Advance Preparation Tasks:

- Bookmark the chart "Education Pays" and set up a computer with internet connection and projector so the chart can be projected for all to see. If a projector is unavailable, make enough copies of the graph for each student before class begins.
- This lesson will refer to Unit 2, Lesson 3. If you have not already taught this lesson, refer to the "Additional Resources" of that lesson to give the students a realistic picture of the cost of living in your city.
- Prepare the game, "Who Wants Future Profits?" (see the game in Activity #2 for further instructions)

Keep in Mind

- This lesson helps put the importance of education into perspective in contrast to the difficulty of living on a minimum wage income.
- Some students may see education as a hindrance to making fast money, which is desirable because the present need for money seems urgent.
- Education can occur outside of the traditional academic setting where students may have been bored or unable to make connections to "reality," and thus done poorly.

This lesson will continue the focus on minimum wage — specifically how a person's wage is usually related to his or her level of education. Some may believe that the minimum wage is a decent wage to receive. This lesson helps students to see the practical comparison of income for a minimum wage earner, and expenses for an average-income individual. Because the students have previously learned the concept of "How much your life costs" from Unit 2, Lesson 3, this element may be familiar, but it is a concept that cannot be reviewed enough, as many students are not paying for all of their expenses.

The goal of this lesson is to help students see the value of learning — not only through higher education, but also through learning a trade or particular skill that will help students succeed. A "reality" for many students who grow up in poverty is the need for fast money. As a result, some students may see education as a hindrance to making fast money. When the present need for money is great, it is difficult to remember that education can lead to earning more money in the long run.

Throughout this unit education is defined as the knowledge obtained to help grow one's skills and abilities. Education includes the options of trade school or certification programs. It is important that students understand that education can occur outside the traditional setting where they may have been bored or unable to make connections to "reality," and thus done poorly. This lesson brings out the importance of how education now relates to "reality" and how important it is to pursue education to give students more opportunities and choices in life. It also helps students take education out of the box they may have put it in, and realize that there are forms of education to which they may be able to relate more than the typical school system.

Lesson Snapshot

Review (3 minutes)
- Meaning of minimum wage
- Current minimum wage amount where you live and in the nation
- Why it varies state to state

Introduction (2 minutes)
- Does minimum wage give enough income to survive?
- How education relates to income

Lecture #1: Minimum Wage (5 minutes)
- Brief history of minimum wage
- Define inflation
- Why law was set up
- Define sweat shops

Activity #1: Reality Check Review (5 minutes)
- Write the annual income of a minimum wage earner on the board
- Brainstorm with students expenses and average costs per month
- Total the cost of expenses and multiply by 12 (months) to get an annual expense total for the year
- How would living on a minimum wage income impact your options in life?

Optional Discussion: Start-up Costs *(10 minutes)*
- *Define transition to independence expenses*
- *Discuss and define contracts, deposits, and fees with the students*
- *Have each student list expenses they expect to pay when they live on their own and number the expenses based on priority*
- *It is important to decide now on these expenses before falling into debt in the future "by accident"*

Activity #2: Who Wants Future Profits? (25 minutes)
- Collect students' names
- Explain rules
- Draw first contestant and play game

Lecture #2: Income Related to Education (5 minutes)

- Draw a correlation between the game and real life
- Explain and discuss "Education Pays" chart
- What types of jobs they want and the requirements for those jobs
- Why statistics show there is a relation between education and income (skills and completion of tasks)
- Define education
- Does this information change how they feel about school or education?

Wrap Up (5 minutes)

- While looking at chart, ask students, "How much education would you like to obtain?"
- Reinforce the concept that the term education in the following lessons will be defined more holistically by including other forms of learning and completion, which will be explored later.

Review (suggested time: 3 minutes)

1. Begin the class by asking the class if they remember the meaning of "minimum wage." After taking answers, remind the class that it is the amount of money per hour that employers are required by federal law to pay employees.
2. Ask the class what the minimum wage is in the state in which you live, along with the nation as a whole. Remind students that the minimum wage varies from state to state depending on the cost of living in that state. Transition by telling the students that this lesson continues to focus on cost of living.

Introduction (suggested time: 2 minutes)

Ask the students if they think that the minimum wage gives individuals enough income to survive. During this lesson, students will be learning more about the practical cost of living and relate it to the income a person receives. Students will also look at how current choices regarding education impact future incomes.

Lecture #1: Minimum Wage (suggested time: 5 minutes)

1. Give a brief history of minimum wage. Ask students how much they think the original minimum wage was. After some answers, tell students that the minimum wage laws were first enacted in 1938 after President Franklin D. Roosevelt signed the Fair Labor Standards Act. The first minimum wage began at $0.25 per hour. Over the years, to keep up with inflation, minimum wage has been gradually increased.

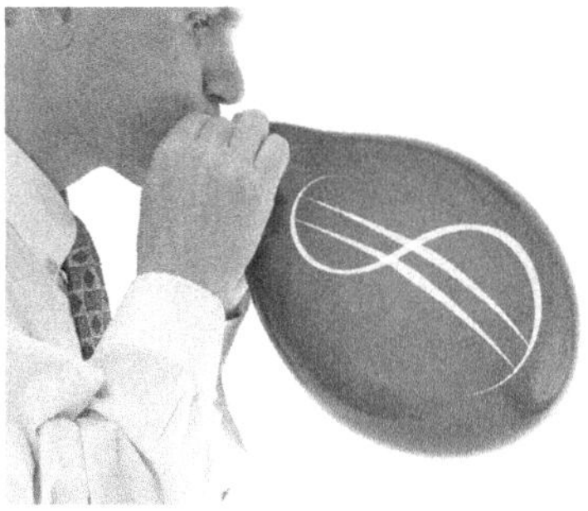

2. Ask the students if they know what **inflation** is. After students have shared some answers, explain that inflation is when the price of goods and services rises over time. Like inflating a ball or balloon, which increases in size with each pump or blow, prices rise every few years.
3. Explain to students why minimum wages were first created. The intent was to control the growth of sweat shops in manufacturing industries. Ask students what **sweat shops** are. After students have shared some answers, explain that sweat shops are factories or workshops, especially in the clothing industry, where manual workers are employed at very low wages for long hours and under poor conditions. The sweat shops employed large numbers of women and young workers, paying them what were considered to be low-quality wages. A minimum wage was proposed as a means to make shop owners pay "fairly." Over time, the focus of minimum wage changed to involve helping

people, especially families, become more self sufficient. Today, minimum wage laws cover workers in most low-paying fields of employment.[1]

Activity #1: Reality Check Review (suggested time: 5 minutes)

The purpose of this activity is to compare the income of a full-time minimum wage job to the cost of living locally.

> **Note to Teacher**
>
> *If you have not yet taught Unit 2, allow for this activity to take longer than 5 minutes. This activity is a review from Unit 2, specifically Lesson 3: "How Much Does Your Life Cost?" Please refer to Activity #3: Local Reality Check and the "Additional Resources" in that lesson for websites to collect information about the cost of living in your city.*

1. Write the annual income for a minimum wage earner on the board. This will have been calculated in Unit 2 as the McDonald's worker. If you did not teach that unit, an easy way to approximately figure this number is to multiply the minimum wage in your state by 40 (hours per week) by 52 (weeks per year) to get a rounded number for the amount an individual may earn if working minimum wage full time. Ask the students if they think that number is enough to survive on. (Their answers may be different when they see a number in the thousands rather than seeing an hourly wage.)
2. If you have previously taught Unit 2 of the *FutureProfits* curriculum, your students will already have learned about the cost of living in their city. Ask the students to think back to the budgets they created during Unit 2, and what they imagined their lives to look like at 25 years old. Pick different expense categories from the budget worksheets (see Budget Simulation Worksheet Before Emergency – 2.2.1). For each category, ask students to share the cost of this expense per month. There may be different answers, but pick an "average" number that is realistic for a low- to average-paying job for a college graduate. Write on the board the expense and the approximate amount per month next to that expense.
3. Add up the total of all the expense categories on the board and multiply that number by 12 (for the number of months in a year). This should give a total for annual expenses that is higher than the annual income for a minimum wage earner. Compare the two amounts with your class and ask the students how they think living on a minimum wage income would impact their options in life.

[1]Neumark, David; William L. Wascher (2008). Minimum Wages. Cambridge, Massachusetts: The MIT Press. ISBN 978-0-262-14102-4. http://mitpress.mit.edu/catalog/item/default.asp?ttype=2&tid=11659.

Optional Discussion: Start-up Costs *(suggested time: 10 minutes)*

Many of the students will eventually need to create a transition plan for when they graduate or move out of their parents'/guardians' house, so they won't easily fall into debt. If your students are close to the age where they are making these types of decisions (specifically seniors in high school), and if time allows, this optional discussion is strongly recommended and fits well at this point in the lesson.

After the students have a more realistic picture of the cost of living in comparison to working a full-time minimum wage job, tell the students there is still one element that was not covered in-depth during the Budget Simulation: **your transition to independence expenses**. Explain that transition to independence expenses are the additional expenses that an individual pays when he or she is transitioning to living independently, specifically start-up costs such as deposits and fees. These costs come up in various expenses such as renting a house or apartment, signing up for a cell phone plan, getting internet, cable/Direct TV, joining a gym, parking permits, or school fees such as tuition and book payments.

- **Contracts**: Ask the students what happens when they sign up for a new cell phone plan. They should eventually tell you that they have to sign a new contract. Ask what a contract is. After some students answer, tell students that a **contract** is a written agreement, especially one concerning employment, sales, or tenancy, that is intended to be enforceable by law. Because cellular carriers have different rates and contracts, the students may debate over amounts or time frames, but in general almost every company will create a contract. Ask the students why they think this contract is made. They should say something about people making payments monthly and not being able to back out of that payment. Then ask what happens if that contract is broken. Usually there is some kind of fee (which will be defined following deposits). A cancellation fee means a company can charge someone extra for breaking the contract.
- **Deposits:** Ask the students what happens when they want to live on their own — away from their parents and not in a college dorm room. Inform the students that any time you begin a "contract" or lease to rent an apartment, you need to give a deposit. This kind of deposit is different from putting money into a bank (which was covered in Unit 3). A **deposit** is an amount of money paid as a pledge for a contract, the balance being payable later. This means that if the contract is upheld, the deposit will most likely be returned later. These deposits are usually seen as a security deposit for renting an apartment or house, but they

are also common later on in life as down payments for cars and homes.

- **Fees:** Finally, when moving into a new place, whether it's a school or an apartment, there may often be start-up costs, school fees such as tuition and book payments, or parking permits. A **fee** is a payment made in exchange for some kind of service. They are often paid at the beginning of a year or semester, but paying them all at once can be difficult financially.

Have each student make a list of the different expenses on which they see themselves needing to spend money when they transition to independence. Then have them number the expenses from most important to least important so they can decide where their priorities now lie.

Conclude the discussion by emphasizing to students the importance of making choices when they are transitioning to independence. Tell them this is a crucial time because it is easy to fall into debt while making these choices. Many students will have to experience delayed gratification while choosing what is most important to them. For example, they may need to choose whether or not living at home and saving for a car is more important than moving out and living on their own while using public transportation. They may also need to make decisions regarding their living situation, choosing whether they want to live with a roommate or two to have money for other things.

Activity #2: Who Wants Future Profits?

(suggested time: 25 minutes)

The purpose of this activity is to interactively teach students about the correlation between education and income. Although the questions in the game do not directly show this correlation, the following lecture will help to show the correlation based on the progression of this game. The questions in the game cover the following categories: FutureProfits, math, science, and history.

Note to Teacher

This game requires advance preparation. It is adapted from the TV show "Who Wants to be a Millionaire." Many students will be familiar with this game, so it will help to provide an interactive and fun way of communicating one of the key concepts of this lesson.

Advance Preparation:

Go to www.futureprofitsresources.org and download the PowerPoint game show, "Who Wants Future Profits?" (4.2.2) to familiarize yourself with the game. Alternatively, you can follow the directions below to create your own PowerPoint game show.

1. There are multiple online sites that provide templates for popular TV show games so you can play the same game with your own questions. Go to www.google.com and search for "Who Wants to be a Millionaire PowerPoint Template." Then click on any that lead to a "PPT file format." This means that you will be downloading a PowerPoint template onto your computer to plug in your own questions.
2. Once you download the PowerPoint template, fill in the 15 questions and answers that are provided in the material titled, "Questions for Who Wants Future Profits?" PPT template (4.2.1).
3. Test the PowerPoint game show to make sure the game will run smoothly.

In-Class Instructions:

1. Have each student write his or her name on a small piece of paper and put their name in a hat or cup.
2. Explain rules of the game to the students (see below).
3. Draw the first contestant's name from the hat or cup, and call them up to the "stage."
4. Go through each question until the contestant gets a question wrong. If a student gets a question wrong, draw another name from the hat or cup and have a new contestant come to the stage. Because this is a variation of the actual game show, the new contestant will get three new lifelines, and will need to start with the first question, even if the first question has already been answered. Continue until one final contestant reaches the final million-dollar question. That student should receive a prize.

Rules:

1. The game show host (the teacher) will read the question, and each of the four answers.
2. The audience - the other students and co-teacher(s) - must refrain from shouting out answers.
3. The contestant (the student) will have a chance to state which multiple-choice answer he or she thinks is correct. The contestant may also use one of three lifelines. Once a lifeline is used, it cannot be used again. The three lifelines are as follows:
   a. 50/50 — When this lifeline is chosen, 2 of the wrong answers will be taken away from the contestant's 4 options. This gives the contestant a 50/50 chance of getting the question right.
   b. Phone a friend — When this lifeline is chosen, the contestant can pick one person from the audience (a student or teacher who is not hosting the game) to help them with answering the question correctly. The student will have one minute to talk through the question and answer with that person.

c. Poll the audience — When this lifeline is chosen, the contestant will be able to poll the audience on which answer they think is correct. Once this lifeline is chosen the host of the game will ask the audience to raise their hands if they believe the answer is A, B, C, or D.

4. If the contestant gets the answer right, he/she will move on to the next question. If not, he/she must go back to his/her seat and a new contestant's name will be drawn out of the hat or cup.

Lecture #2: Income Related to Education

(suggested time: 5 minutes)

The purpose of this lecture is to spend time discussing the correlation between education and annual income. It is important to reinforce the fact that more education usually results in higher income.

1. Transition to the lecture by drawing a correlation between the game and real life: In the game, the number of questions you answer propels you to get more money in the end. As in the game, the amount of education you receive propels you to earn more money in a year.
2. Then show the class the chart entitled, "Education Pays" to show statistically how education is related to annual salary. Use a projector to display this graph that shows the average of what a person made weekly in 2008 related to his or her level of education. Show the students what the average annual salary is for a person without a high school diploma, then move up the list showing that with more education or degrees, the more a person earned weekly. Also show the opposite side of the chart, the more education (or degrees) a person had, the lower the unemployment rate usually was for that person.
3. It will be easier for the students to understand this correlation of income to education by thinking about the requirements it takes to obtain higher paying jobs. While looking at the chart with students, give some examples of how this plays out in real life. Ask a few students what types of jobs they want when they get older. (If you have already discussed this in previous lessons, refer back to some of the jobs the students mentioned or refer to jobs from the Budget Simulation in Unit 2.) After taking answers, ask those same students what the requirements are for getting those jobs.
4. Ask the students why they think that statistics show a relation between education and income. After some answers, explain to students that the skills you attain from graduating show that you know how to complete something and follow through on a task you started. It also develops your skill to be able to do whatever job you are trained to do.
5. Tell the students how education will be defined throughout this unit, and write the definition

on the board. You can say something like, "Although the chart gives statistics of education through the path of college degrees and higher education, throughout this unit we define **education** as the knowledge you obtain that helps grow your skills and abilities, including the options of trade school or certification programs."

6. Ask the class if knowing the relationship between education and salary makes a difference in how much education they want. Ask if it changes how they feel about school.

Wrap Up (suggested time: 5 minutes)

End this lesson on a positive note by encouraging the students to think about how they can profit both educationally and financially in the future. While the graph is being displayed, ask the class how much education they want to obtain. Tell the class that what they do in school today will have an effect on what they decide to do after high school. Reinforce the fact that more education usually results in higher income due to skills and degrees obtained through education. State the importance of having an educational and professional goal, and pursuing it the best they can. This concept will be expanded in future lessons in this unit.

Finally, remind the students that throughout this unit, education will include not only high school or college, but also other forms of learning that will provide them with skills to grow in their abilities. There are many success stories of people who did not graduate from college but pursued their passions and dreams wholeheartedly. Share with the students some examples of successful people who did not go to college. Choose from the following list: Simon Cowell (American Idol), Mary Kay Ash (Mary Kay cosmetics), Walt Disney (successful career in animation), Henry Ford (Ford Motor Company), Bill Gates (Microsoft Corporation), or Steve Jobs (Apple, Inc.).[2] Ask the students why they think these people may have been successful.

The next class will focus on stories of everyday people who made choices for a successful future even in the midst of struggle.

Note to Teacher

It may be a delicate balance to not discourage students from a four-year college degree, but it is important to encourage other options or alternatives for a viable or successful future. These options will be discussed in greater depth in Lesson 4.

[2]College Startup. Nov 5 2007. "15 Successful Entrepreneurs Who Didn't Need College." Retreived May 4 2010 from http://www.college-startup.com/college/15-successful-entrepreneurs-who-didnt-need-college/.

Thank the class for their attention and participation.

Vocabulary:

- inflation
- sweat shops
- *optional: transition to independence expenses*
- *optional: contracts*
- *optional: deposits*
- *optional: fees*
- education

Additional Resources:

For additional resources on the history of federal minimum wage, characteristics of minimum wage workers in 2009, the Fair Labor Standards Act, and the "Education Pays" chart, go to www.futureprofitsresources.org.

Attitude is a little thing
that makes a big difference.
– Winston Churchill,
Former Prime Minister of Great Britain

Materials needed:

- Computer with internet connection, projector, and speakers
- Keisha Woods' video*
- Dr. Luis Carlo's video*
- "Homeless to Harvard" DVD or links to video online*
- Optional extended version of "Homeless to Harvard" clips – 4.3.1*

Key Concepts:

1. Success comes in different forms. A variety of examples helps students relate to success and often makes success feel attainable.
2. A strong sense of purpose and a positive mindset will help you gain success in life and overcome obstacles standing in the way of your goals.

Prep Time: 60 minutes

Advance Preparation Tasks:

- Bookmark the video on Keisha Woods' story (see Video #1 for specifics)
- Bookmark the video on Dr. Luis Carlo's story (see Video #2 for specifics)
- Buy the "Homeless to Harvard" DVD for $19.95 (plus shipping and tax) or bookmark the "Homeless to Harvard" video clips (see Video #3 for specifics)
- Watch the video stories beforehand so you are familiar with the stories and what kind of discussion will come from it
- Set up a computer with internet connection to the projector and speakers so the videos are ready to show

**For all additional resources, including handouts, video links and helpful websites, see www.futureprofitsresources.org*

Keep in Mind

- Stories of real, everyday people to whom students can relate provide a great learning tool.
- Many students may feel that the options available to others are not available to them.
- Success comes from a combination of factors. These factors are not to be mentioned as a formula for success, but rather as guidelines for success.

Stories of real, everyday people to whom students can relate provide a great learning tool. This lesson gives the students a chance to observe and discuss stories of everyday people who have achieved success in their lives. It was intentional not to discuss the lives of "famous" people so students could relate to the stories they hear.

In a clip from the video, "Homeless to Harvard," the main character puts it well when she says, "Sometimes I feel like there's skin on the world, and those of us who are born under it can see through it. We just can't get through it." Many students may feel this way, thinking that the options that are available to others just aren't available to them. Therefore, before we discuss the specific options that are paths to success, it is important to show that others to whom the students relate have "broken through the skin."

In beginning the discussion of success, which will be continued and defined in the following lesson (Unit 4, Lesson 4), it is important to communicate to students that success comes from a combination of factors: hard work, perseverence, timing, access to resources, etc. These lessons are not designed to be a formula for success, but instead guidelines to point the students toward success. Be careful to not talk about the students' success in absolutes or promises. For example, instead of saying, "If you go to college, you will be successful," say something like, "If you go to college, you will be much better positioned for success." Success is not guaranteed, but choices made can often set people up to experience success or failure.

Lesson Snapshot

Review (1 minute)
- Relation of Income to Education

Introduction (1 minute)
- Stories of everyday people

Video #1: Keisha Woods' Story (5 minutes)
- Give a brief biography of Keisha and show the video

Discussion #1: Keisha Woods' Story (3 minutes)
- Discuss obstacles in her life and how she overcame them
- Discuss why she is successful and personal characteristics that add to success

Video #2: Luis Carlo's Story (5 minutes)
- Give a brief biography of Dr. Carlo and show the video

Discussion #2: Luis Carlo's Story (2 minutes)
- Discuss obstacles in his life and how he overcame them
- Discuss why he is successful and personal characteristics that add to success

Video #3: "Homeless to Harvard" (25 minutes)
- Give a brief biography of Liz and show the video

Discussion #3: "Homeless to Harvard" (7 minutes)
- Discuss obstacles in her life and how she overcame them
- Discuss why she is successful and personal characteristics that add to success

Wrap Up (1 minute)
- Next class: Possible future paths for success

Review (suggested time: 1 minute)

As we discussed last class, one of the strongest ways to set yourself up for success is by pursuing education. Statistics show that education is directly related to the amount of income we can earn. This is because education allows people to develop specific talents and characteristics needed for success.

Note to Teacher

Each video in this lesson is followed by a discussion. The purpose of the discussions are to direct students to process what is most important to remember. When asking questions for each discussion, make sure to interact with the students and drive home the most important points of their story, particularly the points to which the students might relate the most.

Introduction

(suggested time: 1 minute)

Success is attainable for everyone, regardless of your life circumstances. This lesson involves looking at stories of people who made choices for a successful future. Their character, positive mindset, and help from others were central in pulling them through tough circumstances.

Video #1: Keisha Woods' Story (suggested time: 5 minutes)

The purpose of this video is to show that no matter what mistakes we make, we can always make choices that will bring success in our lives. Keisha's story includes success even though she dropped out of high school due to family struggles and soon after became a teenage mom. She made a choice to pursue education a few years later, and to pursue a job that she would enjoy. She shares about her experience developing her business and what it took to get there.

Introduce the video by giving a brief biography of Keisha Woods. Keisha grew up in Austin, Texas, and moved to East Palo Alto, California, in 1997, where she met and married her husband, David Woods. David Woods is an active real estate broker and local politician. She has over 10 years of experience working in the real estate arena as a realtor, mortgage consultant and NeighborWorks Certified Counselor. She currently works for the non-profit, Northern California Urban Development, as the Housing Program Manager. She has a passion for educating the consumer on the value of homeownership.

Go to www.futureprofitsresources.org and find the link to the video, "Keisha Woods' Success Story." Show the video to the students and move on to the following discussion.

Discussion #1: Keisha Woods' Story (suggested time: 3 minutes)

- Ask the students what obstacles Keisha faced.
    - Point out that Keisha lacked a support system as a student in high school, but she knew she needed to take care of herself and her daughter so she did whatever it took.
- Ask the students how Keisha overcame her obstacles.
- Ask the students why Keisha's story is viewed as a successful story.
- Ask the students what kind of characteristics Keisha demonstrated that led to her success.

Video #2: Dr. Luis Carlo's Story (suggested time: 5 minutes)

The purpose of this video is to show that even in intense pressure with multiple responsibilities, we can always make choices that will bring success in our lives. Although Dr. Carlo had the responsibility of providing for his family, working a full-time job, and pursuing education full-time, he was still successful. He made a choice to pursue education, knowing that whatever work it took to complete his degree would be worth it. He shares about his experiences and how he made choices to succeed.

Introduce the video by giving a brief biography of Dr. Luis Carlo. Dr. Carlo is a Puerto Rican from New York City who served and retired as a Paramedic with the Fire Department of New York (FDNY) for over 27 years. He was pastor of Wounded Healer Fellowship, Bronx, New York for 13 years. Currently he is Associate Dean and Professor of Urban Studies and Religion & Education at Alliance Theological Seminary, New York City Campus, since 1997. He has received multiple educational degrees that contribute to his knowledge, wisdom, and success. His degrees are as follows: B.A. from Southeastern University, M.A. from Logos Bible College and Graduate School, M.Div. from Alliance Theological Seminary, Doctor of Education from Columbia University and Union Theological Seminary, and D.Min. from Bakke Graduate School. He has been married to Elsa Cornier Carlo for 35 years. They have two children: Luis Albert and Elsa-Marie.

Go to www.futureprofitsresources.org and find the link to the video, "Dr. Luis Carlo's Success Story." Show the video to the students and move on to the following discussion.

Discussion #2: Dr. Luis Carlo's Story (suggested time: 2 minutes)

- Ask the students what obstacles Dr. Carlo faced.
- Ask the students how Dr. Carlo overcame his obstacles.
- Ask the students why Dr. Carlo's story is viewed as a successful story.
- Ask the students what kind of characteristics Dr. Carlo demonstrated that led to his success.

Video #3: "Homeless to Harvard" (suggested time: 25 minutes)

The purpose of this video is to show that even when we come from backgrounds of intense struggle, we can always make choices that will bring success in our lives. "Homeless to Harvard" gives the story of Liz Murray, who found herself living on the streets at 15 after her mentally ill, drug-addicted parents could not keep the family together. Not having much of an education, she gets to a point in her life where she decides to give education her all, and she makes determined choices for a life of success.

Introduce the video by giving a brief biography of Liz Murray. Liz Murray grew up knowing no other income but welfare, as she lived with her mentally ill and drug-addicted parents. At age 15, she found herself living on the streets. This is the story of the choices she made in order to seek success for her future.

YouTube Instructions:
Go to YouTube and search for the title, "Homeless to Harvard Part 1." The video on YouTube is split up into nine parts, so the times will be separated into these nine parts. Bookmark Part 1 and Parts 5 through 9 so that each clip is ready to show. Links to these clips can also be found at www.futureprofitsresources.org.

Note to Teacher

The video, "Homeless to Harvard," is 90 minutes long. Therefore, the following are 23 minutes of specific clips of her story in order to get across the main points. If the class has more than 50 minutes, consider showing an extended version of this film (see www.futureprofitsresources.org). Either show the clips from YouTube or buy the DVD to show sections of the film (instructions for both below). If you choose to buy the DVD, you can order it online at www.mylifeline.com.

Show Part 1, 1:05 to 4:34, as an introduction to Liz Murray's life. *(3.5 minutes)*

- We are skipping over Parts 2-4; give a brief summary of each part:
  - Part 2 shows Liz doing well in school, even though she hasn't been there in months. She finds out that her mother contracted AIDS.
  - Part 3 is when she's taken from her home and put in a group home, where she has a negative experience). Then she goes back to her grandpa's home and visits with her mom. When she starts attending school again, she meets her best friend, Chris.
  - Part 4 shows Liz taking care of her mom. While living with her grandpa, he hits her so she leaves, becomes homeless, and stops going to school. She hangs with her friends, sleeps on their couches, and sleeps on the subway.

Show Part 5, 1:23 to 3:59, where she takes care of her mom while she's still homeless. *(2.5 minutes)*

- Inform students of the parts skipped: Liz finds out that her mom dies, and goes to meet her grandpa and sister to bury her. Her friends come with her to show their support.

Show Part 5, 6:04 to 7:32 *(1.5 minutes)*

Show Part 6, 2:29 to 3:27, then 4:56 to 8:28, which shows the part where her life changes and she decides to go back to school. *(4.5 minutes – If more time, show Part 6, 0:00 to 8:28.)*

- Inform students of the parts skipped: The rest of Part 6 and the beginning of Part 7 (0 to 5:04) show Liz getting her dad to give the school an address so the school wouldn't know she is homeless. She also finds out that her dad has AIDS as her mom did.

Show Part 7, 7:17 to the end and then Part 8, 0 to 5:11, which shows Liz working hard in school. She runs into her best friend, Chris, and tries to help her get into school. This shows the difference in mindsets of the two girls. Liz also gets to go on a trip to Harvard with her school. *(8 minutes)*

- Inform students of the parts skipped: The rest of Part 8 and the beginning of Part 9 shows her applying for a scholarship from the New York Times to go to Harvard and getting it, enabling her to go to college.

Show Part 9, 0:36 to 1:13, then 4:50 to 6:55, which shows Liz's acceptance of the New York Times scholarship and starting at Harvard. *(2.5 minutes)*

"Homeless to Harvard" DVD Instructions:

- Begin at Chapter 1, Fast-forward to 1:15
  - Show 1:15 - 4:51 *(3.5 minutes)*
  - Inform students of the parts skipped: Liz has success in school, even though she hasn't been there in months. She finds out that her mother contracted HIV AIDS. She is taken from her home and put in a group home, where she has a negative experience. Then she goes back to her grandpa's home and visits with her mom. When she starts attending school again, she meets her best friend, Chris. Liz often takes care of her mom. While living with her grandpa, he hit her so she leaves, becomes homeless, and stops going to school. She hangs with her friends, sleeps on their couches, and sleeps on the subway.
- Skip to Chapter 9, Fast-forward to 41:24
  - Show 41:24 - 44:06 *(3 minutes)*
  - Inform students of the parts skipped: Liz finds out that her mom dies, and goes to meet her grandpa and sister to bury her. Her friends come with her to show their support.

- Skip to Chapter 10, Fast-forward to 46:17
  - Show 46:17 - 47:49 *(1.5 minutes)*
- Skip to Chapter 11, Fast-forward to 52:36
  - Show 52:36 - 53:37 *(1 minute)*
- Skip to Chapter 12
  - Show 55:00 - 58:49 *(4 minutes)*
  - Inform students of the parts skipped: Liz gets her dad to give the school an address so the school doesn't know she is homeless. She finds out that her dad has AIDS as her mom did.
- Skip to Chapter 14, Fast-forward to 1:05:39
  - Show 1:05:39 - 1:13:38 *(8 minutes)*
- Skip to Chapter 16, Fast-forward to 1:18:53
  - Show 1:18:53 – 1:19:32 *(40 seconds)*
  - Inform students of the parts skipped: Liz applies for a scholarship from the New York Times to go to Harvard. She gets it and gives her acceptance speech.
- Skip to Chapter 17, Fast-forward to 1:23:17
  - Show 1:23:17 - 1:25:28 *(2 minutes)*

Discussion #3: "Homeless to Harvard" (suggested time: 7 minutes)

- Ask the students what were some of the obstacles that Liz faced.
  - Point out that one of the obstacles she faced was the differing goals of her best friend. Ask the students what they may have done if they were in her place.
- Ask the students what choices Liz made to overcome her obstacles.
- Ask the students why Liz's story is viewed as a successful story.
- Ask the students what kind of characteristics Liz demonstrated that led to her success.

Wrap Up (suggested time: 1 minute)

Wrap up the class by reflecting on the lesson:

"Each story seen today represents a story of success for an everyday person like you and me. Our next class will focus more specifically on what those paths to success might look like."

Thank the class for their attention and participation.

Vocabulary:
None

Additional Resources:
For additional information on the "Homeless to Harvard" movie, go to www.futureprofitsresources.org.

Focusing your life solely on making a buck
shows a poverty of ambition.
It asks too little of yourself.
And it will leave you unfulfilled.
–President Barack Obama

Materials needed:

- Magazines (enough for at least one magazine per student)
- Glue or glue sticks (Mod Podge® or decoupage works best for this activity. Students can use their fingers to spread the Mod Podge or use paint brushes.)
- Scissors for students to share (at least one pair of scissors for every two students)
- Paper or cardboard for each student (can be varying sizes, but must be big enough to make a collage, around 8″ by 8″)
- Job Cards from Unit 2, Lesson 2 (use as a reference) – 2.2.2 or 2.2.3*
- Whiteboard and pen, or chalkboard and chalk, or poster paper and pen
- *Optional: Job Facts Sheet – 4.4.1**

Key Concepts:

1. Financial success is having the power to choose opportunities for your future.
2. Although college is most likely the best option for students to take in our society today, it is not the only path post-high school that will bring a future of success.
3. Choosing your desired future path now will set you up for a successful future. The choices you make today are steps that will move you forward on a path.

Prep Time: 15 minutes

**For all additional resources, including handouts, video links and helpful websites, see www.futureprofitsresources.org*

Advance Preparation Tasks:

- Buy or find magazines for students that would have graphics and words inside that may express the students' view of success for their futures
- Set up the materials for the Success Collage Activity so that it runs smoothly
- *Optional: Make copies of Job Facts Sheet to hand out to students at the end of class*

Keep in Mind

- Many students who come from a disadvantaged background feel that they don't deserve success, or that success is something the rich have and is not an option for the poor.
- Some students may not attend college or even graduate high school.
- It is important to encourage a variety of career options that can lead to financial success.
- The more practical job options given to the students, along with personal experiences shared, the more students will begin to dream about jobs that would be best for them.

In this lesson, students will continue to learn about success through the lens of employment opportunities. Success may be a term that comes with a lot of baggage for some students. Many students who come from a disadvantaged background feel as though they don't deserve success, or that success is something to which the rich have access and is not available to the poor. This lesson strives to make success an attainable and desirable option for students who may feel this way. Students will learn about different types of career paths that can set them on a path of success. It will always be a delicate balance in a broad group of students to encourage other options or alternatives for a viable or successful future, while not discouraging students from obtaining a four-year college degree. It also is important to not be tied to college as the only way to be financially successful in life. Some students may not attend college or even graduate high school. This may discourage some of them from pursuing options that could lead to a successful future. Students should be aware of the various career opportunities available. In America, college is the most secure path to follow in order to have a successful future. Even though it is the intention of this curriculum to encourage all students to go to college, they should also be aware of other paths.

Although there are many possible paths students' lives can take after high school, this lesson will focus on four paths students may choose that could potentially lead to success. The four paths are **college, trade school, entrepreneurship**, and **immediate work**. There are more paths available to students, but this lesson focuses only on these four. Many students will not know what they want to do when they enter the workforce, or some may have an idea of what they want, but no idea how to get there. The more practical job options described to the students, the more they will begin to dream about jobs that would be best for them. Any personal experiences you can share with the students will help them see future available options for themselves. Consider going on a field trip with your students to a place where the workers can share about their different jobs and where students can ask questions, or bring guest speakers with different skills or jobs into the classroom to share their journey with the students. The students must begin or continue to think about their futures, both financially and educationally. This lesson will also set up the following lessons to personalize and discuss these paths for their lives in greater depth.

Lesson Snapshot

Review (3 minutes)
- Video stories — what students remember most
- How they would define success

Introduction (2 minutes)
- Define success using dictionary definition and FutureProfits definition
- What success is and is not

Activity: Success Collages (15 minutes)
- Instruct students to make collages that define personal success for their futures
- Distribute materials to students
- Draw four paths on the board to prepare the following discussion and lectures

Discussion: Potential Paths (5 minutes)
- Ask students what options they may have after they graduate from high school
- State the four paths this lesson will discuss

Lecture #1: The Path of College (8 minutes)
- Typical jobs and salaries that require a college degree
- This path can include the option of Graduate School (name jobs that require graduate school or a Master's degree)
- Discuss advantages and obstacles
- Ask students how many of them would need to go to college to obtain the job they want in the future.

Lecture #2: The Path of a Trade (5 minutes)
- Define trade
- Define apprenticeship
- Typical trade routes include apprenticeship, community college, trade school, or vocational school
- Typical jobs and salaries that require trade school
- Discuss advantages and obstacles

Lecture #3: The Path of Entrepreneurship (5 minutes)
- Define entrepreneurship
- Typical jobs that are included in entrepreneurship
- Discuss advantages and obstacles
- Define start-up capital and entrepreneurial mindset

Lecture #4: The Path of Immediate Work (5 minutes)
- Typical jobs that are included in entering the workforce immediately
- Discuss advantages and obstacles
- Encourage taking classes part-time if possible, and using the job to develop skills needed for future jobs

Wrap Up (2 minutes)
- Ask students about most appealing path and why
- Preview next class about decision making

Review (suggested time: 3 minutes)

The last class focused on hearing stories of other people whose lives resemble success in some way. Ask the students what they remember most from the stories from last class, and how they would define success after seeing their stories.

Introduction (suggested time: 2 minutes)

Begin the lesson by defining **success**. The dictionary defines success as the accomplishment of an aim or purpose. Although success can be perceived differently, the *FutureProfits* curriculum defines success financially by referring back to the definition of power in Unit 1. Power is when an individual has the ability to make choices about his or her own destiny. Therefore success financially means that an individual has the ability to make choices that give him or her more options for the future, options that will give him or her the opportunity to do what he or she loves to do. Students need to understand both what success is and what success is not.

- Success is not something we fall into. When we look at the dictionary definition, it is accomplishing something you are aiming for. Success usually doesn't happen by accident, but is made up of intentional choices.
- Success is not defined by a certain amount of money made each year. If an individual is doing something he/she loves, is able to choose that occupation, and it is able to bring in an income that covers the individual's cost of living, it can be a success financially.

This lesson will focus on the idea of financial success by looking at pathways that can set up our lives to be successful in the end.

Activity: Success Collages (suggested time: 15 minutes)

The purpose of this activity is to give the students an opportunity to express themselves through art by creating a collage that defines what success might look like in their lives.

1. Because success involves choice, students will create a collage as a reminder of how they personally desire success in their lives. Give each student a magazine and a pair of scissors. Tell students to cut pictures and words out of the magazine that best describe what they want success to look like in their futures. Instruct them to trade magazines with other students once they are done cutting pictures out of their magazine.

2. As students cut out pictures and words from their magazines, distribute the glue or glue sticks for the students to share, along with a piece of paper or cardboard for each student. Instruct students to glue the pictures and words they cut out onto this paper or cardboard.

3. As students continue to work on their collage, draw on the white board four paths that lead to separate end points. Do not write the words at the end of the paths yet. The drawing will set you up for the following discussion and lectures in which you will write the name of each path as each lecture begins. Make the left-center path look wider than the other paths.

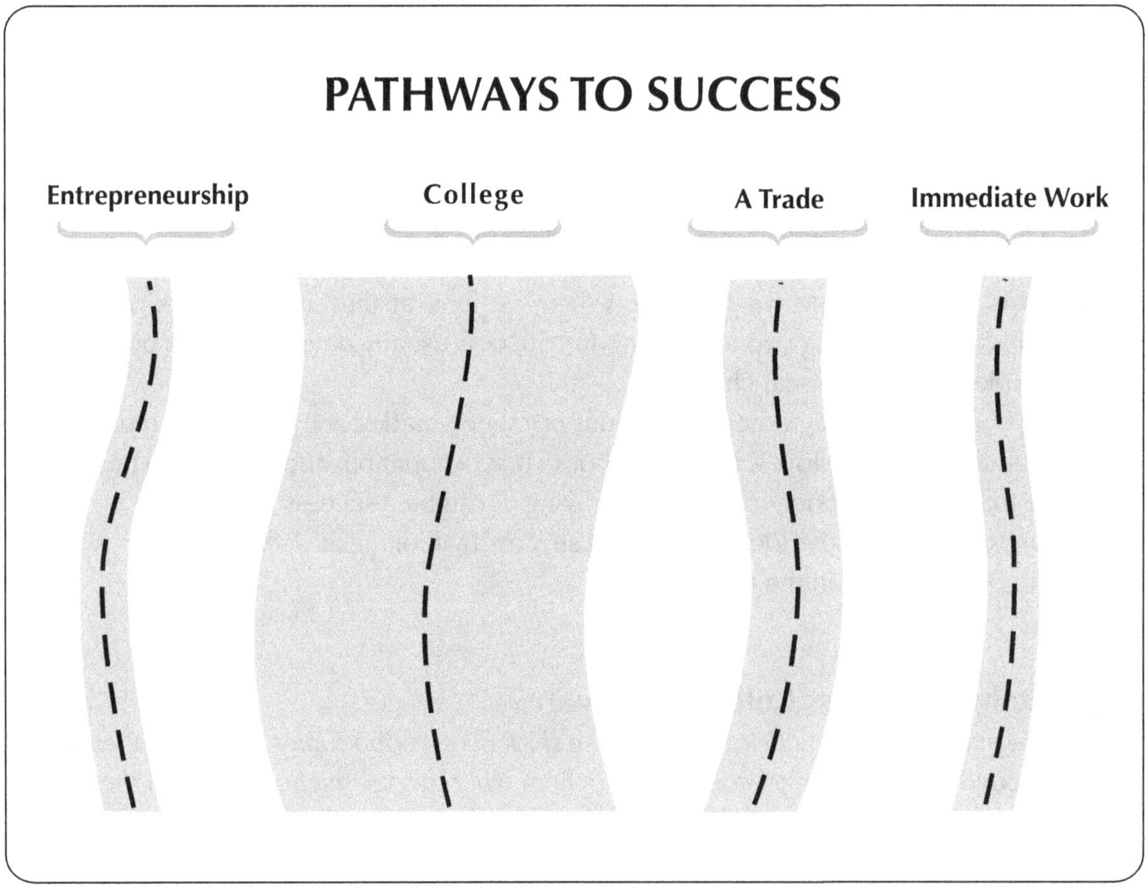

Discussion: Potential Paths (suggested time: 5 minutes)

After students have had a chance to work on their collages, have students put aside their collages and materials for the rest of the lesson, even if they have not finished with their collage. This will help the class focus on the following discussion and lectures.

Ask the class to name some potential career paths they can take after they graduate from high school. Specify that you are not asking about different jobs they might have, but paths they can take that lead to different jobs. After students share, explain that the focus will be on four potential paths that can lead to success: College, Trade School, Entrepreneurship and Immediate Work.

Note to Teacher

Although there is a lot that can be said about each path, focus on sharing the main description along with the advantages and obstacles of each path. Feel free to point back to the videos from the last lesson to give an example of a story of the different paths. If time permits, feel free to share the path you chose, and how you made the decision to go down that path.

Lecture #1: The Path of College (suggested time: 8 minutes)

The purpose of this lecture is to focus on the advantages of a college degree, the potential end points of a college degree (including further education and salaries of jobs), and the potential road blocks that are on that path of getting a college degree.

Begin by reminding the students about the information in Lesson 2: going to college and attaining an education is directly related to income, and can be very important for a successful career. Before describing anything about college, write college on the wide, left-center path drawn on the board.

1. Give the students some examples of typical jobs and salaries that require a college degree. Use some examples from the Budget Simulation, specifically Unit 2, Lesson 2. Pick examples that students would find appealing, or that they would personally desire in their futures.
2. Mention that this path also includes further education past a college degree, such as graduate school. These jobs and salaries are often the most competitive around, which is why they require more schooling. Some examples from the Budget Simulation include the psychologist, the lawyer, and the doctor.
3. Then ask the students what the advantages are of having a college degree. Some advantages may include:
   a. **More opportunities** — A college degree opens up a variety of career opportunities throughout life.
   b. **Time to decide future career** — If students are not sure what they want as a job, classes in college will help them to narrow down their options and help them decide on a path to pursue.

c. **Better competition** — A college degree will make them more competitive in the job market. Many desirable places to live have a highly competitive work field because a lot of people want to live there, so businesses will hire the best of the best. The best of the best is often seen as those who have been academically successful.

d. **Resume help** — A college degree looks good on their resumes. A resume is a document that contains a summary of an individual's education, achievements, and previous job experience for specific employment search. A college degree is often the first thing that employers look for as they sort through large piles of resumes.

e. **Many options available** — The college path is wide, meaning there are many options when it comes to choosing a college. The options include a junior college, a state college, a private college, or obtaining an online degree. This provides several choices for individuals of different academic and economic backgrounds when planning a route to higher education. There is an opportunity for almost any student with a high school diploma to go to college.

f. **Motivates work in school now** — If students set career-related educational goals early, it is easier for them to achieve their goals as they will try to maintain a good grade point average (GPA). Students who end up with a low GPA may not have as good a chance to get into the college or university of their choice straight out of high school. However, that doesn't mean it's not possible. They can attend a junior college regardless of their GPA and work toward transferring to their ideal school or university. Attending a junior college could also help students decide what college or university they would like to attend.

4. Ask the students what some of the obstacles or roadblocks are when one is traveling down the college path. As they name some obstacles, discuss them with the students. Make sure that if the students do not name the following obstacles, that you discuss them before moving on to the next part of the lesson.

a. **Takes too much time** — It may seem like four years to get a college degree is too long to wait. Encourage the students with the idea that college may seem like a long path, but it can also have the greatest pay off.

b. **Too expensive** — There may be some financial obstacles in affording college. Students may not have a college fund set up or the money available to pay for the average cost of going to college, especially state schools and private schools. Inform the students that many colleges will do as much as possible to help students come to their school. There is financial aid available to students whose families have lower incomes. Students can apply for financial aid by filling out a FAFSA (Free Application for Federal Student Aid). There are also many scholarships available for college, and the students' ability to obtain a scholarship is based on choices they make now. Also inform the students that many junior colleges will charge less for classes than state colleges. In fact, many students take the junior college route because it gives them time to save up money to pay for a four-year school.

c. **Other financial obligations** — Some students may have other financial obligations, requiring them to work full-time and go to school full-time. Finishing college may take longer if an individual needs to work full-time.

A suggested concluding comment: "Having only a high school diploma may still limit you when trying to find a job. Although there may be obstacles, there is usually nothing stopping you from attending college. Even if one makes really big mistakes in high school, or believes they cannot afford it, college is still a possible opportunity. The junior college route often helps students afford to go to college. Even if you start out with a few classes, the path to finishing college may be a longer path, but it's better than not going to college at all."

Finally ask the students how many think a college education is necessary to have the kind of job they want. Tell the students it's important to remember that what they do today in school will directly affect their future schooling. That's why it's so important to make the most of their present situation.

Lecture #2: The Path of a Trade (suggested time: 5 minutes)

The purpose of this lecture is to focus on the advantages of working a trade, the potential end points of working a trade (including salaries of potential trades), and the potential road blocks that are on the path of working a trade.

If the college path is not a path that students are interested in following, there is another path of learning a **trade** that can be a positive option. A trade is a skilled job, typically one requiring manual skills and special training. The path of working a trade is obtained either through gaining an apprenticeship or attending community college, a trade school or a vocational school. An **apprenticeship** is a training program under the supervision of a journey-level craftsperson or a trade professional. Apprenticeships are preferrable because people are often paid through the training process. Through becoming an apprentice or attending these schools, people will learn the specific skill of their choice. Students must be intentional to think about a vocation that would sustain their financial needs and wants, and follow the appropriate training options. There are many trades students can learn that will help obtain good-paying jobs. Write the words "A Trade" on the path to the right of "College."

1. Ask the students what kind of careers or jobs are understood to be a trade. Write students' answers on the board next to the trade path. Some examples may be a plumber, electrician, painter, nursing assistant, dental hygienist, welder or mechanic. These are all very good professions that do not require a college degree. They can obtain the skill to perform these types of jobs by becoming an apprentice or going to a trade school. Pull an example or two from the job cards from Unit 2 (attachment 2.2.2 or 2.2.3) and tell the students some of the salaries they might be able to earn following trade school. Some examples from the Budget Simulation include the Emergency Medical Technician, the auto mechanic, the dental hygienist, the contruction project manager, the barber or hair dresser, or the electrician.
2. Then ask the students what the advantages of working a trade are. Some advantages may include:
   a. **Less time than obtaining a college degre**e — Working a trade can possibly set you up with a high-paying job in a shorter amount of time than a college degree may take. Some people who know a trade are able to make a lot of money. This is because people always need a mechanic, plumber, painter, etc. These are specific skills that the average person does not possess. Therefore, people will pay good money for these kinds of services.
   b. **Sometimes paid while learning** — If taking the route of an apprentice, you can often get paid while learning.
3. Ask the students what some of the obstacles or roadblocks are if traveling down the trade path. As they name some obstacles, discuss them with the students. Make sure if the students do not name the following obstacles, that you discuss them with your students before moving on to the next part of the lesson.
   a. **Limited opportunities** — Having a trade without a college degree limits them to that one trade. If they start off as a mechanic at the age of 22 and then at the age of 32 they no longer want to be a mechanic, it will be very difficult to change careers. However, if they have a college degree more opportunities are available.
   b. **Difficult first few years** — When entering a trade, they will spend the first few years doing menial, laborious tasks while learning and making their way through an apprenticeship.
   c. **Much competition** —There is often competition among other skilled workers, so they frequently need to be "the best" in the city in that specific trade. They will also need to be the best in advertising their services.

Conclude this section by encouraging the students to remember the following points if they are interested in pursuing trade school:

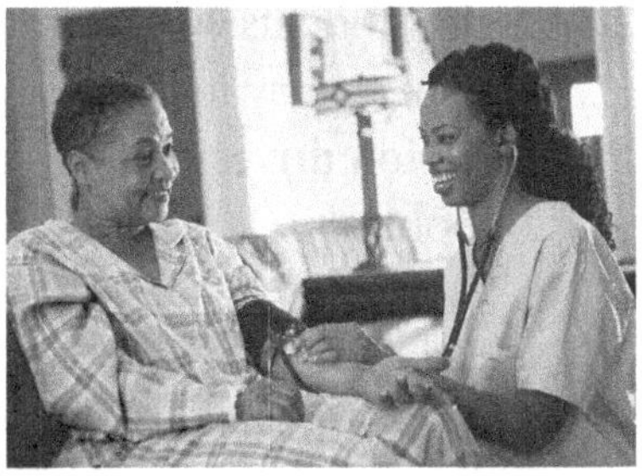

1. They are always better off going through an "official" apprenticeship (i.e., a union apprenticeship) than an informal one. A common apprenticeship happens through a labor union. If they are interested in obtaining an apprenticeship, they should go to their local union hall and ask about the process of becoming an apprentice for their trade of choice.
2. A good resource to take advantage of is a career center at a local junior college. A career center will help them see a variety of career options and give them the steps to follow that path.
3. There are many classes that can be taken at a junior college for low cost instead of going to a for-profit school like ITT Tech, Devry, or any regional example. Many people go to these schools and leave with debt.
4. Construction trades are subject to economic factors. When the economy slows, jobs can be scarce, so good money management is extremely important.

Lecture #3: The Path of Entrepreneurship

(suggested time: 5 minutes)

The purpose of this lecture is to focus on the advantages of being an entrepreneur, the potential end points of entrepreneurship (including different kinds of jobs), and the potential road blocks that are on the path of being an entrepreneur.

Entrepreneurship is another path that can be a positive option. Entrepreneurship is when an individual starts his or her own business. Write the word "Entrepreneurship" on the path to the left of College.

1. Ask the students what kind of careers or jobs one might get if they were an entrepreneur. Write students' answers on the board next to the entrepreneurship path. Some examples may include a real estate agent, a retaurant owner or salon owner. In general, an **entrepreneur** is anyone who creates a new product to sell that could be its own business. The classic example of entrepreneurship is a child setting up a lemonade stand to make some extra money. Although the competition and risk is much greater as an adult, entrepreneurship is the same sort of idea. The salaries for an entrepreneur range dramatically based on what type of business one starts. The extreme

example used in the Budget Simulation was the co-founder of a rising social networking site, like Facebook, making $3,000,000 a year. Entrepreneurship requires a lot of work but can also have a lot of rewards.

2. Ask the students what they think might be some advantages to being an entrepreneur. Some advantages may include:
   a. **Passion drives them** — Entrepreneurs often do something they love and are passionate about.
   b. **Shot-callers** — Entrepreneurs will be their own boss and therefore decide what hours they work.
   c. **Money-makers** — Entrepreneurs can make a lot of money in the long run.

3. Ask the students what some of the obstacles or roadblocks are if traveling down the entrepreneurship path. As they name some obstacles, discuss them with the students. Make sure if the students do not name the following obstacles, that you discuss them before moving on to the next part of the lesson.
   a. **Hard work** — Despite the great outcomes of entrepreneurship, people who start their own business work very hard and long hours when they first open their business. It usually takes a couple of years before they even make a profit. Therefore being an entrepreneur requires great vision and motivation.
   b. **Great financial cost in the beginning** — There is often a great financial cost in the beginning. An entrepreneur would need start-up capital and some kind of business sense and expertise to be successful in entrepreneurship. **Start-up capital** often comes from someone who likes the idea the entrepreneur has for starting a business and thinks the business might make some profit. The person will contribute a sum of money, with the hope that he/she will have some part in the future financial return.
   c. **Greater risk** — In general, the financial risk is greater with starting a new business. An individual never knows how the business will do financially until he/she starts it, usually because an entrepreneur is creating a new idea or product. Because of the great financial risk, many small businesses fail.

A suggested concluding comment: "If you plan to open your own business, you don't always need a college degree, but you definitely will need to have a strong business ethic and entrepreneurial mindset. An entrepreneurial mindset is when a person will do whatever it takes to help the business succeed. It means having a mindset that takes initiative to make things happen and perseveres through many obstacles. The best way to set yourself up to be a successful entrepreneur is to go to college and get a degree that will help you run your business. This also provides a backup plan if the business is unsuccessful."

Lecture #4: The Path of Immediate Work

(suggested time: 5 minutes)

The purpose of this lecture is to focus on the advantages of immediate work, the potential end points of immediate work (including different kinds of jobs), and the potential road blocks that are on the path of immediate work.

The last path many students might choose is going into the workforce immediately. Write the words "Immediate Work" on the path to the right of "Trade School."

1. Ask the students what kind of careers or jobs one might get if they went into the workforce immediately. Some of these jobs may start out as minimum wage (such as the McDonald's job from the Budget Simulation). Other examples from the Budget Simulation include the Starbucks barista, the receptionist, or possibly a daycare center teacher. Note to the students that the salaries of these jobs tend to be in a lower range.
2. Ask the students what they think are some advantages to entering the workforce immediately. Some advantages may include:
   a. **Immediate money** — They can make money immediately, which can help provide for more immediate financial needs.
   b. **College is a more sustainable option** — College may be a more sustainable option later on once they have taken a few years in the workforce to earn and save money.
   c. **Develop skills** — It can help develop their skills for future jobs.
3. Ask the students what some of the obstacles or roadblocks are traveling down the immediate work path. As they name some obstacles, discuss them with the students. Make sure if the students do not name the following obstacles, that you discuss them before moving on to the next part of the lesson.
   a. **Less money** — they may not make as much money in the long run.
   b. **Limited opportunities** — they may be more limited in your future opportunities by not having a college degree or a marketable skill.
   c. **Emergencies happen** — it is much harder to have a back-up plan to help support them financially during that emergency.

Although this can be a successful path, it requires having an entrepreneurial mindset to be able to have success in whatever job they have. Through hard work and initiative, many people can move to higher positions within their company and make a decent living. Encourage students to pay attention to the way hard work is rewarded within the company, to watch what is required of people who are in positions of leadership, and to take leadership in any position they may have in their company, regardless of how menial the job may seem. Employers and managers take notice of good character and high standards.

Suggest to your students that even if they desire to take this route for practical reasons, they should think about taking classes part-time while working full time, just to keep college in their minds as an option for the future. Also suggest that students use this job strategically to develop their skills for future jobs.

Wrap Up (suggested time: 2 minutes)

Ask the students what path sounds most appealing to them at this point and why.

Tell the class that they have many options when it comes to their future, but to be successful in any of them, they must make choices even now as to what they want to pursue and begin working hard toward that path. Remind students that what they choose today will directly affect how they profit in the future. In order to make successful choices now, they will need to understand the process of making even the small decisions in a wise manner so they can have success in the future. Decision making will be the topic for the next class.

If helpful for your students, give each student a copy of the Job Facts Sheet for more information on the four paths so they can reference them in the future see www.futureprofitsresources.org.

Thank the class for their attention and participation.

Vocabulary:

- success
- resume
- trade
- apprenticeship
- entrepreneurship
- start-up capital
- entrepreneurial mindset

Additional Resources:

For additional resources on student financial aid, apprenticeships, entrepreneurship, and college information, go to www.futureprofitsresources.org.

In a moment of decision,
the best thing you can do
is the right thing to do.
The worst thing you can do is nothing.
–Theodore Roosevelt, Former U.S. President

Materials needed:

- The "Little Choices" Worksheet – 4.5.1*
- The Scenario #1 and #2 Worksheets – 4.5.2 and 4.5.3*
- Whiteboard and pen, or chalkboard and chalk, or poster paper and pen

Key Concepts:

1. The process of making wise decisions is similar for both minor and major decisions.
2. Even the little decisions we make in our present can often impact our future.

Prep Time: 15 minutes

Advance Preparation Tasks:

- Make enough copies of the Little Choices Worksheet for each student
- Make enough copies of either/both the Scenario #1 and #2 Worksheets for each student

For all additional resources, including handouts, video links and helpful websites, see www.futureprofitsresources.org

Keep in Mind

- Many students struggle with overcoming obstacles because they have not been given structure to help them get back on the right path after making a mistake.
- It is most important to help students learn critical thinking skills because every decision they make can impact their futures.

This lesson is meant to communicate the importance of critical thinking. It is difficult for many students who come from low-income neighborhoods to overcome the obstacles they face because many have not been given the structure or support to help them get back on the right path after making a mistake. Many need to understand and attain the skills to overcome obstacles.

When an obstacle gets in the way on any of the paths to success, it is easy to feel overwhelmed and not know how to deal with it. Part of the difficulty is trying to manage time wisely. Critical thinking skills are important with time management. It is important for students to think for themselves and not rely on others to tell them what is right or to make the decisions for them. This is especially true in regard to peer pressure. The desire to belong and fit in is so strong in high school that when a decision comes their way — especially decisions that seem to be "insignificant" — most students don't stop to think about how the decision will impact their future. They often follow along with what the majority is doing.

Critical thinking deeply impacts an individual's future. When anyone makes a decision without thinking about future implications, it is easy to be manipulated into making a decision that could be harmful in the future. Therefore, learning the process of decision making is just as important as a college education. Once one learns how to make wise decisions, he or she can know how to navigate through the systems that exist in the world and use common sense to choose what is best.

Another benefit of the decision making process is that students learn more about themselves. Becoming more self-aware helps them understand not only why they make the decisions they do, but what decisions are in line with their visions, dreams, and values. Most importantly, it allows students to hope and dream for a better future for their lives.

Lesson Snapshot

Review (2 minutes)
- Review definition of success and the four main paths discussed last class

Introduction (3 minutes)
- Topic: making decisions
- Share a story about an important decision you made

Activity #1: The Little Choices (10 minutes)
- Hand out worksheet and explain
- Discuss a couple of the "little choices"

Discussion: How Do You Make Decisions? (5 minutes)
- Discuss different ways people make decisions
- Define wisdom and the importance of making wise decisions

Lecture: Tools of Decision Making (5 minutes)
- Write the five steps on the board and explain

Activity #2: Decision Making Scenarios (10 minutes)
- Break into groups of four to five students; give each student a worksheet of either scenario #1 or #2
- Have students follow the decision making process outlined on the worksheet, brainstorming options with their group

Discussion: Scenario #1 (5 minutes)
- Go through each step of the decision making process concerning Scenario #1 with the students

Discussion: Scenario #2 (5 minutes)
- Go through each step of the decision making process concerning Scenario #2 with the students

Wrap Up (5 minutes)

- Remind students what making a wise decision means
- Next class: Life map

Review (suggested time: 2 minutes)

Ask the students to define success from the last lesson. Remind them that success is not making a certain amount of money per year, but it's having the ability to make choices that give us more options for our future.

Ask the students what the four main paths were that were discussed in the last lesson. Point out that our choices today impact the paths we take in our future.

Introduction (suggested time: 3 minutes)

This lesson is about making decisions. Ask the students why it would be important to think through making decisions. After receiving some answers, share a real life story about one of the most important decisions you made. Choose a story that is a major decision, but point out to the students how a lot of little decisions led up to the major decision. Then tell the students that the decision making process is usually the same for both seemingly minor decisions and major decisions, and that understanding the process helps us make wise decisions.

Activity #1: The Little Choices (suggested time: 10 minutes)

The purpose of this activity is to help students see how the little choices in life can impact their future.

Hand out the "Little Choices" Worksheet. Explain to students that in life, even though it doesn't seem like it, the little choices are often what will most impact their futures. These choices can lead them to having more control when it comes to the bigger choices further down the road. This is especially true in high school before they enter the workforce and before they rely on their own income to support financial needs.

The "Little Choices" Worksheet is a list of choices one might make during high school.

> **Note to Teacher**
>
> *Use the teacher's guide* for "The Little Choices" to quickly see which "little choices" listed could have a negative effect or positive effect. The bolded choices will potentially have a negative effect on their futures.*

*See www.futureprofitsresources.org for downloadable teacher's guide

Direct students to mark the choices in the list that they think may have a negative effect on their life by making an "X" in the box next to the choice. After they go through the worksheet, go over a couple of the choices with the class and discuss how this choice might affect their future either in a positive or a negative way.

Discussion: How Do You Make Decisions? (suggested time: 5 minutes)

Ask the students if they make decisions based on what they know or what they feel. Our personalities affect the way we make decisions. Many people tend to make decisions based on their feelings. When people critically think through their options and decide based on what they know, instead of what they feel, they can make the best decision. This is one way that wisdom grows. Ask the students what wisdom means. After some students answer, tell them that **wisdom** is applying experience, knowledge, and good judgment to the choices we make. Many know it as learning from our mistakes, or learning from others' mistakes. An easy way to remember it is to think of the best possible solution, in the best possible way, for the largest number of people, for the longest length of time. When we think about how to make good decisions, it's helpful to answer those questions by going through a five-step decision making process.

Lecture: Tools of Decision Making (suggested time: 5 minutes)

It can be helpful to learn how to make wise decisions by using a process to determine what the best decision is. We make decisions every day "without thinking." When we don't think about how the decision will impact our future and the future of others, we are prone to making a poor decision. Here is a five-step process to help us remember tools for decision making (write these five steps on the board):

1. List your options
2. List what's important to you
3. List the pros and cons of each option
4. List people who could give you good advice
5. Decide and act

Explain each step a little more in-depth.

1. **List your options.** When confronted with a decision that needs to be made, we often think there is only one option – the first option that comes to our minds. But when we stop to list our options (even the negative options), we gain confidence that the decision we are making is the best.

2. **List what's important to you.** Our values, passions, and dreams will often affect the way we make decisions. It is important to make sure our decision is aligned with our values, passions and dreams, since we will be the ones who deal with the outcomes of that decision. Many of our decisions now will impact our dreams for the future. So if our dreams are not considered in the decision making process, our decisions are likely to impact our future dreams negatively.
3. **List the pros and cons of each option.** This may involve research at times. Researching doesn't always mean looking in a book; it does mean putting thought into the outcomes of the decision. One decision may look more appealing to you, but may not be the best decision to make in the end, once you think through the cons of that decision and the pros of other options. This step helps to expose the unforseen consequences that may happen because of our decisions.
4. **List people who could give you good advice.** These people are often mentors, experts, or those who know you well. When taking this step, it is important to not ask everyone — only the core people who will help you make the best decision. These are the people who want the best for you, and do not have ulterior motives or biases in helping you make a choice. It is similar to the "Who Wants Future Profits?" game we played during Lesson 2. When you need help with figuring out an answer, you have people "on call" who will help answer your questions with the correct answers so you can win.

5. **Decide and act.** This means that you make an action plan with steps so you will actually make it from Point A to Point B. If there is no action, you are still making a passive decision to not act. Therefore, when you intentionally make a decision, there will be an action that follows it.

Activity #2: Decision Making Scenarios (suggested time: 10 minutes)

The purpose of this activity is to go through the tools of decision making (the five-step process) with a sample decision that the students may have to make during high school. The example decisions included are somewhat common to teenagers and provide several options for students to consider in order to determine what the best decision would be. If there is a different decision that you think would be more specific or helpful for your students to think through, go through the five steps of decision making using that decision instead.

1. Split the class into groups of four to five students. Distribute to each group one of the two different scenarios. Each student should have his or her own worksheet to write on.
2. Tell the groups to read the scenario they have been given, and then go through the decision making process on the worksheet. They should work as a group to brainstorm, but can come to separate individual decisions if they desire. After each group has gone through the worksheet, have students share their decision making process with the class using the following discussions.

Discussion: Scenario #1 (suggested time: 5 minutes)

1. Ask one of the students to read aloud Scenario #1.
2. Have the students share the options they brainstormed and write all the options on the board. They may be surprised at how many options there are. If the students haven't brainstormed many options, feel free to add to the discussion by suggesting these options:
   a. Miss the party of the year. Stay at home and study for your English test. Go to bed early and get a good night's sleep.
   b. Drive your mom's car to the party. Stay up late and have the time of your life. Do not study for your English test.
   c. Drive your mom's car to the party, stay for a couple of hours, then come home to stay up late and study for the test.
   d. Get to the party without driving your mom's car (bus or walk). Stay up late and have the time of your life. Walk home after the party and crash.
3. Ask the groups if their values, passions, and/or goals were the same for each person in the group, or if they were different. Then ask the students what some of those values, passions, and/or goals were and write them on the board.
4. Pick two of the main options and write the pros and cons for each on the board. The following two have been provided, but their lists of pros and cons are not comprehensive.

a. Drive your mom's car to the party, stay for a couple of hours, then come home to stay up late and study for the test.

PROS	CONS
Show up in style (and promptly)	May get grounded for driving mom's car
Get to study some	May miss some answers on the test
Have a blast at the party	You'll miss out on some of the party
You get the best of both worlds...party, and at least a "better" grade...if not the best grade.	A number of things could happen driving your mom's car and it would be a worse night than expected (accident, pulled over, etc.)
	You don't get a lot of sleep so you're tired when you take your test the next morning

b. Get to the party without driving your mom's car (bus or walk). Stay up late and have the time of your life. Walk home after the party and crash.

PROS	CONS
Have a blast at the party	Embarrassment of getting off at the bus stop right in front of the house where the party is
Don't get in trouble with your mom for using the car.	Walking 10 blocks to the party will probably make you sweaty when you get to the door
	You won't have time to study and you get a bad grade on the test
	The party could get busted. You're pretty sure that alcohol will be there, so the cops could get everyone in trouble, even if you're not drinking.
	You don't get a lot of sleep so you're tired when you take your test the next morning

5. Ask the students to name the people they listed to give them good advice. List these people on the board.
6. Ask the students to share their decision, and what actions would follow that decision. Hopefully some of the students will have come up with creative options. Encourage them to think creatively in all their decisions, to think through what is the best decision for everyone involved, and to consider how the choice will affect their future.

Discussion: Scenario #2 (suggested time: 5 minutes)

1. Ask one of the students to read aloud Scenario #2.
2. Have the students share the options they brainstormed and write all the options on the board. If the students haven't brainstormed many options, feel free to add to the discussion by suggesting these options:
   a. Celebrate your mom's birthday and buy her a present, but don't get your video game and don't do anything for your significant other.
   b. Celebrate your one-year anniversary with your significant other, and buy him/her a present, but don't get your video game and don't do anything for your mom.
   c. Celebrate your mom's birthday with her and buy your significant other an expensive present to make up for not being with him/her, but don't get your video game.
   d. Get your video game, make presents for your mom and significant other, and spend some time with each of them.
   e. Get your video game, make presents for your mom and significant other, and spend all day playing the game.
   f. Celebrate your one-year anniversary with your significant other and buy your mom an expensive present to make up for not being with her, but don't get your video game.
3. Ask the groups if the values, passions, and/or goals were the same or different for each person in the group. Ask students to name some of those values, passions, and/or goals; write them on the board.
4. Pick two of the main options and write the pros and cons for each option on the board. The following two have been provided, but their lists of pros and cons are not comprehensive.
   a. Celebrate your mom's birthday with her and buy your significant other an expensive present to make up for not being with him/her, but don't get your video game.

PROS	CONS
Your significant other will feel loved and probably won't break up with you.	You don't get your video game, and the surprises of the game are ruined by your friends, who have all played it.
Your mom will feel loved and may be easier on you with your significant other.	Although you are spending time with your mom, you didn't get her a present, so she may be annoyed with you all day.

b. Get your video game, make presents for your mom and significant other, and spend some time with each of them.

PROS	CONS
Both mom and significant other got to spend time with you.	Mom and significant other may be annoyed that they had to share that day with someone else, so the time with them may not be that great.
Not all of the features are ruined because at least you got to play the game for a little while. Now you'll be able to contribute to the excitement with your friends.	Don't get time to play a lot of the game, even though you were able to buy it, so some of the new features are ruined for you.
Your gifts were thoughtful.	Your mom or significant other may have expensive taste and are upset that you didn't spend more money on them.

5. Ask the students to name the people they listed to give them good advice. List these people on the board.
6. Ask the students to share their decision, and what actions would follow that decision. Hopefully some of the students will have come up with creative options in making this decision.

Wrap Up (suggested time: 5 minutes)

A suggested concluding comment:

"We are constantly bombarded with choices. Every day we make decisions: from the simplest decisions to get out of bed or clean our rooms, to the bigger decisions, like where to go to college. It is important to have a process for making wise decisions. Remember that making a wise decision means considering what is the best possible solution, in the best possible way, for the most people, for the longest length of time. This should cause us to consider how that decision would affect our own future."

Next class, we will create a life map that will help set ourselves up for success.
Thank the class for their attentiveness and participation.

Vocabulary:

- wisdom

Whenever you see a successful business, someone once made a courageous decision.
–Peter Drucker,
Author and Management Expert

Materials needed:

- Local map or laptop with internet access, projector, and whiteboard
- Markers or whiteboard pens in three colors
- Legal size white paper for each student
- Markers, crayons, or colored pencils (enough for all students)

Key Concepts:

1. You must plan ahead to discover the most direct route to accomplish your goals.
2. There are consequences of making "wrong turns" in the journey of life, but you can still make a "right turn" to point you back to your original goal.

Prep Time: 15 minutes

Advance Preparation Tasks:

- Bookmark a Google map on your computer of the local area and project it on a whiteboard, so you can draw on the white board map, OR
- Copy a large map of the local area that the students will be able to see at the front of the room
- Buy or collect enough materials for each student
- Prepare a Life Map to show to the students during Step 6 of the Activity, and consider a story to share during the Wrap Up

Keep in Mind

- This lesson is meant to break the common misconception that if one makes a lot of money, all their problems will disappear.

Because of the allure and influence the media has on many students, there is a common misconception that if you make a lot of money, all your problems will disappear. Some students may have the attitude of, "I don't need to learn how to be wise about money. I just need to get a job that pays a lot so I don't have to worry about being wise with my money." This attitude will not help them succeed financially. This lesson is meant to break that thinking by helping students see that even if they want a job that makes a lot of money they will have to work hard and take necessary steps to get that job. If the students just say or think, "Some day, I'll have a job that makes a lot of money," they will most likely never make it to that point. Achieving that goal in the future takes intentional planning, setting and meeting short-term goals along the way.

Lesson Snapshot

Review (5 minutes)
- Why it's important to think through how to make decisions
- Have several students share decisions they have made since the last class and if they used any part of the decision making process

Introduction (5 minutes)
- Ask students, if they could go anywhere in the world, where would it be and why
- Ask what they would need to do to get ready for a journey
- Draw out similarities between traveling a route to a specific destination and traveling through life

Lecture: From Point A to Point B (10 minutes)
- Project map on board or use a large copy of a map on which to draw steps
- Pick two points for the students to travel to and have the students take you through the 4-7 steps it takes to get from Point A to Point B
- What happens if I make a wrong turn?
- What happens if I make multiple wrong turns because I'm in a new area?
- Relate example back to real life

Activity: Life Maps (15 minutes)
- Distribute materials
- Have students pick a goal that takes a minimum of five years to attain:
    - Label Point A on far left side of the paper with today's date and a brief description of their life right now
    - Label Point B on far right side of the paper with future date and a brief description of the goal they would like to achieve
    - Fill in the space between with 8-10 dots that represent steps they will need to take in order to get to Point B as directly as possible
    - Demonstrate with an example
    - Encourage students to be creative

Discussion: Right and Wrong Turns (10 minutes)

- Have several students share the goal they chose
- Have several students share steps they included
- Brainstorm "wrong turns"
- Use your previously demonstrated map to demonstrate a wrong turn, and how you can make a couple of right turns to point you back to your destination

Wrap Up (5 minutes)

- Ask students what they do to "bounce back" or gain motivation after they've made "wrong turns" in life and are dealing with the consequences
- Share a story about making a wrong turn, specifically the habits that help you stay motivated and keep moving forward after you made that "wrong turn"
- Encourage students to keep moving forward

Review (suggested time: 5 minutes)

Ask the students why it would be important to think through how to make decisions.

Remind students that an important step in making decisions is considering how each option will impact the future. Ask the students to share some of the decisions they've made since the last class if there were any consequences that came that they didn't foresee. Then review the five steps of decision making by asking the students if they included any of the five steps in making their decisions, and reminding students of what the five steps are if they don't remember.

Introduction (suggested time: 5 minutes)

Ask students if they could go anywhere in the world, where would it be and why. Then ask the students what they would need to do to get ready for a journey. After students answer, remind them that it takes a lot of preparation to be ready for a journey. Point out that we go on little journeys every day from home to school, school to home, and everywhere in between. We get there by walking, or taking bikes, buses, trains, subways and cars. We drive on roads, lanes, streets, highways, and freeways. Each road presents different obstacles along the way. We are highly dependent on the mode of transportation and its features to provide us with safe travel and arrival at our destination. Each route we travel can give us a picture of the journey of life. And just like there are several options for traveling to specific destinations, we have all arrived in our present place in life by a variety of routes, coming from different beginnings, or backgrounds.

Remind the students that throughout this unit, a lot of paths and options for success have been discussed. We've even looked at other people's lives to learn from their triumphs and mistakes. Today, this unit, which discusses what is needed to succeed, will conclude with looking both at what our lives look like currently and what we hope our futures will look like.

Lecture: From Point A to Point B (suggested time: 10 minutes)

The purpose of this lecture is to introduce the basic idea that while there are many routes from Point A to Point B, there is one route that is most direct, and therefore better than other routes. The idea of following directions and making wrong turns is an analogy that will set up today's main activity.

Use two locations with which your students are familiar – landmarks, hangouts, the school or other locations where your students go often. Ask a student to give you directions from Point A to Point B. The two locations should be far enough apart to require four to seven steps on the directions. It is generally helpful to have a map of the local area — either a printed map on which you can draw or a Google map projected on a whiteboard where you can draw. Trace the route on the map as the student gives you instructions. After the student has directed you all the way to your destination (Point B), summarize by saying, "So, this is pretty straightforward, right? We can all agree that if I follow these steps, I will get where I want to go, without wasting time or energy in the process. There probably isn't a way I can get from here to there much faster or more easily."

Then ask the students, "What happens if I make a wrong turn?" Demonstrate on the map by using a second color to draw a line (only 1-2 blocks) that departs from the agreed-upon route. Allow for one to two student responses, then summarize by saying something like: "If I realize it right away, I can get back on track pretty quickly. I can either make a U-turn and get right back on my route, or I can make a couple of extra turns and meet up with my original route a block or two away. (For example, if I made a right turn when I was supposed to go straight, I can make a left at the next street, make another immediate left, and then a right turn back onto the street where I started puts me back on track.) It may add a minute or two to my travel time, but it's not too big a deal." Using the second color, trace a route that gets you back on track on the map.

Then ask, "What if I'm traveling in a place I don't know very well, and I make two or three wrong turns in a row?" Use a third color, and trace three to five turns on the map that lead toward a completely different end-point, preferably in the opposite direction from your original Point B.

Draw from the following to address this issue: "By the time I realize I'm not following my route, I may have gone a long way in the wrong direction, and I may be headed toward a completely different place from where I originally wanted to go. It may be that I will be so far off track that I'm no longer sure how to get back. By the time I get back to where I started, or figure out a new set of directions to get to my desired destination, I've wasted a lot of time, energy, and gas. I also probably feel frustrated, irritable, and discouraged."

Draw from the following to make the connection between map routes and life map routes: "Life works a lot like this. Everyone starts out somewhere. Let's say this class is Point A and everyone has dreams about where they would like to end up. The life that you imagine for yourself in 10 or 20 years is your Point B. Although directions may be different because our destinations are different, it is still true that for every one of us there is a most direct way to get from Point A to the Point B that we can choose. There is a set of steps we can take, like the turns in a set of directions, and if we follow the steps, we will get to Point B. In life, each time we make a decision, it's like making a turn in the car. That turn can get us closer to our desired destination, but a wrong turn can take us out of the way and make the trip longer and more complicated. It is extremely important to think now about where you want to end up, and to plan ahead for the steps you need to take to get there. Every time you make a decision, you can ask yourself whether it is a right turn or a wrong turn — in other words, 'Will this choice take me closer to or further away from Point B?'"

Activity: Life Maps

(suggested time: 15 minutes)

Explain to the students that they are going to begin mapping out the steps to take to get from Point A (now) to Point B (our future goal).

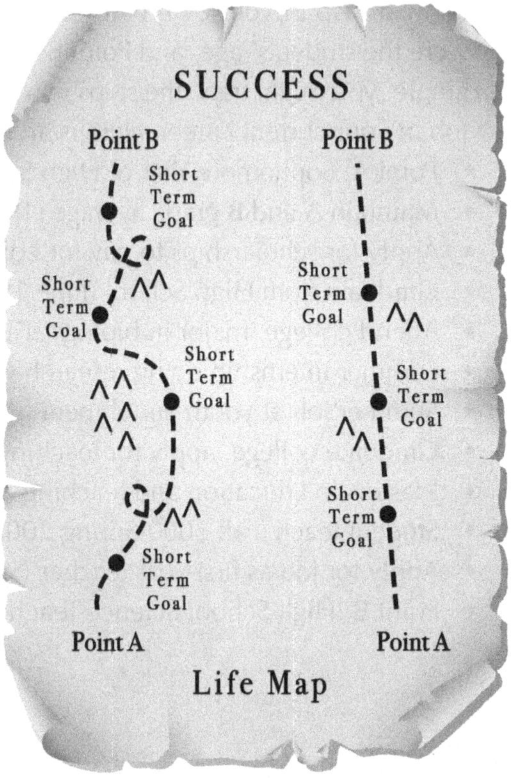

1. Hand out a piece of legal-size white paper to each student, and distribute pens, crayons, or colored pencils so each student has access to a few colors.

2. Tell the students to pick a goal that would take a minimum of five years to attain. The most obvious goals are education or career-based, but a student could also pick a goal like owning a home. There is no need to define for the students what qualifies as an acceptable goal, as long as the goal they choose does not involve illegal or dangerous activities and can be broken down into a series of steps over an extended period of time.

3. At the far left of the paper, each student should draw a dot, and label it Point A. Ask them to write today's date and a brief description about their life right now. For example, a student might write "2010, sophomore in high school."

4. At the far right of the paper, each student should draw a second dot, and label this one Point B. Ask them to write a date and a brief description of the goal they want to achieve. For example, a student might write, "2025, lawyer." The length of time between Point A and Point B will vary, depending on what is appropriate for the specific goal. Students should pick a realistic time frame. If they aren't sure how much time they will need, they can leave the date blank for now and add it at the end after they have filled in the steps and calculated how long each step would take to accomplish.

5. Direct the students to fill in the space between the two dots by drawing a map that shows the steps they should follow to get from Point A to Point B. Each dot is like a turn, representing a point where completing a step will bring them closer to Point B, but missing the step could take them off track. Every student should include at least 8-10 "turns" on their map, and label them with the appropriate time frame and a brief description. Demonstrate with an example before they begin (see Step 6).

6. Draw a map of your own path on the board as an example. Point A should be when you were the students' age, and Point B should be a major accomplishment in your life. For example, you might trace the steps you took from sophomore year of high school to your first job in your current career. Here is an example:
   - Point A: Sophomore Year of High School (1994)
   - Maintain A and B grade average (1994-1996)
   - Apply for scholarships to pay for college (Fall 1995-Spring 1996)
   - Graduate from High School (June 1996)
   - Attend college, major in biology (Fall 1996-Spring 2000)
   - Summer internship doing research with a biology professor (Summer 1998)
   - Summer job at youth enrichment program (Summer 1999)
   - Graduate college, apply for teaching programs (June 2000)
   - Masters in Education and teaching credential program (Fall 2000-Spring 2001)
   - Student teach (Fall 2000-Spring 2001)
   - Apply for job as first-year teacher (Spring 2001)
   - Point B: High School Science Teacher (Fall 2001)

For each bullet point, you would draw a dot on the board, and then connect the dots from Point A to Point B. The dots don't need to be drawn in a straight line, like a timeline, but instead can be staggered, so that the end result looks like the route you would draw on a map, with a series of left and right turns leading from Point A to Point B. Leave your map on the board so you can refer back to it again at the end of the discussion.

The sample timeline includes things like internships, enrichment programs and student teaching that are all career enriching for the teacher. Help the students figure out those same types of steps for their point B decision.

7. Encourage students to be creative in making their maps. They can choose to illustrate some of the steps or decorate the map in other ways.

Discussion: Right and Wrong Turns (suggested time: 10 minutes)

The purpose of this discussion is (1) to encourage students to think ahead about the consequences of their decisions so they might decide to avoid "wrong turns" and (2) to help students recognize that a wrong turn does not have to completely take them off course. Students are encouraged to recognize that they always have the power to begin making right turns that will eventually lead them to their goals.

Ask for a couple of volunteers to share their responses to the following questions:
- What goal did you use as Point B on your map?
- What is one step you included to help you get from Point A to Point B?

Ask the rest of the class if anyone else included a similar step on his/her map. Repeat this process several times, until students have shared a variety of steps they included on their maps. Then consider saying, "We've spent most of our time today talking about the right turns that we should take to get ourselves where we want to be. But just like when we're following directions on a road map, there are also plenty of times when we might make a wrong turn. Let's take a few minutes to brainstorm some examples of wrong turns. Remember, wrong turns are the decisions that take us in a different direction or make it more complicated for us to get to Point B." Take notes on the board as students brainstorm their ideas about decisions that would take them off of their desired route. Examples might include: drug or alcohol use, getting arrested, cutting class, not passing a class, unsafe sexual activity that results in a sexually-transmitted disease or an unplanned pregnancy, etc.

Consider saying, "Most of us make at least a few wrong turns during our lives. Sometimes those decisions only affect our lives in small ways, and it's easy to get back on track. Other times those decisions have big consequences, like when we make so many wrong turns that we aren't quite sure how to find our way back to our planned route. Even when we get ourselves far off track, we can always plan a new route to lead back to Point B. Let's use my map as an example again. What if I had been arrested for drug use while I was still in high school?" (You can choose any example of a "wrong turn" that you want. An arrest for drug use is only one option, provided here as an example.) Using a second color, draw a line from the "Maintain an A and B average" dot that leads away from Point B. Draw a new dot and label it "Arrest." Ask the students why getting arrested for drug use would take you off of your route. Reasons include:

- It is harder to maintain good grades if you're using drugs.
- An arrest on your record might make it harder to get scholarships, get into college, or get the jobs you want.
- If you have to spend time in jail, it would be difficult to graduate from high school on time.

Note to Teacher

Be aware that this will likely be a delicate conversation. Many of your students have likely already made one or more "wrong turns" and may already feel like they are way off track. Encourage students to recognize that they always have the power to start making "right turns" instead. The route may be more difficult, more complicated, and longer, but it is definitely possible to correct a wrong turn and start heading toward Point B.

Tell the class, "Let's assume that this isn't the first time I've been caught with drugs, and this time I have to spend a month in juvie. By the time I get out, I can't finish the semester at school. But, I have stopped getting high, and I'm ready to work hard again. What can I do?" Lead the students in brainstorming some steps you could take that would get you back on track. Make a dot for each step, and connect the dots, drawing a line that eventually reconnects with your original map. For example, you might list the following steps:

- Finish classes at a continuation school and graduate (December 1996)
- Enroll at local community college for two years, and maintain A or B grade average (1997-1999)
- Apply for transfer to four-year college and for scholarships (Spring 1999)
- Connect back to the original map at "Attend college, major in biology," but change the dates to Fall 1999-Spring 2001.

Point out to the students that you can now continue toward Point B, but you are a year behind and getting this far has been more complicated. It probably took more energy and work on your part, and felt more frustrating and discouraging. Maybe there were times when you were more likely to give up because Point B seemed harder to get to. Emphasize that it would have been an easier journey if you had stuck to the original map, and that it is possible to plan a new route when you get off track. Detours take longer, but they don't block us from reaching our destination.

Wrap Up (suggested time: 5 minutes)

Ask the students if there is anything they do that helps them keep moving forward when they've made a wrong turn in the past. Then share the habits that help you stay motivated and keep moving forward when you made a wrong turn in your past. Explain the story, what the wrong turn was, and how you made decisions to help you get back on the most efficient path toward your goal.

End this lesson by encouraging the students to keep moving forward on the path. At some point, almost everyone struggles with how to get back on track when a decision doesn't go according to plan, or when a wrong turn is made. Encourage the students to fight for motivation to keep moving forward, especially during the times of struggle, and they will grow in character and perseverance as they do. Also encourage them to surround themselves with positive people who want good things for their future and who will encourage them along the path if or when they make a wrong turn.

Thank the class for their attentiveness and participation.

Glossary

Annual Income (or Gross Annual Income) – The total wages or salary a person earns in a year, usually before taxes are taken out of the pay.

Apprenticeship – An on-the-job training program under the supervision of a journey-level craftsperson or a trade professional.

ATM Card – A card that allows a person to deposit and withdraw money from his/her account without going inside the bank, usually at an ATM (Automated Teller Machine). It does not allow a person to withdraw money from his/her account when making purchases at stores.

ATM Fees – ATM (Automated Teller Machine) allows a person to withdraw cash at any time. Banks will usually charge customers from other banks a fee to use their ATM.

Bankruptcy – When a person goes to court and asks the court to declare that it is impossible for this person to pay back what he or she owes.

Budget – A tool or plan for how an individual will spend his/her money over a specified future period of time. A budget can be made for a person, family, or group of people, a business, government, country or multinational organization or any other entity that makes and spends money.

Business Loan – A loan in which an individual borrows money to start a new business or make an existing business bigger.

Capitalism – An economic and political system that determines how the businesses in a country operate. The prices, production, and distribution of goods are determined mainly by competition in a free market. The country's trade and industry are controlled by private owners for profit, rather than by the state.

Car Loan – A loan in which an individual borrows money to purchase a car or other vehicle.

Check Cashing Outlet – A business that will cash an individual's personal check for a fee. The fee usually ranges from 1%-3% of the check amount.

Checking Account – An account at a bank against which checks can be drawn by the account depositor. It usually pays the lowest amount of interest, if any. It allows a person to spend his/her money anytime and almost anywhere using checks or a debit card.

Consumer Loan – A loan in which an individual borrows money to purchase a personal item that is often expensive, like a big screen TV, laptop computer, furniture, etc. A consumer loan is usually obtained by using a credit card, although it is possible to get a consumer loan from a bank.

Contract – A written agreement, especially one concerning employment, sales, or tenancy, which is intended to be enforceable by law.

Cost of Living – The average cost of food, clothing, and other necessary or usual goods and services paid by a person.

Credit – The borrowing capacity of an individual or company.

Credit Card – A card received through a contractual agreement in which a borrower receives money now, and agrees to repay the lender in the future, with interest. Credit cards often charge very high interest rates, and require the consumer to pay back only a minimum monthly payment.

Credit Score – A numerical expression based on an analysis of a person's credit files to indicate to lenders how likely that individual is to repay a loan on time. A credit score is primarily based on credit report information, typically sourced from credit bureaus.

Debit Card – A card the bank gives a person that allows one to transfer money electronically from his/her bank account to make purchases, allowing a person to not have to carry cash or a checkbook.

Debt – When one owes money to a company or person.

Delayed Gratification – The mindset one has of waiting to obtain something one wants. Delayed gratification is experienced when one "saves up" over time before purchasing a special item. (see Instant Gratification)

Deposit – An amount of money paid as a pledge for a contract, the balance being payable later.

Direct Deposit – When the employer electronically sends an employee's paycheck amount to his or her bank account instead of giving the employee a paycheck to deposit.

Documentary – A film of people involved in real events, created to be a factual report of the event. Some portions of documentaries may be re-enacted if original footage is not available.

Education – The knowledge you obtain that improves your skills and abilities, whether by trade school, certification programs or academic schooling.

Entrepreneur – A person who organizes, operates, and assumes the risk for a business venture.

Entrepreneurship – When an individual starts his or her own business from a new idea or innovation.

Entrepreneurial Mindset – When a person will do whatever it takes to help the business succeed. It means taking the initiative to make things happen and persevering through many obstacles, staying focused on the goal, and working hard. An employee with these characteristics is appreciated by a wide variety of employers.

Expenses – The money exiting our lives when we spend it. It is used more frequently to describe the costs a person doesn't choose, like utilities, housing, and transportation, but it also includes entertainment and other optional purchases.

Federal Deposit Insurance Corporation (FDIC) – A government company that guarantees that money deposited in banks will be safe, up to $250,000 per individual account.

Fee – A payment made in exchange for some kind of service.

Financial Literacy – The knowledge and skills to make informed judgments and effective decisions regarding earning, spending and managing money and credit. Financial literacy

helps an individual fulfill personal, family, social and governmental responsibilities.
Gross Income – The amount of money a person earns before taxes are deducted from the pay.
Home Loan (or Mortgage) – A loan in which an individual borrows money, usually from a bank, to purchase a house, condo, mobile home, or other type of residence.
Income – The money coming into one's life, from any source, including wages earned and gifts received.
Inflation – When the price of goods and services rises over time without increasing in size or quality.
Instant Gratification – The act of giving oneself what one desires immediately, often at future expense. A person who practices instant gratification regularly will not want to invest in or wait for anything that takes time to acquire, often suffering future negative consequences. (see Delayed Gratification)
Interest – A percentage of money either paid or received on a repeating set schedule.
Interest Rate – The percentage individuals have to pay each year in addition to the money borrowed.
Loan – Borrowed money, paid back with interest.
Loan Shark – A lender who charges extreme amounts to the borrower, who is usually in dire need.
Minimum Payment – The minimum amount a credit card holder is required to repay each billing period on an open balance. A cardholder can make a payment that is in excess of the minimum payment due. However, a payment cannot be for less than the minimum payment due without incurring additional fees.
Minimum Wage – The amount of money per hour that employers are required by federal law to pay employees. The minimum wage rate fluctuates between countries, and sometimes between states or counties. The minimum wage attempts to protect employees from exploitation, allowing them to afford the basic necessities of life.
Monthly Charge / Fee – The fee a bank charges its customers for keeping an account open at that bank. Some bank accounts do not have a monthly fee; other banks require customers to meet certain account conditions in order to be exempt from monthly fees.
Monthly Income - The amount a person gets paid each month.
Need - An expense that is necessary for the most basic level of survival. This includes food, shelter, and clothing. An item can also be considered a need if it is necessary to help us earn our income.
Negative Cash Flow – When a person has more money going out (expenses) than he/she has coming in (income).
Negative Interest - The charge for the privilege of borrowing money, typically expressed as an annual percentage rate. It is considered negative because it causes him/her to pay more money than he / she borrowed.

Overdraft fees – Fees charged each time a person spends more money than what is available in his / her account. No matter how small the overdraft, the fee is usually the same.

Payday Loan – A small, short-term loan that a borrower uses to cover expenses until the next payday. The borrower agrees to pay the amount of the loan plus a fee in interest by his/her next payday.

Percentage – A ratio, expressed as a number divided by 100; a smaller amount taken from the whole amount.

Positive Cash Flow – When there is more money coming into a person's life (income) than going out of his/her life (expenses).

Positive Interest – The amount a person can accumulate in interest through various investments. It is considered positive because it helps a person's money work for him/her, and he/she receives more money over time than he/she originally invested.

Power – When an individual has the ability to make choices about his or her own destiny.

Powerlessness – When an individual has or feels a lack of opportunities and choices about his or her future.

Predator – An organism that lives by preying on other organisms.

Predatory Lending – An unscrupulous lending practice that targets low-income or otherwise vulnerable people. Predatory lending involves companies or people making high-cost loans to borrowers based on their level of assets and not on their ability to repay the debt. This practice also may require a borrower to refinance the loan repeatedly, which lets the lender charge high points and fees. Another predatory practice is using fraud or deceit to conceal the true cost of the loan from an unsophisticated borrower.

Predatory Loan – When money is lent to the borrower with excessively high interest rates or fees for urgent or emergency circumstances such as medical expenses, rent, utility bills, or food. These loans are not provided by banks or credit card companies, but are offered by businesses willing to take advantage of people with no other choices. It is nearly impossible to pay the money back in the time required.

Privilege – When certain people start with advantages due solely to circumstances outside of their control.

Profit – A financial gain, especially the difference between the amount earned and the amount spent in buying, operating, or producing something.

Rent-to-own – An arrangement that starts off as a traditional rental agreement, in which a person pays monthly for the use of an item. It is different because the two parties agree to transfer ownership at the end of a specified period of time. At the end of this agreement, consumers are often left paying twice as much, if not more, for owning the rented goods than they would have if they had bought them outright.

Resources – The supply of money, education, connections with people, transportation, health care, or personal skills and capabilities that can be drawn on in order to function effectively.

Resume – A document that contains a summary of an individual's education, achievements, and previous job experience. It is used to tell potential employers about a job candidate.

Saving Account – A bank account that earns interest, usually more interest than checking accounts. These accounts are associated with ATM cards, which are only used at an ATM machine.

Simulation – An experience when people pretend to be someone or something other than themselves.

Slave – When a person is the legal property of another person or company and is forced to obey the owner.

Slavery – The condition of not being in control of one's own life, of having to act according to someone else's commands, resulting in lack of freedom, opportunities and choices.

Start-up Capital – A sum of money often contributed to an entrepreneur to begin a new business. It is given by a person who likes the idea and believes the entrepreneur will make a profit. This money is given with the hope that the donor will have some part in the future financial return.

Student Loan – A loan in which an individual borrows money, usually from the government or a bank, to pay for college tuition and other school-related expenses.

Success – The accomplishment of an aim or purpose. Financial success is measured by the ability an individual has to make choices that broaden his/her opportunities for the future – opportunities that will give him/her the option of doing what he or she loves.

Sweatshops – Factories or workshops, especially in the clothing industry, where manual workers are employed at very low wages for long hours and under poor conditions.

Take-Home Income (or Net Income) – The amount of money a person actually receives after taxes are deducted from gross income.

Tax Brackets – The percentage of money paid to the state or government based on the income a person receives. People with lower incomes pay a lower percentage, and people with higher incomes pay a higher percentage.

Trade – A skilled job, typically one requiring manual skills and special training.

Transition to Independence Expenses – The additional expenses that an individual pays when he or she is transitioning to living independently, specifically start-up costs such as deposits and fees.

Utilities – Commodities or services, such as water, electricity, gas, and garbage pick-up, provided by a public utility company.

Want – Any expense not considered a need; an item that may make life more comfortable, but is not necessary for survival.

Wisdom – Applying experience, knowledge, and good judgment to the choices we make. An easy way to remember it is to think of the best possible solution, in the best possible way, for the largest number of people, for the longest duration of time.

NORTHERN CALIFORNIA
URBAN DEVELOPMENT

Northern California Urban Development (NCUD) was established in 2005 with the mission of transforming Northern California's urban communities through economic empowerment and community development. NCUD seeks to break the cycle of poverty in local residents' lives by contributing needed resources, services, and financial education. Beginning in East Palo Alto, California, NCUD has fostered initiatives that encourage economic empowerment, leadership development, financial literacy and life skills education, and home ownership education.

NCUD offers support and consulting services to assist community-based organizations, schools and churches that seek to implement programs similar to ours. Our staff has over 20 years of experience in their respective fields, and a wealth of knowledge to impart. If you need guidance in the overarching vision, development or implementation of the *FutureProfits* curriculum (school-based or afterschool program-based), community housing questions or information regarding credit union development, please visit our website at www.norcaludc.org or call us directly at (877) 824-NCUD.

Northern California Urban Development and Christian Community Development Association would like to thank you for purchasing this curriculum. We welcome your questions, comments and input as we strive to improve this resource. Feel free to contact us at info@futureprofitsresources.org.

CHRISTIAN COMMUNITY DEVELOPMENT ASSOCIATION

Restoring under-resourced communities

In 1989, Dr. John Perkins called together a group of Christian leaders who were bonded by one significant commitment – mobilizing the churches of the United States to get fully engaged in the work of restoring under-resourced communities, not at arms length, but at the grassroots level. An association was formed, and the Christian Community Development Association (CCDA) held its first annual conference in Chicago.

Today, CCDA is made up of over 3,000 individuals and more than 500 organizations from grassroots, community based groups to some of the largest relief and development organizations in the world. Nationally, CCDA members are redeveloping under-resourced urban, rural and suburban communities utilizing the philosophy of Christian Community Development. This ministry philosophy of Christian Community Development (CCD) is a Biblical approach to working in under-resourced communities comprised of Eight Key Components:

- Relocation (Presence in the Community)
- Reconciliation
- Redistribution
- Church-Based
- Listening to the Community
- Wholistic Ministry (addressing the needs of the whole person)
- Leadership Development
- Empowerment

The vision of CCDA is clear – to see wholistically restored communities with Christians fully engaged in the process of transformation. Our mission – to inspire, train, and connect Christians who seek to bear witness to the Kingdom of God by reclaiming and restoring under-resourced communities – supports the efforts of the growing number of individuals and organizations who are working to rebuild their communities, turning them from places of devastation into places of hope.

The following Chinese proverb, often quoted by Dr. Perkins, captures the heart of CCD:

Go to the people,
Live among them,
Learn from them,
Love them,
Start with what they know,
Build on what they have:
But of the best leaders,
When their task is done,
The people will remark
"We have done it ourselves."

For more information about CCDA, our National Conference, Institute, and Curriculum, contact us at info@ccda.org.